Taste of Home
TEST KITCHEN
FAVORITES

TASTE OF HOME BOOKS • RDA ENTHUSIAST BRANDS, LLC • MILWAUKEE, WI

Taste *of* Home

International Standard Book Numbers:
D 978-1-61765-965-2
U 978-1-61765-966-9
International Standard Serial Number:
2690-3792
Component Numbers:
D 119700100H
U 119700102H

Executive Editor: Mark Hagen
Senior Art Director: Raeann Thompson
Editor: Amy Glander
Assistant Art Director: Courtney Lovetere
Designer: Jazmin Delgado
Copy Editor: Ann Walter

Cover Photography: *Taste of Home* Photo Studio

Pictured on front cover:
Citrus Cranberry Pie, p. 213
Chicken Parmesan Slider Bake, p. 25
Lentil Taco Cups, p. 117
Mixed Berry French Toast Bake, p. 58
Chocolate Peanut Butter Shakes, p. 33

Pictured on title page:
The Best Chicken & Dumplings, p. 107

Pictured on back cover:
Honey Cornbread, p. 83
Chocolate Bavarian Torte, p. 226
Best Ever Sweet Pickles, p. 11
Shrimp Tortellini Pasta Toss, p. 128

Printed in USA

1 3 5 7 9 10 8 6 4 2

More ways to connect with us: 🇫 🇹 🇮 🇵

Simply the Best

Family time is truly special in my house, so I always try to set the table with the best foods possible—the tastiest, the prettiest and the most memorable. As executive culinary director of the *Taste of Home* Test Kitchen, I get a sneak peek at (and taste of) all the wonderful recipes that our readers share with us.

Over the past 25 years, our Test Kitchen has tested, tasted and approved more than 75,000 recipes. From all-time standbys to trendy new bites, we've seen and tasted them all! (Tough job, huh?) That's why I'm so excited about this incredible all-new collection of 314 recipes that our staff happily deemed the best of the best!

We asked our Test Kitchen pros which dishes made their list of all-time favorites—which recipes they actually took home and served their own families. Next, we put those tasty specialties into this handy resource. Now you can find these top-notch appetizers, entrees, soups, desserts and more in one spot.

This book begins with a collection of recipes from the *Taste of Home* staff. I'll introduce you to some of the talented folks I work with and share their all-time best dishes. Turn to page 20 and you'll find the stunning three-layer Best Vanilla Cake shared by Margaret Knoebel, a culinary assistant on our team. And I'm obsessed with the Pressure-Cooker Fabulous Fajitas on page 138 and the Caramel-Pecan Monkey Bread on page 184. Both of these eye-opening dishes were the result of team efforts in our Test Kitchen.

Not only will you discover a host of mouthwatering sensations developed by our own experts, but also must-try dishes sent in by our readers. On page 150, Saturday Afternoon Oven Pot Roast is a dish you won't want to wait for the weekend to try. It was submitted by Colleen Delawder, a home cook from Herndon, Virginia. It instantly became a hit with all of us!

You'll also find chapters featuring our breakfast favorites, five-star appetizers, savory entrees and, of course, the heavenly sweets we adore.

Your family deserves the best, so why not serve tried-and-true winners every night of the week? With *Taste of Home Test Kitchen Favorites* at your fingertips, I know our most-loved dishes are going to become new standbys in your home as well.

Happy cooking,

Sarah Farmer

DISHING WITH

Sarah Farmer
Taste of Home *Executive Culinary Director*

Take a Peek Inside Our Test Kitchen

Family cooks sharing their all-time best recipes—that's long been the hallmark of *Taste of Home*. And while we couldn't do what we do without these gracious home cooks, it's our Test Kitchen team that makes sure each recipe we receive will turn out perfect in kitchens from coast to coast.

Each year the *Taste of Home* Test Kitchen staff receives about 6,000 recipes, and tests about half of those.

Every recipe submission is reviewed by our team of professional food editors and culinary assistants. They check that each recipe is complete, calls for common ingredients, offers easy-to-follow directions and fits with the *Taste of Home* family of recipes. In addition, they check to be sure *Taste of Home* has not published a similar recipe in the past.

Once it gets the initial stamp of approval, a recipe is scheduled for testing and the cooking begins! It should come as no surprise that every weekday our Test Kitchen is busy baking, frying, simmering, mixing and preparing all sorts of delicious dishes. Just consider these facts:

• The Test Kitchen uses 382 pounds of butter per year.

• The cooks go through 600 pounds of flour per month.

• Roughly 98 pounds of bacon sizzle to perfection in the Test Kitchen annually.

• Our prep cooks slice and dice about 441 onions and 294 lemons each year.

On average, the Test Kitchen hosts two taste-testing sessions per day for a panel of test cooks and editors. After tasting an item, they discuss it in detail—flavor, texture, cooking method, visual appeal and more.

Every recipe needs a thumbs-up approval from the panel before it's designated as "ready for publication" in the *Taste of Home* database. There are more than 229,000 recipes in our extensive collection. In fact, if we wrote each recipe on a 3x5-inch index card laid end to end, the cards would cover 318 football fields!

Once a recipe is scheduled for publication, it's slated to appear on a set in the *Taste of Home* Photo Studio. Another kitchen, located within the studio, ensures our team of creative food stylists will have each dish ready for its time in the spotlight. Our team of talented photographers shoot foods an average of eight hours per day.

In addition to appearing in *Taste of Home* magazine, recipes are posted on *TasteofHome.com* as well as social media sites, where they can receive up to 20 million page views.

Similarly, recipes are published in our cookbooks as well as special-interest publications found at grocery stores and wherever cooking magazines are sold.

Why do so many people send their recipes to *Taste of Home?* Many are entries for contests and others are submitted for particular magazine features. Most, however, come from home cooks who simply want to share their love of food with families just like yours!

CONTENTS

FAVORITE...

**MOM'S SUPER STUPENDOUS
POTATO SALAD, PAGE 10**

Staff Recipes

At *Taste of Home*, we're all about authentic family-pleasing meals. Here are some of our very own recipes—the dishes we've tasted, tested and perfected in our own home kitchens. For us, these are the recipes that conjure up heavenly aromas, stir up sweet memories of Sunday dinner, and bring our loved ones happily dashing to the table. Whether you're feeding a crowd or just your own hungry crew, dig in to these staff creations that capture the essence of home cooking.

GREEN CHILE
CHEESEBURGERS

DISHING WITH

James Schend
Deputy Editor

A diner outside of Albuquerque, New Mexico, served the most amazing burgers topped with roasted green chiles. They had a smoky flavor and a bit of a bite. Here's my take on the juicy specialties.

GREEN CHILE CHEESEBURGERS

—James Schend, Deputy Editor

- -

Prep: 20 min. • **Cook:** 15 min.
Makes: 6 servings

- 3 whole green chiles, such
     as Anaheim or Hatch
- 2 lbs. ground beef
- 1 tsp. salt
- ½ tsp. pepper
- 6 slices slices sharp cheddar cheese
- 6 hamburger buns, split and toasted
     Optional toppings: Lettuce leaves
     and sliced tomato

1. Grill peppers, covered, over high heat until all sides are blistered and blackened, about 8-10 minutes, turning as needed. Immediately place peppers in a small bowl; let stand, covered, 20 minutes. Reduce grill temperature to medium heat.
2. Meanwhile, in a large bowl, combine beef, salt and pepper; mix lightly but thoroughly. Shape into six ¾-in.-thick patties.
3. Peel off and discard charred skin from peppers. Cut peppers lengthwise in half; carefully remove stems and seeds. Cut into slices or coarsely chop.
4. Grill burgers, covered, over medium heat until a thermometer reads 160°, 5-7 minutes on each side. Top with cheese and chiles; grill, covered, until the cheese is melted, 1-2 minutes longer. Top bun bottoms with burgers and, if desired, lettuce and tomato.
1 burger: 482 cal., 26g fat (11g sat. fat), 116mg chol., 552mg sod., 23g carb. (4g sugars, 1g fiber), 36g pro.

CALIFORNIA
ROLL IN A JAR

CALIFORNIA ROLL IN A JAR

I'm a big sushi fan but don't always have time to make those intricate rolls at home. This jar is layered with my favorite California roll ingredients—I get all the flavor but none of the fuss.

—James Schend, Deputy Editor

- -

Prep: 20 min. • **Cook:** 15 min. + standing
Makes: 4 servings

- 1 cup uncooked sushi rice
- 1 cup water
- ½ tsp. salt
- 1 Tbsp. rice vinegar
- 1 Tbsp. sugar
- 2 medium ripe avocados,
     peeled and cubed
- 1 cup lump crabmeat, drained
- 1 cup chopped cucumber
- 2 nori sheets, thinly sliced
     Optional: Pickled ginger slices, soy
     sauce and toasted sesame seeds

1. Wash rice in a colander until water runs clear. Combine rice, 1 cup water and salt in a large saucepan; bring to a boil. Reduce heat; cover. Simmer until water is absorbed and rice is tender, 15-20 minutes. Remove from heat. Let stand 10 minutes. Combine rice vinegar and sugar, stirring until the sugar is dissolved. Stir into rice.
2. Place ⅓ cup rice into each of four 1-pint wide-mouth canning jars; layer with half of the avocados, crabmeat, cucumber and nori. Top with remaining rice and repeat layers. Cover and refrigerate until serving. Transfer into bowls; toss to combine. If desired, serve with optional ingredients.
1 serving: 349 cal., 11g fat (2g sat. fat), 33mg chol., 562mg sod., 52g carb. (6g sugars, 7g fiber), 11g pro.

TEST KITCHEN TIP
Imitation crabmeat is an acceptable substitution for the more costly lump crabmeat.

MOM'S SUPER STUPENDOUS POTATO SALAD
—Ellie Martin Cliffe, Deputy Editor

- -

Prep: 20 min. • **Cook:** 15 min. + chilling
Makes: 12 servings

- 1 garlic clove, peeled
- 3 lbs. small red potatoes, quartered
- 2 Tbsp. cider vinegar, divided
- 1½ tsp. salt, divided
- 6 hard-boiled large eggs, divided use
- 1 cup mayonnaise
- ½ cup sour cream
- 1 Tbsp. Dijon mustard
- ½ tsp. paprika, plus extra for garnish (optional)
- ¼ tsp. pepper
- 1 medium sweet onion, finely chopped
- 2 celery ribs, finely chopped
- 2 Tbsp. minced fresh parsley

1. Skewer garlic with a toothpick (to make it easy to find after cooking). Place potatoes, 1 Tbsp. vinegar, 1 tsp. salt and skewered garlic in a Dutch oven; add water to cover. Bring to a boil. Reduce heat; simmer until tender, 10-12 minutes. Drain the potatoes, reserving garlic; remove skewer and crush garlic clove.
2. Meanwhile, chop 5 eggs. Whisk together mayonnaise, sour cream, mustard, paprika, pepper, garlic and remaining vinegar and salt. Stir in potatoes, chopped eggs, onion and celery. Refrigerate 4 hours or until cold.
3. Just before serving, slice remaining egg. Top salad with egg; sprinkle with parsley and, if desired, additional paprika.
¾ cup: 281 cal., 19g fat (4g sat. fat), 107mg chol., 472mg sod., 20g carb. (2g sugars, 2g fiber), 6g pro.

DISHING WITH

Ellie Martin Cliffe
Deputy Editor

In college, my best friend and I debated whose mom made the best potato salad. Turns out they were almost identical! Even though I've since tweaked our recipe, it still takes me home again.

MOM'S SUPER
STUPENDOUS
POTATO SALAD

BEST EVER SWEET PICKLES

When I was a kid, I always looked forward to the homemade jams and jellies my granny made from her farm-grown berries. Our urban backyard doesn't have room for a berry patch, but we do have a trellis for growing cucumbers. I pack away these sweet pickles every summer.
—Ellie Martin Cliffe, Deputy Editor

- -

Prep: 1 hour + standing • **Process:** 10 min.
Makes: 4 pints

- 9 cups sliced pickling cucumbers
- 1 large sweet onion, halved and thinly sliced
- ¼ cup canning salt
- 1 cup sugar
- 1 cup water
- 1 cup white vinegar
- ½ cup cider vinegar
- 2 Tbsp. mustard seed
- 1 tsp. celery seed
- ½ tsp. whole peppercorns
- 4 bay leaves
- 12 garlic cloves, crushed

1. In a large nonreactive bowl, combine cucumbers, onion and salt. Cover with crushed ice and mix well. Let stand 3 hours. Drain; rinse and drain thoroughly.

2. In a Dutch oven, combine the sugar, water, vinegars, mustard seed, celery seed and peppercorns. Bring to a boil, stirring to dissolve sugar. Add cucumber mixture; return to a boil, stirring occasionally. Reduce heat; simmer, uncovered, 4-5 minutes or until heated through.

3. Carefully ladle hot mixture into 4 hot wide-mouth 1-pint jars, leaving ½-in. headspace. Add 3 garlic cloves and 1 bay leaf to each jar. Remove air bubbles and, if necessary, adjust the headspace by adding hot pickling liquid. Wipe the rims. Center lids on jars; screw on bands until fingertip tight.

4. Place jars into canner with simmering water, ensuring that they are completely covered with water. Bring to a boil; process for 10 minutes. Remove jars and cool.
¼ cup: 35 cal., 0 fat (0 sat. fat), 0 chol., 175mg sod., 8g carb. (7g sugars, 0 fiber), 0 pro.

PORT WINE CRANBERRY SAUCE

This crimson sauce has just the right amount of tartness to complement poultry, pork and game.
—Ellie Martin Cliffe, Deputy Editor

- -

Takes: 20 min. • **Makes:** 2 cups

- 1 pkg. (12 oz.) fresh or frozen cranberries
- 1¼ cups sugar
- ¼ cup port wine or grape juice
- 2 tsp. cornstarch
- 2 Tbsp. cold water

In a small saucepan, cook cranberries, sugar and wine over medium heat just until berries begin to pop, 10-12 minutes. Combine the cornstarch and water until smooth; stir into cranberry mixture. Bring to a boil; cook and stir until berries pop and sauce is thickened, about 2 minutes. Serve sauce warm or cold. Refrigerate leftovers.
¼ cup: 146 cal., 0 fat (0 sat. fat), 0 chol., 1mg sod., 38g carb. (34g sugars, 2g fiber), 0 pro.

BEST EVER SWEET PICKLES

CRUNCHY HONEY-GLAZED
BUTTERNUT SQUASH

THE BEST EVER TOMATO SOUP
—Josh Rink, Food Stylist

Prep: 20 min. • **Cook:** 30 min.
Makes: 16 servings (4 qt.)

- 3 **Tbsp. olive oil**
- 3 **Tbsp. butter**
- ¼ **to ½ tsp. crushed red pepper flakes**
- 3 **large carrots, peeled and chopped**
- 1 **large onion, chopped**
- 2 **garlic cloves, minced**
- 2 **tsp. dried basil**
- 3 **cans (28 oz. each) whole peeled tomatoes**
- 1 **container (32 oz.) chicken stock**
- 2 **Tbsp. tomato paste**
- 3 **tsp. sugar**
- 1 **tsp. salt**
- ½ **tsp. pepper**
- 1 **cup heavy whipping cream, optional Fresh basil leaves, thinly sliced, optional**

1. In a 6-qt. stockpot or Dutch oven, heat oil, butter and pepper flakes over medium heat until butter is melted. Add carrots and onion; cook, uncovered, over medium heat, stirring frequently, until the vegetables are softened, 8-10 minutes. Add garlic and dried basil; cook and stir 1 minute longer. Stir in tomatoes, chicken stock, tomato paste, sugar, salt and pepper; stir well. Bring to a boil. Reduce heat; simmer, uncovered, to let flavors blend, 20-25 minutes.

2. Remove pan from heat. Using a blender, puree the soup in batches until smooth. If desired, slowly stir in heavy cream, stirring continuously to incorporate; return to stove to heat through. If desired, top soup with fresh basil.

1 cup: 104 cal., 5g fat (2g sat. fat), 6mg chol., 572mg sod., 15g carb. (10g sugars, 2g fiber), 3g pro. **Diabetic exchanges:** 1 starch, 1 fat.

CRUNCHY HONEY-GLAZED BUTTERNUT SQUASH

I'm now required to bring this to every family gathering during the holidays because it's so awesome! Why not start a new tradition for your family?
—Sarah Farmer, Executive Culinary Director

Prep: 20 min. • **Bake:** 45 min.
Makes: 10 servings

- ½ **cup honey**
- 1 **tsp. dried thyme, divided**
- 1 **large butternut squash (about 5 lbs.), peeled, halved, seeded and thinly sliced**
- 3 **Tbsp. water**
- ¼ **cup plus 2 Tbsp. olive oil, divided**
- 1½ **tsp. salt, divided**
- 1½ **tsp. pepper, divided**
- ½ **cup panko bread crumbs**

1. Preheat oven to 375°. In a large saucepan, heat the honey and ½ tsp. thyme, stirring occasionally, over low heat until fragrant, 3-4 minutes.

2. Meanwhile, in a large microwave-safe dish, combine the squash and water; microwave, covered, on high 6-8 minutes or until squash is tender. Drain. Add ¼ cup olive oil, 1 tsp. salt and 1 tsp. pepper; toss to coat.

3. On a flat surface, stack the squash slices. Arrange stacks on their sides in a greased 9-in. square baking dish. (To make stacking easier, set baking dish on end; fill with squash stacks. When dish is full, return to original position.) Drizzle 3 Tbsp. honey mixture over the squash.

4. Bake until squash is tender, 45-50 minutes. In a small skillet, heat the remaining oil over medium heat. Add bread crumbs; toss with remaining thyme and remaining salt and pepper. Cook and stir until golden brown, about 5 minutes. Sprinkle over the baked squash; if desired, drizzle with additional honey mixture.

1 serving: 237 cal., 8g fat (1g sat. fat), 0 chol., 373mg sod., 43g carb. (20g sugars, 8g fiber), 3g pro.

THE BEST EVER
TOMATO SOUP

DISHING WITH

Josh Rink
Food Stylist

Creamy, rich and bursting
with brightness, this soup
is the ultimate sidekick to
a grilled cheese sandwich.

DISHING WITH

Peggy Woodward
Senior Food Editor

A kid-friendly wrap is a fantastic way to use leftover chicken and get them to eat more veggies. Using colorful, thin strips of vegetables adds visual interest when the wrap is cut into slices. Suddenly, spinach is too pretty to turn down.

LUNCHBOX CHICKEN WRAP
—Peggy Woodward, Senior Food Editor

- -

Takes: 10 min. • **Makes:** 1 serving

- ¼ cup hummus
- 1 whole wheat tortilla (8 in.), room temperature
- ½ cup fresh baby spinach
- ⅓ cup shredded cooked chicken breast
- 2 carrot sticks
- 2 sweet red pepper strips

Spread the hummus over tortilla; top with spinach. Place the chicken, carrot and red pepper in a row near center of tortilla; roll up tightly. If desired, cut crosswise into slices. Wrap securely or pack in an airtight container; refrigerate until serving.

1 wrap: 324 cal., 10g fat (1g sat. fat), 36mg chol., 441mg sod., 35g carb. (3g sugars, 7g fiber), 23g pro.

SPICED BUTTERNUT SQUASH CHILI

I love how a hint of heat with a touch of sweetness from the Gustus Vitae spicy chocolate cinnamon cane sugar adds another layer of flavor to this contest-winning chili recipe from Jeanne Larson of Rancho Santa Margarita, California.
—Peggy Woodward, Senior Food Editor

- -

Prep: 20 min. • **Cook:** 30 min.
Makes: 8 servings (2 qt.)

- 1 lb. ground beef or turkey
- ¾ cup chopped red onion
- 5 garlic cloves, minced
- 3 Tbsp. tomato paste
- 1 Tbsp. chili powder
- 1 tsp. ground cumin
- ½ to 1 tsp. salt
- 1¾ to 2 cups water
- 1 can (15 oz.) black beans, rinsed and drained
- 1 can (15 oz.) pinto beans, rinsed and drained
- 1 can (14½ oz.) diced tomatoes
- 1 can (14½ to 15 oz.) tomato sauce
- 1 Tbsp. Gustus Vitae spicy chocolate cinnamon cake sugar
- 3 cups peeled butternut squash, cut into ½-in. cubes
- 2 Tbsp. cider vinegar
  Optional: Chopped avocado, plain Greek yogurt and shredded mozzarella cheese

1. In a Dutch oven over medium heat, cook the ground beef and onion, crumbling meat, until the beef is no longer pink and onion is tender, 6-8 minutes.
2. Add next 5 ingredients; cook 1 minute longer. Stir in water, both types of beans, diced tomatoes, tomato sauce and spicy chocolate cinnamon sugar. Bring to a boil; reduce heat. Stir in squash; simmer, covered, until squash is tender, 20-25 minutes. Stir in the vinegar.
3. If desired, serve the chili with chopped avocado, plain Greek yogurt and shredded mozzarella cheese.

1 cup: 261 cal., 8g fat (3g sat. fat), 35mg chol., 704mg sod., 32g carb. (6g sugars, 8g fiber), 18g pro.

SPICED BUTTERNUT SQUASH CHILI

SLOW-COOKER DOUGHNUT BREAKFAST BAKE
—Rashanda Cobbins, Food Editor

Prep: 15 min. • Cook: 4 hours + standing
Makes: 12 servings

- 24 cake doughnuts, cut into bite-sized pieces
- 2 apples, peeled and chopped
- 1 cup heavy whipping cream
- 4 large eggs
- 1 Tbsp. vanilla extract
- ½ cup packed brown sugar
- 1 tsp. ground cinnamon
  Optional: Whipped cream and fresh berries

1. Line inside of 5-qt. slow cooker with a double layer of heavy duty foil; spray insert and foil with cooking spray. Layer half the doughnut pieces in slow cooker; top with half the apples. Repeat with remaining doughnuts and apples. In large bowl, whisk together cream, eggs and vanilla; pour over doughnut pieces and apples. In a small bowl, mix together the brown sugar and cinnamon; sprinkle over doughnut mixture.
2. Cook, covered, on low until set, 4-5 hours. Remove insert. Let stand, uncovered, for 20 minutes. If desired, serve with whipped cream and fresh berries.

1 serving: 609 cal., 36g fat (17g sat. fat), 95mg chol., 547mg sod., 64g carb. (32g sugars, 2g fiber), 8g pro.

SLOW-COOKER DOUGHNUT BREAKFAST BAKE

DISHING WITH

Rashanda Cobbins
Food Editor

This extravagant dish will be the star of the brunch table. Try serving it with sausage, fresh berries and yogurt.

SPICY FRIED OKRA

This fried vegetable is a southern delicacy. It's sure to add excitement to any warm-weather meal.
—Rashanda Cobbins, Food Editor

Takes: 30 min. • Makes: 4 servings

- 3 cups sliced fresh or frozen okra, thawed
- 6 Tbsp. buttermilk
- 2 tsp. Louisiana-style hot sauce
- ¼ cup all-purpose flour
- ¼ cup cornmeal
- ½ tsp. seasoned salt
- ¼ tsp. cayenne pepper
  Oil for deep-fat frying
  Additional salt and pepper, optional

1. Pat the sliced okra dry with paper towels. Place buttermilk and Louisiana-style hot sauce in a shallow bowl. In another shallow bowl, combine the flour, cornmeal, salt and pepper. Dip okra in buttermilk mixture, then roll in cornmeal mixture.
2. In a cast-iron or other heavy skillet, heat 1 in. of oil to 375°. Fry okra, a few pieces at a time, until golden brown, 1½-2½ minutes on each side. Drain on paper towels. If desired, season with additional salt and pepper.

¾ cup: 237 cal., 16g fat (1g sat. fat), 1mg chol., 326mg sod., 20g carb. (4g sugars, 3g fiber), 5g pro.

TEST KITCHEN TIP
Okra is a rich source of vitamins K and C. Prior to breading and frying, it's low in calories and naturally fat-free.

DOUBLE CHOCOLATE
ESPRESSO POUND CAKE

DISHING WITH

Rachel Bernhard Seis

Senior Editor

Two of my biggest loves in life—
chocolate and coffee—come
together in this rich pound cake.
Grate some extra chocolate on
top and thank me later.

DOUBLE CHOCOLATE ESPRESSO POUND CAKE

—Rachel Bernhard Seis, Senior Editor

Prep: 20 min. • **Bake:** 80 min. + cooling
Makes: 16 servings

- 5 oz. milk chocolate, chopped
- ¼ cup brewed espresso
- 1 cup butter, softened
- 3 cups sugar
- 5 large eggs, room temperature
- 2 tsp. vanilla extract
- 3 cups all-purpose flour
- 1½ tsp. baking powder
- ½ tsp. salt
- ⅔ cup 2% milk
- 1 cup (6 oz.) dark chocolate chips

FROSTING
- ¼ cup butter, softened
- 3 cups confectioners' sugar
- 3 Tbsp. 2% milk
- 3 tsp. vanilla extract
- ½ tsp. salt

1. In a double boiler or metal bowl over hot water, melt milk chocolate in espresso; stir until smooth. Remove from the heat.
2. In a large bowl, beat butter and sugar until crumbly, about 2 minutes. Add eggs, 1 at a time, beating well after each addition. Beat in vanilla. Combine the flour, baking powder and salt; add to creamed mixture alternately with milk, beating well after each addition. Stir in the dark chocolate chips and melted chocolate mixture.
3. Transfer batter to a greased and floured 10-in. fluted tube pan. Bake at 325° until a toothpick inserted near the center comes out clean, 80-90 minutes. Cool cake for 10 minutes before removing from pan to a wire rack to cool completely.
4. In a large bowl, beat butter until light and fluffy. Beat in the confectioners' sugar, milk, vanilla and salt; frost cake.
1 slice: 573 cal., 22g fat (14g sat. fat), 100mg chol., 344mg sod., 91g carb. (71g sugars, 2g fiber), 6g pro.

PULLED PORK PARFAIT

THAI PEANUT NAAN PIZZAS
To get my Thai-food fix, I top naan bread with a ginger-peanut sauce, veggies, cilantro and a bit of Sriracha.
—Rachel Bernhard Seis, Senior Editor

Takes: 25 min. • **Makes:** 4 servings

- ¼ cup creamy peanut butter
- 3 Tbsp. sesame ginger salad dressing
- 1 Tbsp. water
- 1 tsp. soy sauce
- 2 naan flatbreads
- 1 cup shredded part-skim mozzarella cheese
- 1 small sweet red pepper, julienned
- ½ cup julienned carrot
- ½ cup sliced baby portobello mushrooms
- ¼ cup chopped fresh cilantro
  Sriracha chili sauce, optional

1. Preheat oven to 425°. For sauce, mix first 4 ingredients until blended. Place naan on a baking sheet; spread with sauce. Top with cheese and vegetables.
2. Bake until cheese is melted and crust is golden brown, 8-10 minutes. Top with cilantro and, if desired, drizzle with Sriracha chili sauce.
½ pizza: 316 cal., 19g fat (6g sat. fat), 21mg chol., 698mg sod., 25g carb. (8g sugars, 2g fiber), 13g pro.

PULLED PORK PARFAIT
I tried a version of this meaty parfait at Miller Park, home of my favorite baseball team, the Brewers. I take it up a notch by layering in corn and creamy macaroni and cheese, so it truly is a full barbecue meal you can take on the go.
—Rachel Bernhard Seis, Senior Editor

Takes: 15 min. • **Makes:** 4 servings

- 1 pkg. (16 oz.) refrigerated fully cooked barbecued shredded pork
- 1 cup frozen corn
- 2 cups refrigerated mashed potatoes
- 2 cups prepared macaroni and cheese

In each of four 1-pint wide-mouth canning jars, divide and layer the ingredients in the following order: pulled pork, corn, mashed potatoes, and macaroni and cheese. Cover and freeze or refrigerate until ready to serve. When ready to serve, remove the lid and microwave until heated through. To serve from freezer, partially thaw in refrigerator overnight before microwaving.
1 serving: 349 cal., 8g fat (4g sat. fat), 45mg chol., 1116mg sod., 41g carb. (20g sugars, 1g fiber), 17g pro.

DISHING WITH

Susan Stetzel
Associate Food Editor

This cran-raspberry cocktail is great any time of year. In winter, the cranberry makes it a good fit for holiday parties; on a warm summer's night, the refreshing raspberry flavor shines through. It's a favorite for our girls' night!

CRANBERRY SPARKLER

—Susan Stetzel, Associate Food Editor

- -

Takes: 5 min. • **Makes:** 3 servings

- ¾ **cup raspberry rum**
- ½ **cup cranberry juice**
- ¼ **cup lime juice**
  Ice cubes
- ¾ **cup ginger ale or lemon-lime soda, chilled**
  Optional: Fresh raspberries and cranberries

Combine rum and juices. Fill three rocks or old-fashioned glasses with ice. Divide rum mixture evenly among glasses; top each with 2 oz. ginger ale. If desired, serve with fresh raspberries and cranberries.

1 serving: 174 cal., 0 fat (0 sat. fat), 0 chol., 6mg sod., 12g carb. (11g sugars, 0 fiber), 0 pro.

EASY MEXICAN BROWNIES

EASY MEXICAN BROWNIES

I was hosting a fun Mexican-themed cocktail party and needed a quick dessert. Dressing up a box brownie mix was easy!
—Susan Stetzel, Associate Food Editor

- -

Prep: 10 min. • **Bake:** 20 min. + cooling
Makes: 2 dozen

- 1 **pkg. fudge brownie mix (13x9-in. pan size)**
- 2 **tsp. ground cinnamon**
- 1 **tsp. ground ancho chili pepper**
- ¾ **cup dark chocolate chips**

ADDITIONAL INGREDIENTS

- 2 **large eggs, room temperature**
- ½ **cup canola oil**
- ¼ **cup water**

1. Whisk together brownie mix and spices. Transfer mixture to a 1-qt. glass jar. Top with chocolate chips. Cover and store in a cool dry place up to 3 months.

2. To prepare brownies: Preheat oven to 350°. Whisk eggs, oil and water until blended. Gradually add chocolate chips and brownie mix, mixing well. Spread into a greased 13x9-in. baking pan.

3. Bake 20-25 minutes or until a toothpick inserted in center comes out clean (do not overbake). Cool brownies completely in pan on a wire rack.

1 brownie: 173 cal., 10g fat (3g sat. fat), 16mg chol., 92mg sod., 21g carb. (15g sugars, 1g fiber), 2g pro.

STRAWBERRY CUPCAKES WITH WHIPPED CREAM FROSTING

—Lisa Kaminski, Associate Editor

Prep: 20 min. • **Bake:** 20 min. + cooling
Makes: 16 cupcakes

- ½   cup seedless strawberry jam or preserves, warmed
- ¾   cup butter, softened
- 1   cup sugar
- 3   large egg whites, room temperature
- 1   tsp. vanilla extract
- 1   cup 2% milk
- ½   cup sour cream
- 1⅔ cups all-purpose flour
- 1   tsp. baking powder
- ¼   tsp. baking soda
- ¼   tsp. salt
       Red food coloring, optional

FROSTING
- 2   cups heavy whipping cream
- ⅓   cup confectioners' sugar
- ⅓   cup seedless strawberry jam or preserves
- ½   tsp. vanilla extract
       Fresh strawberries, optional

1. Preheat oven to 350°. Line 16 muffin cups with paper or foil liners. Press warm jam through a fine-mesh strainer. Discard pulp.
2. In a large bowl, cream butter and sugar until light and fluffy, 5-7 minutes. Add egg whites, 1 at a time, beating well after each addition. Beat in strained jam and vanilla. In a small bowl, whisk milk and sour cream until smooth. In another bowl, whisk the flour, baking powder, baking soda and salt; add to creamed mixture alternately with milk mixture, beating well after each addition. If desired, stir in food coloring.
3. Fill prepared muffin cups three-fourths full. Bake until a toothpick inserted in center comes out clean, 20-25 minutes. Cool for 10 minutes before removing to wire racks to cool completely.
4. In a large bowl, beat cream until it begins to thicken. Add confectioners' sugar, jam and vanilla; beat until stiff peaks form. Spread or pipe over cupcakes. Refrigerate leftovers. If desired, garnish with fresh strawberries.
1 cupcake: 353 cal., 21g fat (13g sat. fat), 60mg chol., 184mg sod., 38g carb. (27g sugars, 0 fiber), 4g pro.

STRAWBERRY CUPCAKES WITH WHIPPED CREAM FROSTING

DISHING WITH

Lisa Kaminski
Associate Editor

Fresh strawberries are full of water, so they have a tendency to weigh down cake batters and make soggy cakes. That's why these strawberry cupcakes rely on strawberry jam or preserves. The concentrated flavor is just right for light and tender cupcakes.

BEST VANILLA CAKE

FREEZER BREAKFAST SANDWICHES
—Christine Rukavena, Editor

Prep: 25 min. • **Cook:** 15 min.
Makes: 12 sandwiches

- 12 large eggs
- ⅔ cup 2% milk
- ½ tsp. salt
- ¼ tsp. pepper

SANDWICHES
- 12 English muffins, split
- 4 Tbsp. butter, softened
- 12 slices Colby-Monterey Jack cheese
- 12 slices Canadian bacon

1. Preheat oven to 325°. In a large bowl, whisk eggs, milk, salt and pepper until blended. Pour into a 13x9-in. baking pan coated with cooking spray. Bake until set, 15-18 minutes. Cool on a wire rack.
2. Meanwhile, toast English muffins (or bake at at 325° for 12-15 minutes or until lightly browned). Spread 1 tsp. butter on each muffin bottoms.
3. Cut eggs into 12 portions. Layer muffin bottoms with an egg portion, a cheese slice (tearing cheese to fit) and Canadian bacon. Replace muffin tops. Wrap the sandwiches in foil; freeze in a freezer container or bag.
4. To use frozen sandwiches: Remove foil. Wrap the sandwich in a paper towel and microwave at 50% power until thawed, 1-2 minutes. Turn sandwich over; microwave at 100% power until hot and a thermometer reads at least 160°, 30-60 seconds. Let stand 2 minutes before serving.
1 sandwich: 334 cal., 17g fat (9g sat. fat), 219mg chol., 759mg sod., 26g carb. (3g sugars, 2g fiber), 19g pro.

TEST KITCHEN TIP
Not only is it possible to freeze cooked eggs, but they actually taste better when frozen and reheated than cooked eggs stored in the refrigerator. Cooked eggs can be frozen for up to 1 year, but we find they taste best within 3 to 6 months of the freezing date.

BEST VANILLA CAKE

There's a reason why this vanilla cake recipe is the best. Adding some creamy vanilla bean paste into this moist, rich cake batter creates a power-packed vanilla flavor unlike any other.
—Margaret Knoebel, Culinary Assistant

Prep: 20 min. + standing
Bake: 30 min. + cooling • **Makes:** 16 servings

- 1½ cups sour cream
- 1 Tbsp. vanilla bean paste
- 1 Tbsp. vanilla extract
- 4 cups cake flour
- 2½ cups sugar
- 4½ tsp. baking powder
- 2 tsp. salt
- 1 cup unsalted butter, softened
- ¼ cup canola oil
- 6 large egg whites, room temperature
- 2 large eggs, room temperature

1. Preheat oven to 350°. In a small bowl mix sour cream, vanilla paste and vanilla extract until combined. Let stand 10 minutes. Line bottoms of 3 greased 9-in. round baking pans with parchment; grease paper.
2. Sift cake flour, sugar, baking powder and salt together twice into a large bowl. Add butter and canola oil; beat until mixture is crumbly. Add egg whites, 1 at a time, beating well after each addition. Add eggs, 1 at a time, beating well after each addition. Beat in sour cream mixture just until combined.
3. Transfer batter to prepared pans. Bake until a toothpick inserted in center comes out clean, 30-35 minutes. Cool in pans for 10 minutes before removing to wire racks; remove paper. Cool completely. Frost cake as desired.
1 slice: 399 cal., 16g fat (8g sat. fat), 54mg chol., 462mg sod., 59g carb. (32g sugars, 1g fiber), 5g pro.

FREEZER BREAKFAST SANDWICHES

BUFFALO CHICKEN DIP
PAGE 27

Snacks

Whether it's a holiday, the boss's birthday or a retirement farewell, we love to break away from the work for a little laughter, camaraderie and, of course, the chance to indulge in sensational hot bites, finger foods and snacks of all kinds. Give one of our favorite party pleasers a try the next time you gather with friends or family.

CHICKEN PARMESAN
SLIDER BAKE

CHICKEN PARMESAN SLIDER BAKE

Sliders are the perfect finger food for any get-together, and this flavorful chicken Parmesan version won't disappoint.
—Nick Iverson, Denver, CO

- -

Prep: 20 min. • **Bake:** 25 min.
Makes: 1 dozen

24 oz. frozen breaded chicken tenders
 1 pkg. (12 oz.) Hawaiian sweet rolls
 1 pkg. (7½ oz.) sliced provolone
    and mozzarella cheese blend
 1 jar (24 oz.) marinara sauce
TOPPING
 ½ cup butter, cubed
 1 tsp. garlic powder
 1 tsp. crushed red pepper flakes
 ¼ cup grated Parmesan cheese
 2 Tbsp. minced fresh basil

1. Preheat oven to 375°. Prepare chicken tenders according to package directions. Meanwhile, without separating rolls, cut horizontally in half; arrange roll bottoms in a greased 13x9-in. baking dish. Place half of cheese slices over roll bottoms. Bake until cheese is melted, 3-5 minutes.
2. Layer rolls with half of sauce, chicken tenders, remaining sauce and remaining cheese slices. Replace top halves of rolls.
3. For topping, microwave butter, garlic powder and red pepper flakes, covered, on high, stirring occasionally, until butter is melted. Pour over rolls; sprinkle with Parmesan. Bake, uncovered, until golden brown and heated through, 20-25 minutes. Sprinkle with basil before serving.
1 slider: 402 cal., 23g fat (11g sat. fat), 62mg chol., 780mg sod., 34g carb. (10g sugars, 4g fiber), 17g pro.

"What's not to like about this dish? Chicken tenders, cheese, sauce, Hawaiian rolls? Yes, yes and yes! I share this at my book club and family gatherings, and it goes over great every time."

— LISA KAMINSKI, ASSOCIATE EDITOR

GARLIC GARBANZO
BEAN SPREAD

GARLIC GARBANZO BEAN SPREAD

My friends and family always ask me to make this for potlucks and parties. You can serve it as an appetizer or a filling for sandwiches.
—Lisa Moore, North Syracuse, NY

- -

Takes: 10 min. • **Makes:** 1½ cups

 1 can (15 oz.) garbanzo beans or
    chickpeas, rinsed and drained
 ½ cup olive oil
 2 Tbsp. minced fresh parsley
 1 Tbsp. lemon juice
 1 green onion, cut into 3 pieces
 1 to 2 garlic cloves, peeled
 ¼ tsp. salt
    Assorted fresh vegetables and
    baked pita chips

In a food processor, combine the first 7 ingredients; cover and process until blended. Transfer to a bowl. Refrigerate until serving. Serve with vegetables and pita chips.
2 Tbsp.: 114 cal., 10g fat (1g sat. fat), 0 chol., 96mg sod., 6g carb. (1g sugars, 1g fiber), 1g pro. **Diabetic exchanges:** 2 fat, ½ starch.

SPICY EDAMAME

Edamame (pronounced ay-duh-MAH-may) are young soybeans in their pods. In our Test Kitchen, we boiled and seasoned them to create a unique finger food.
—*Taste of Home* Test Kitchen

Takes: 20 min. • **Makes:** 6 servings

- 1 **pkg. (16 oz.) frozen edamame pods**
- 2 **tsp. kosher salt**
- ¾ **tsp. ground ginger**
- ½ **tsp. garlic powder**
- ¼ **tsp. crushed red pepper flakes**

Place edamame in a large saucepan; cover with water. Bring to a boil. Cover and cook until tender, 4-5 minutes; drain. Transfer to a large bowl. Add the seasonings; toss to coat.
1 serving: 52 cal., 2g fat (0 sat. fat), 0 chol., 642mg sod., 5g carb. (1g sugars, 2g fiber), 4g pro.

TEST KITCHEN TIP
Edamame is a popular Asian food produced from the soybean that is harvested early, before the beans become hard. The young beans are parboiled and frozen to retain their freshness.

NUTELLA HAND PIES

NUTELLA HAND PIES

These puff pastry Nutella pies are so good, you may not want to share!
—*Taste of Home* Test Kitchen

Takes: 30 min. • **Makes:** 9 servings

- 1 **large egg**
- 1 **Tbsp. water**
- 1 **sheet frozen puff pastry, thawed**
- 3 **Tbsp. Nutella**
- 1 **to 2 tsp. grated orange zest**

ICING

- ⅓ **cup confectioners' sugar**
- ½ **tsp. orange juice**
- ⅛ **tsp. grated orange zest**
  Additional Nutella, optional

1. Preheat oven to 400°. In a small bowl, whisk egg with water.
2. Unfold puff pastry; cut into 9 squares. Place 1 tsp. Nutella in center of each; sprinkle with orange zest. Brush edges of pastry with egg mixture. Fold 1 corner over the filling to form a triangle; press edges to seal. Transfer to an ungreased baking sheet.
3. Bake until the pastry is golden brown and cooked through, 17-20 minutes. Cool slightly.
4. In a small bowl, mix confectioners' sugar, orange juice and orange zest; drizzle over pies. If desired, warm additional Nutella in a microwave and drizzle over tops.
1 hand pie: 190 cal., 10g fat (2g sat. fat), 21mg chol., 100mg sod., 24g carb. (8g sugars, 2g fiber), 3g pro.

BUFFALO CHICKEN DIP

Buffalo wing sauce, cream cheese and salad dressing make a lively party dip with some real kick. Everywhere I take it, people want the recipe.

—Peggy Foster, Florence, KY

Takes: 30 min. • **Makes:** about 2 cups

1   **pkg. (8 oz.) cream cheese, softened**
1   **cup cooked chicken breast**
½   **cup Buffalo wing sauce**
½   **cup ranch or blue cheese salad dressing**
2   **cups shredded Colby-Monterey Jack cheese French bread baguette slices, celery ribs or tortilla chips**

1. Preheat oven to 350°. Spread cream cheese into an ungreased shallow 1-qt. baking dish. Layer with chicken, wing sauce and salad dressing. Sprinkle with cheese.
2. Bake, uncovered, 20-25 minutes or until cheese is melted. Serve with baguette slices.
2 Tbsp.: 156 cal., 13g fat (7g sat. fat), 38mg chol., 484mg sod., 2g carb. (1g sugars, 0 fiber), 7g pro.

BUFFALO CHICKEN DIP

BERRY MINI CHEESECAKES

There's always room for dessert. These little bites of cheesecake are just enough to satisfy your sweet tooth craving.
—*Taste of Home* Test Kitchen

Prep: 20 min. • **Bake:** 15 min. + chilling
Makes: 1½ dozen

1   **cup graham cracker crumbs**
3   **Tbsp. butter, melted**
8   **oz. cream cheese, softened**
⅓   **cup sugar**
1   **tsp. vanilla extract**
1   **large egg, room temperature, lightly beaten**
18   **fresh raspberries**

1. Preheat oven to 350°. In a small bowl, combine graham cracker crumbs and butter. Press crumb mixture gently onto the bottom of 18 paper-lined miniature muffin cups. In another small bowl, beat the cream cheese, sugar and vanilla until smooth. Add egg; beat on low speed just until combined. Spoon over crusts.
2. Bake 12-14 minutes or until centers are set. Cool 10 minutes before removing from the pan to a wire rack to cool completely. Refrigerate at least 1 hour.
3. To serve, remove paper liners; top cheesecakes with raspberries.
1 mini cheesecake: 100 cal., 7g fat (4g sat. fat), 31mg chol., 83mg sod., 8g carb. (5g sugars, 0 fiber), 2g pro.

HOMEMADE CHURROS

CURRIED CHICKEN MEATBALL WRAPS

We love these easy meatball wraps topped with crunchy veggies and peanuts, sweet raisins and a creamy dollop of yogurt. They are great for picky eaters because everyone can assemble their own.
—Jennifer Beckman, Falls Church, VA

- -

Prep: 25 min. • **Bake:** 20 min.
Makes: 2 dozen

- 1 large egg, lightly beaten
- 1 small onion, finely chopped
- ½ cup Rice Krispies
- ¼ cup golden raisins
- ¼ cup minced fresh cilantro
- 2 tsp. curry powder
- ½ tsp. salt
- 1 lb. lean ground chicken

SAUCE
- 1 cup plain yogurt
- ¼ cup minced fresh cilantro

WRAPS
- 24 small Bibb or Boston lettuce leaves
- 1 medium carrot, shredded
- ½ cup golden raisins
- ½ cup chopped salted peanuts
   Additional minced fresh cilantro

1. Preheat oven to 350°. In a large bowl, combine the first 7 ingredients. Add chicken; mix lightly but thoroughly. With wet hands, shape mixture into 24 balls (about 1¼-in.).
2. Place meatballs on a greased rack in a 15x10x1-in. baking pan. Bake 17-20 minutes or until cooked through.
3. In a small bowl, mix sauce ingredients. To serve, place 2 tsp. sauce and 1 meatball in each lettuce leaf; top with remaining ingredients.
1 appetizer: 72 cal., 3g fat (1g sat. fat), 22mg chol., 89mg sod., 6g carb. (4g sugars, 1g fiber), 6g pro. **Diabetic exchanges:** 1 lean meat, ½ starch.

HOMEMADE CHURROS

These fried cinnamon-sugar goodies are best served fresh and hot. Try them with cups of coffee or hot chocolate. Don't be surprised if people start dunking—and then go back for more.
—*Taste of Home* Test Kitchen

- -

Prep: 15 min. + cooling • **Cook:** 20 min.
Makes: about 1 dozen

- ½ cup water
- ½ cup 2% milk
- 1 Tbsp. canola oil
- ¼ tsp. salt
- 1 cup all-purpose flour
- 1 large egg, room temperature
- ¼ tsp. grated lemon zest
   Additional oil for frying
- ½ cup sugar
- ¼ tsp. ground cinnamon

1. In a large saucepan, bring the water, milk, oil and salt to a boil. Add flour all at once and stir until a smooth ball forms. Transfer to a large bowl; let stand for 5 minutes.
2. Beat on medium-high speed for 1 minute or until the dough softens. Add the egg and lemon zest; beat for 1-2 minutes. Set aside to cool.
3. In a deep cast-iron or heavy skillet, heat 1 in. oil to 375°. Insert a large star tip in a pastry bag; fill with dough. On a baking sheet, pipe dough into 4-in. strips.
4. Transfer strips to skillet and fry until golden brown on both sides. Drain on paper towels. Combine the sugar and cinnamon; sprinkle over churros. Serve warm.
1 churro: 122 cal., 5g fat (1g sat. fat), 17mg chol., 60mg sod., 17g carb. (9g sugars, 0 fiber), 2g pro.

CURRIED CHICKEN
MEATBALL WRAPS

BITE-SIZED APPLE PIES

Kids love to eat—and make—these cute little bites. Simply wrap strips of pastry around apple wedges and shake on some cinnamon-sugar. Then just bake and watch them disappear!
—*Taste of Home* Test Kitchen

- -

Prep: 20 min. • **Bake:** 15 min.
Makes: 16 appetizers

½ **cup sugar**
2 **tsp. ground cinnamon**
2 **sheets refrigerated pie crust**
3 **Tbsp. butter, melted, divided**
2 **medium tart apples**
   Caramel sauce, optional

1. Preheat oven to 425°. In a small bowl, mix sugar and cinnamon; reserve 1 Tbsp. of the cinnamon-sugar. On a lightly floured surface, unroll pie crusts; roll and trim each to an 8-in. square. Brush with 2 Tbsp. butter; sprinkle with remaining sugar mixture. Cut each square into eight 1-in. strips.
2. Cut each apple into 8 wedges; wrap 1 strip of pastry around each wedge, placing sugared side of pastry against the apple.
3. Place on a parchment-lined baking sheet. Brush tops with remaining butter; sprinkle with reserved sugar mixture. Bake until pastry is golden brown, 13-15 minutes. Serve warm, with caramel sauce if desired.
1 appetizer: 163 cal., 9g fat (4g sat. fat), 10mg chol., 108mg sod., 21g carb. (9g sugars, 0 fiber), 1g pro.

BITE-SIZED
APPLE PIES

CHILI CHICKEN STRIPS

Instead of ordinary bread crumbs, seasoned crushed corn chips coat these slightly crunchy chicken fingers. If your family likes food with some heat, use the full 1½ teaspoons of chili powder.
—*Taste of Home* Test Kitchen

- -

Takes: 25 min. • **Makes:** 6 servings

- ¾ cup crushed corn chips
- 2 Tbsp. dry bread crumbs
- 1 Tbsp. all-purpose flour
- 1 to 1½ tsp. chili powder
- ½ tsp. seasoned salt
- ½ tsp. poultry seasoning
- ¼ tsp. pepper
- ¼ tsp. paprika
- 1 large egg
- 1½ lbs. boneless skinless chicken breasts, cut into ½-in. strips
- 4 Tbsp. butter

1. In a shallow bowl, combine the first 8 ingredients. In another shallow bowl, beat egg. Dip chicken in egg, then roll in the corn chip mixture.

2. In a large skillet, cook half of the chicken in 2 Tbsp. butter for 8-10 minutes or until the meat is no longer pink. Repeat with the remaining chicken and butter.

3 chicken strips: 265 cal., 12g fat (6g sat. fat), 119mg chol., 381mg sod., 14g carb. (0 sugars, 1g fiber), 25g pro.

TOMATO & ARTICHOKE BRUSCHETTA

This healthy and delicious bruschetta is great for entertaining. Just mix up the topping and chill until party time.
—Gina Bergamino, Chanhassen, MN

- -

Takes: 30 min. • **Makes:** about 6½ dozen

- 4 cups grape tomatoes, chopped
- 1 cup shredded part-skim mozzarella cheese
- ¾ cup water-packed artichoke hearts, rinsed, drained and chopped
- 3 green onions, chopped
- 3 Tbsp. pine nuts, toasted
- ¼ cup olive oil
- 3 Tbsp. red wine vinegar
- 3 garlic cloves, minced
- ¾ tsp. pepper
- ¼ tsp. salt
- 1 French bread baguette (10½ oz.), cut into ¼-in. slices

1. Preheat oven to 425°. In a large bowl, combine tomatoes, cheese, artichokes, green onions and pine nuts. Whisk the oil, vinegar, garlic, pepper and salt; pour over tomato mixture and toss to coat.

2. Place bread on ungreased baking sheets. Bake 4-5 minutes on each side or until golden brown. Top with tomato mixture.

1 appetizer: 24 cal., 1g fat (0 sat. fat), 1mg chol., 37mg sod., 3g carb. (0 sugars, 0 fiber), 1g pro.

CHILI CHICKEN STRIPS

GRILLED PINEAPPLE WITH LIME DIP

Serve this dish as an appetizer or dessert—the choice is yours! If desired, the pineapple wedges can be rolled in flaked coconut before grilling.
—*Taste of Home* Test Kitchen

Prep: 20 min. + marinating • **Grill:** 10 min.
Makes: 8 servings

    1   fresh pineapple
    ¼   cup packed brown sugar
    3   Tbsp. honey
    2   Tbsp. lime juice
LIME DIP
    3   oz. cream cheese, softened
    ¼   cup plain yogurt
    2   Tbsp. honey
    1   Tbsp. brown sugar
    1   Tbsp. lime juice
    1   tsp. grated lime zest

1. Peel and core the pineapple; cut vertically into 8 wedges. Cut each wedge horizontally into 2 spears. In a bowl or shallow dish, combine the brown sugar, honey and lime juice; add pineapple and turn to coat. Cover and refrigerate for 1 hour.
2. In a small bowl, beat cream cheese until smooth. Beat in the yogurt, honey, brown sugar, lime juice and lime zest. Cover and refrigerate until serving.
3. Coat grill rack with cooking spray before starting the grill. Drain pineapple, discarding marinade. Grill pineapple spears, covered, over medium heat for 3-4 minutes on each side or until grill marks are golden brown. Serve with lime dip.
2 spears with 2 Tbsp. dip: 160 cal., 4g fat (2g sat. fat), 12mg chol., 41mg sod., 32g carb. (28g sugars, 2g fiber), 2g pro.

TURKEY-CRANBERRY BAGELS

Make use of that leftover Thanksgiving turkey in a way your family loves. These are good with all sorts of cranberry sauces and chutneys, so have fun playing around.
—*Taste of Home* Test Kitchen

Takes: 10 min. • **Makes:** 4 servings

    4   plain bagels, split and toasted
    8   oz. thinly sliced cooked turkey
    8   slices provolone cheese
    ½   cup whole-berry cranberry sauce

Preheat broiler. Place bagel halves on a baking sheet; layer with turkey and cheese. Broil 4-6 in. from heat until cheese is melted, 1-2 minutes. Top with cranberry sauce.
2 bagel halves: 469 cal., 16g fat (8g sat. fat), 73mg chol., 645mg sod., 49g carb. (12g sugars, 2g fiber), 34g pro.

GRILLED PINEAPPLE
WITH LIME DIP

CHOCOLATE PEANUT
BUTTER SHAKES

GARDEN SALSA

My mouthwatering salsa is made from ripe garden ingredients and subtle seasonings. It's one of my go-to dishes for parties.
—Michelle Beran, Claflin, KS

- -

Takes: 15 min. • **Makes:** 5 cups

- 6 medium tomatoes, finely chopped
- ¾ cup finely chopped green pepper
- ½ cup finely chopped onion
- ½ cup thinly sliced green onions
- 6 garlic cloves, minced
- 2 tsp. cider vinegar
- 2 tsp. lemon juice
- 2 tsp. olive oil
- 1 to 2 tsp. minced jalapeno pepper
- 1 to 2 tsp. ground cumin
- ½ tsp. salt
- ¼ to ½ tsp. cayenne pepper
  Tortilla chips

In a large bowl, combine the tomatoes, green pepper, onions, garlic, vinegar, lemon juice, oil, jalapeno and seasonings. Cover and refrigerate until serving. Serve with chips. **Note:** Wear disposable gloves when cutting hot peppers; the oils can burn skin. Avoid touching your face.

2 Tbsp.: 17 cal., 0 fat (0 sat. fat), 0 chol., 62mg sod., 3g carb. (0 sugars, 0 fiber), 0 pro.

Three-Pepper Garden Salsa: Broil 6 Anaheim chiles 4 in. from the heat until skins blister, about 2 minutes. With tongs, rotate the peppers a quarter turn. Broil and rotate until all sides are blistered and blackened. Immediately place chiles in a bowl; cover and let stand for 15-20 minutes. Peel off and discard charred skins. Remove stems and seeds. Finely chop peppers. Add to salsa with other peppers.

CHOCOLATE PEANUT BUTTER SHAKES

These rich chocolate peanut butter shakes will make you feel like you're sitting in a 1950s soda fountain. Make it modern with an over-the-top garnish like skewered doughnut holes.
—*Taste of Home* Test Kitchen

- -

Takes: 10 min. • **Makes:** 2 cups

- ¾ cup 2% milk
- 1½ cups chocolate ice cream
- ¼ cup creamy peanut butter
- 2 Tbsp. chocolate syrup
  Optional toppings: Sweetened whipped cream and miniature peanut butter cups, quartered

In a blender, combine the milk, ice cream, peanut butter and syrup; cover and process until smooth. If desired, garnish with some whipped cream, peanut butter cups and additional chocolate syrup.
1 cup: 501 cal., 29g fat (11g sat. fat), 41mg chol., 262mg sod., 51g carb (43g sugars, 3g fiber), 14g pro.

CRAN-ORANGE PIE IN A JAR

Be prepared for compliments when you serve these individual pudding pies. They're cute and have a citrusy twist.
—*Taste of Home* Test Kitchen

- -

Prep: 20 min. + chilling • **Makes:** 4 servings

- 1 cup graham cracker crumbs
- 2 Tbsp. butter, melted
- 2 cups cold fat-free milk
- 1 pkg. (1 oz.) sugar-free instant white chocolate pudding mix
- ½ tsp. grated orange zest
- ½ cup whole-berry cranberry sauce

1. In a small bowl, combine cracker crumbs and butter. Press into the bottom of each of 4 half-pint canning jars.
2. In another bowl, whisk milk and pudding mix for 2 minutes. Stir in orange zest. Let stand for 2 minutes or until soft-set. Spoon over crusts. Top with cranberry sauce. Cover and refrigerate for at least 1 hour.
1 serving: 253 cal., 8g fat (4g sat. fat), 18mg chol., 439mg sod., 40g carb. (21g sugars, 1g fiber), 6g pro.

HOMEMADE
POTATO CHIPS

HOMEMADE POTATO CHIPS

Forget buying the bag of potato chips at the grocery store when you can make these at home. This quick and easy recipe will delight everyone in the family.
—*Taste of Home* Test Kitchen

- -

Prep: 30 min. + soaking **Cook:** 5 min./batch
Makes: 8½ cups

 7 **unpeeled medium potatoes (about 2 lbs.)**
 2 **qt. ice water**
 5 **tsp. salt**
 2 **tsp. garlic powder**
1½ **tsp. celery salt**
1½ **tsp. pepper**
    Oil for deep-fat frying

1. Using a vegetable peeler or metal cheese slicer, cut potatoes into very thin slices. Place in a large bowl; add ice water and salt. Soak for 30 minutes.

2. Drain potatoes; place on paper towels and pat dry. In a small bowl, combine the garlic powder, celery salt and pepper; set aside.

3. In a cast-iron or other heavy skillet, heat 1½ in. oil to 375°. Fry potatoes in batches until chips are golden brown, 3-4 minutes, stirring frequently.

4. Remove with a slotted spoon; drain on paper towels. Immediately sprinkle with seasoning mixture. Store the chips in an airtight container.

¾ cup: 176 cal., 8g fat (1g sat. fat), 0 chol., 703mg sod., 24g carb. (1g sugars, 3g fiber), 3g pro.

TEST KITCHEN TIP
Use a mandoline to slice the potatoes extra thin.

VANILLA
ICE CREAM

VANILLA ICE CREAM

We think that this is the best ice cream recipe ever. With only four ingredients, it just might be the easiest, too. No ice cream maker? No problem.
—*Taste of Home* Test Kitchen

- -

Prep: 5 min. • **Process:** 20 min. + freezing
Makes: 1¼ qt.

 2 **cups heavy whipping cream**
 2 **cups half-and-half cream**
 1 **cup sugar**
 2 **tsp. vanilla extract**

Combine all ingredients, stirring to dissolve sugar completely. Fill cylinder of ice cream maker no more than two-thirds full; freeze according to manufacturer's directions.

(Refrigerate any remaining mixture until ready to freeze.) Serve immediately or store in covered containers in freezer.

Note: To prepare recipe without an ice cream maker, place a 13x9-in. dish in freezer until cold. Prepare cream mixture as directed; transfer to prepared dish. Freeze until edges of mixture begin to set, 20-30 minutes. Using a hand mixer, beat mixture until smooth. Freeze, covered, until firm, about 3 hours longer, beating again every 30 minutes.

½ cup: 308 cal., 22g fat (14g sat. fat), 78mg chol., 37mg sod., 23g carb. (23g sugars, 0 fiber), 3g pro.

CAPRESE SALAD KABOBS

Trade in the usual veggie party platter for these unique kabobs. I often make them for my family to snack on, and it's an awesome way to get kids to join in the fun of assembling the skewers.
—Christine Mitchell, Glendora, CA

Takes: 10 min. • **Makes:** 12 kabobs

- 24 grape tomatoes
- 12 cherry-size fresh mozzarella cheese balls
- 24 fresh basil leaves
- 2 Tbsp. olive oil
- 2 tsp. balsamic vinegar

On each of 12 appetizer skewers, alternately thread 2 tomatoes, 1 cheese ball and 2 basil leaves. To serve, whisk together oil and vinegar; drizzle over kabobs.

1 kabob: 44 cal., 4g fat (1g sat. fat), 5mg chol., 10mg sod., 2g carb. (1g sugars, 0 fiber), 1g pro. **Diabetic exchanges:** 1 fat.

FAIR-FAVORITE CORN DOGS

FAIR-FAVORITE CORN DOGS

Bring the county fair home to your kitchen with these summer-ready corn dogs. A tip for dipping: Pour the batter into a tall Mason jar and then dunk your hot dogs for an even all-over coating.
—*Taste of Home* Test Kitchen

Prep: 15 min. + standing • **Cook:** 5 min./batch
Makes: 10 corn dogs

- 1 pkg. (8½ oz.) cornbread/muffin mix
- ⅔ cup all-purpose flour
- 1 tsp. ground mustard
- ½ tsp. onion powder
- ½ tsp. chili powder
- ½ tsp. paprika
- ⅛ tsp. ground cumin
- 1 large egg
- 1 cup 2% milk
- 10 hot dogs
- 10 wooden skewers
  Oil for deep-fat frying

1. In a large mixing bowl, combine the first 7 ingredients. In another bowl, whisk milk and egg; stir into dry ingredients just until moistened. Let stand for 15 minutes. Insert skewers into hot dogs; dip into batter.

2. In an electric skillet or deep-fat fryer, heat oil to 375°. Fry corn dogs, a few at a time, until golden brown, 2-3 minutes, turning occasionally. Drain on paper towels.

1 corn dog: 352 cal., 23g fat (7g sat. fat), 53mg chol., 682mg sod., 26g carb. (7g sugars, 1g fiber), 9g pro.

TEST KITCHEN TIP

Don't forget to let the batter stand before coating the hot dogs. It thickens up a bit and clings better after 15 minutes. Make sure the oil temperature returns to 375° between batches.

PINA COLADA DIP

If you like pina coladas, you've gotta try this fluffy fruit dip. Scooped up with a slice of fresh pineapple, it tastes just like the classic beachside drink.
—*Taste of Home* Test Kitchen

- -

Prep: 10 min. + chilling • **Makes:** 20 servings

1¼ cups cold 2% milk
¾ cup pineapple yogurt
1 pkg. (3.4 oz.) instant coconut cream pudding mix
1 carton (8 oz.) frozen whipped topping, thawed
 Optional: Toasted unsweetened coconut flakes and maraschino cherries
 Fresh pineapple wedges
 Vanilla wafers

1. In a large bowl, whisk milk, yogurt and pudding mix 2 minutes (mixture will be thick). Fold in whipped topping. Refrigerate, covered, at least 2 hours.
2. If desired, top with coconut and cherries before serving. Serve with pineapple wedges and vanilla wafers.

¼ cup dip: 68 cal., 3g fat (3g sat. fat), 2mg chol., 64mg sod., 8g carb. (8g sugars, 0 fiber), 1g pro.

ROASTED RED PEPPER TAPENADE

When entertaining, I often rely on my pepper tapenade recipe because it takes only 15 minutes to whip up and pop in the fridge. You can use walnuts or pecans instead of almonds.
—Donna Magliaro, Denville, NJ

- -

Prep: 15 min. + chilling • **Makes:** 2 cups

3 garlic cloves, peeled
2 cups roasted sweet red peppers, drained
½ cup blanched almonds
⅓ cup tomato paste
2 Tbsp. olive oil
¼ tsp. salt
¼ tsp. pepper
 Minced fresh basil
 Toasted French bread baguette slices or water crackers

1. In a small saucepan, bring 2 cups water to a boil. Add garlic; cook, uncovered, just until tender, 6-8 minutes. Drain and pat dry. Place red peppers, almonds, tomato paste, olive oil, garlic, salt and pepper in a small food processor; process until blended. Transfer to a small bowl. Refrigerate at least 4 hours to allow flavors to blend.
2. Sprinkle with basil. Serve with French bread baguette slices.

2 Tbsp. dip: 58 cal., 4g fat (0 sat. fat), 0 chol., 152mg sod., 3g carb. (2g sugars, 1g fiber), 1g pro. **Diabetic exchanges:** 1 fat.

PINA COLADA DIP

PRESSURE-COOKER LIGHT DEVILED EGGS

Our updated version of a classic appetizer uses only half the egg yolks of traditional deviled eggs and calls for soft bread crumbs to help firm up the filling. Light ingredients lower the fat grams even more.
—*Taste of Home* Test Kitchen

- -

Prep: 20 min. • **Cook:** 5 min. + releasing
Makes: 16 servings

  8 **large eggs**
 ¼ **cup fat-free mayonnaise**
 ¼ **cup reduced-fat sour cream**
  2 **Tbsp. soft bread crumbs**
  1 **Tbsp. prepared mustard**
 ¼ **tsp. salt**
     Dash white pepper
  4 **pimiento-stuffed olives, sliced**
     Paprika, optional

1. Place trivet insert and 1 cup water in a 6-qt. electric pressure cooker. Set eggs on trivet. Lock lid; close pressure-release valve. Adjust to pressure-cook on high for 5 minutes. Let pressure release naturally for 5 minutes; quick-release any remaining pressure. Immediately place eggs in a bowl of ice water to cool. Remove shells.
2. Cut eggs lengthwise in half. Remove yolks; refrigerate 8 yolk halves for another use. Set whites aside. In a small bowl, mash remaining yolks. Stir in mayonnaise, sour cream, bread crumbs, mustard, salt and pepper. Stuff or pipe into egg whites. Garnish with olives. If desired, sprinkle with paprika.
1 stuffed egg half: 32 cal., 2g fat (1g sat. fat), 46mg chol., 132mg sod., 1g carb. (1g sugars, 0 fiber), 3g pro.

GLAZED CHICKEN WINGS

I received this recipe from a cousin while visiting her on Vancouver Island. The wings are an appealing appetizer, but also make a fun meal when served with rice and a salad.
—Joan Airey, Rivers, MB

- -

Prep: 15 min. • **Bake:** 50 min.
Makes: 2 dozen

 2½ **lbs. chicken wings**
 ½ **cup barbecue sauce**
 ½ **cup honey**
 ½ **cup soy sauce**

Cut chicken wings into 3 sections; discard wing tip section. Place in a greased 13x9-in. baking dish. Combine the barbecue sauce, honey and soy sauce; pour over wings. Bake, uncovered, at 350° for 50-60 minutes or until chicken juices run clear.
Note: Uncooked chicken wing sections (wingettes) may be substituted for whole chicken wings.
1 chicken wing: 86 cal., 4g fat (1g sat. fat), 15mg chol., 380mg sod., 8g carb. (8g sugars, 0 fiber), 6g pro.

TEST KITCHEN TIP

Always make sure the pressure-release valve on your pot is closed before you start cooking. Even the pros at the *Taste of Home* Test Kitchen have forgotten to close the valve and returned to see the pot venting instead of building pressure.

PRESSURE-COOKER
LIGHT DEVILED EGGS

TANGIER ISLAND VIRGINIA CRAB CAKES

I grew up eating these crab cakes. They're crispy on the outside and tender on the inside. They're absolutely delicious every time I make them.
—Ann Girucky, Norfolk, VA

- -

Prep: 20 min. • **Cook:** 5 min./batch
Makes: 12 crab cakes

    1   large egg, beaten
    1   Tbsp. mayonnaise
    1   tsp. ground mustard
    1   tsp. seafood seasoning
    1   tsp. prepared mustard
    1   tsp. minced fresh parsley
    ½   tsp. salt
    ¼   tsp. pepper
    1   lb. lump crabmeat, drained
    2   slices white bread, finely
        crumbled (about 1½ cups)
    3   Tbsp. canola oil

1. In a large bowl, mix the first 8 ingredients until blended. Fold in crab until well coated. Gently stir in the breadcrumbs until well blended. Shape mixture into twelve ½-in.-thick patties.
2. In a large skillet, heat oil over medium-high heat. Add crab cakes in batches; cook the cakes for 2-3 minutes on each side or until dark golden brown.

1 crab cake: 90 cal., 5g fat (1g sat. fat), 52mg chol., 407mg sod., 3g carb. (0 sugars, 0 fiber), 8g pro.

TEST KITCHEN TIP

Crabmeat has a delicate and sweet taste. There are four grades: claw, special, lump and jumbo lump. Using blue lump crabmeat in the above recipe will result in the best texture and flavor.

**TANGIER ISLAND
VIRGINIA CRAB CAKES**

9-LAYER GREEK DIP

Instead of the same taco dip at every family event or potluck, try this light, cool and refreshing Greek dip. It looks and tastes delicious—and it's healthy, too.
—Shawn Barto, Winter Garden, FL

Takes: 20 min. • **Makes:** 5½ cups

- 1 carton (10 oz.) hummus
- 1 cup refrigerated tzatziki sauce
- ½ cup chopped green pepper
- ½ cup chopped sweet red pepper
- ½ cup chopped peeled cucumber
- ½ cup chopped water-packed artichoke hearts, drained
- ½ cup chopped pitted Greek olives, optional
- ¼ cup chopped pepperoncini
- 1 cup crumbled feta cheese
  Baked pita chips

In a 9-in. deep-dish pie plate, layer the first 6 ingredients; top with olives, if desired, and pepperoncini. Sprinkle with feta cheese. Refrigerate until serving. Serve with baked pita chips.

Note: For that fresh-from-the-kitchen taste, make your own tzatziki sauce by combining ½ cup peeled, seeded and finely chopped cucumber with ½ cup plain Greek yogurt, 4 tsp. lemon juice, 1 Tbsp. chopped dill, 1 minced garlic clove, and salt and pepper to taste. Refrigerate.

¼ cup: 60 cal., 4g fat (1g sat. fat), 5mg chol., 210mg sod., 4g carb. (1g sugars, 1g fiber), 3g pro. **Diabetic exchanges:** ½ starch, ½ fat.

BUFFALO WING DIP

If you like spice, you'll love this dip. It's super cheesy, full of rich flavor and has that Buffalo wing taste you know and love!
—*Taste of Home* Test Kitchen

Prep: 20 min. • **Cook:** 2 hours
Makes: 6 cups

- 2 pkg. (8 oz. each) cream cheese, softened
- ½ cup ranch salad dressing
- ½ cup sour cream
- 5 Tbsp. crumbled blue cheese
- 2 cups shredded cooked chicken
- ½ cup Buffalo wing sauce
- 2 cups shredded cheddar cheese, divided
- 1 green onion, sliced
  Tortilla chips

1. In a small bowl, combine the cream cheese, dressing, sour cream and blue cheese. Transfer to a 3-qt. slow cooker. Layer with chicken, wing sauce and 1 cup cheese. Cover and cook on low for 2-3 hours or until heated through.

2. Sprinkle with remaining cheese and onion. Serve with tortilla chips.

¼ cup dip: 167 cal., 14g fat (8g sat. fat), 47mg chol., 348mg sod., 2g carb. (0 sugars, 0 fiber), 8g pro.

9-LAYER
GREEK DIP

SAUSAGE, EGG & CHEDDAR
FARMER'S BREAKFAST, PAGE 46

Breakfasts

At *Taste of Home*, we're no strangers to busy schedules and hectic workdays. To keep our energy going all day long, we start with a satisfying breakfast. Here are our top picks for the best morning meals—everything from easy egg dishes and perfect pancakes to heart-healthy grain bowls and warm oatmeal.

BLT GRAIN
BOWLS

BLT GRAIN BOWLS

I absolutely love a BLT with sliced avocado and a poached egg. Lately I've been trying grain bowls, and I thought the flavors of my favorite sandwich would work well in one. My family agreed!
—Elisabeth Larsen, Pleasant Grove, UT

- -

Prep: 15 min. • **Cook:** 20 min.
Makes: 4 servings

- 1 cup quinoa, rinsed
- 4 Tbsp. olive oil, divided
- 2 Tbsp. minced fresh basil
- 2 Tbsp. white wine vinegar, divided
- 1 Tbsp. lemon juice
- 4 large eggs
- 8 oz. cherry tomatoes
- 3 cups fresh arugula
- 1 small ripe avocado, peeled and sliced
- 4 bacon strips, cooked and crumbled

1. Prepare quinoa according to the package directions. Combine 3 Tbsp. olive oil, basil, 1 Tbsp. vinegar and lemon juice. Add to the cooked quinoa; stir to combine.
2. Place 2-3 in. of water in a large skillet with high sides; add remaining vinegar. Bring to a boil; adjust heat to maintain a gentle simmer. Break 1 cold egg at a time into a small cup; holding cup close to surface of water, slip egg into water. Cook, uncovered, until whites are completely set and yolks begin to thicken but are not hard, 3-5 minutes. Using a slotted spoon, lift eggs out of water. Keep warm.
3. In a large skillet, heat remaining oil over medium heat. Cook tomatoes until they begin to release their juices, 8-10 minutes. Add arugula; cook and stir just until arugula is wilted, 1-2 minutes.
4. To serve, divide quinoa evenly among 4 bowls. Add cherry tomatoes, arugula, avocado slices and crumbled bacon. Top each with a poached egg.
1 serving: 446 cal., 28g fat (5g sat. fat), 194mg chol., 228mg sod., 33g carb. (2g sugars, 6g fiber), 17g pro.

TEST KITCHEN TIP
Heating the cherry tomatoes brings out their rich, tomato-y flavor. It yields a homegrown taste any time of year.

APPLE PIE
STEEL-CUT OATMEAL

APPLE PIE STEEL-CUT OATMEAL

Dessert for breakfast? Try this slow-cooker oatmeal that tastes just like apple pie. The steel-cut oats have so much flavor and texture. We sprinkle toasted pecans on top.
—Angela Lively, Conroe, TX

- -

Prep: 10 min. • **Cook:** 6 hours
Makes: 8 servings

- 6 cups water
- 1½ cups steel-cut oats
- 1½ cups unsweetened applesauce
- ¼ cup maple syrup
- 1½ tsp. ground cinnamon
- ½ tsp. ground nutmeg
- ⅛ tsp. salt
- 1 large apple, chopped
  Optional: Sliced apples, toasted pecans and additional maple syrup

In a 4-qt. slow cooker, combine the first 7 ingredients. Cover and cook on low for 6-8 hours or until liquid is absorbed. Stir in chopped apple. If desired, top servings with apple slices, pecans and syrup.
1¼ cups: 171 cal., 2g fat (0 sat. fat), 0 chol., 39mg sod., 36g carb. (13g sugars, 4g fiber), 4g pro.

PRESSURE-COOKER RAISIN NUT OATMEAL

There's no better feeling than starting off the day with a great breakfast. I love that the oats, fruit and spices in this homey meal cook together on their own.
—Valerie Sauber, Adelanto, CA

- -

Prep: 10 min. + standing
Cook: 5 min. + releasing • **Makes:** 6 servings

- 3 cups vanilla almond milk
- ¾ cup steel-cut oats
- ¾ cup raisins
- 3 Tbsp. brown sugar
- 4½ tsp. butter
- ¾ tsp. ground cinnamon
- ½ tsp. salt
- 1 large apple, peeled and chopped
- ¼ cup chopped pecans

1. In a 6-qt. electric pressure cooker, combine the first 7 ingredients. Lock lid; close pressure-release valve. Adjust to pressure-cook on high for 5 minutes. Let pressure release naturally. Press cancel.
2. Stir in apple. Let stand for 10 minutes before serving (oatmeal will thicken upon standing). Spoon the oatmeal into bowls; sprinkle with pecans.
¾ cup: 272 cal., 9g fat (2g sat. fat), 8mg chol., 298mg sod., 47g carb. (29g sugars, 4g fiber), 4g pro.

SAUSAGE, EGG & CHEDDAR FARMER'S BREAKFAST

SAUSAGE, EGG & CHEDDAR FARMER'S BREAKFAST

This hearty combination of sausage, hash browns and eggs will warm you up on a cold winter morning.
—Bonnie Roberts, Newaygo, MI

- -

Takes: 30 min. • **Makes:** 4 servings

- 6 large eggs
- ⅓ cup 2% milk
- ½ tsp. dried parsley flakes
- ¼ tsp. salt
- 6 oz. bulk pork sausage
- 1 Tbsp. butter
- 1½ cups frozen cubed hash brown potatoes, thawed
- ¼ cup chopped onion
- 1 cup shredded cheddar cheese

1. Whisk eggs, milk, parsley and salt; set aside. In a 9-in. cast-iron or other heavy skillet, cook sausage over medium heat until no longer pink; remove and drain. In same skillet, heat butter over medium heat. Add potatoes and onion; cook and stir until tender, 5-7 minutes. Return sausage to pan.
2. Add egg mixture; cook and stir until almost set. Sprinkle with cheese. Cover and cook until cheese is melted, 1-2 minutes.
1 cup: 330 cal., 24g fat (11g sat. fat), 364mg chol., 612mg sod., 9g carb. (3g sugars, 1g fiber), 20g pro.

TEST KITCHEN TIP
If you don't have frozen hash brown potatoes handy, use par-cooked cubed potatoes.

THE BEST EVER PANCAKES

I'm not exaggerating when I say I make pancakes every weekend. I love them in any form and variation, and this is one of my favorite recipes. I hope it will be one of yours, too!

—James Schend, Deputy Editor

- -

Prep: 15 min. • **Cook:** 5 min./batch
Makes: 12 pancakes

- 1½ cups all-purpose flour
- 2 Tbsp. sugar
- 1 tsp. baking powder
- ½ tsp. baking soda
- ½ tsp. salt
- 1 cup buttermilk
- 2 large eggs, room temperature
- ¼ cup butter, melted
- 1 tsp. vanilla extract

1. In a large bowl, whisk together the first 5 ingredients. In another bowl, whisk the remaining ingredients; stir into the dry ingredients just until moistened.
2. Preheat griddle over medium heat. Lightly grease griddle. Pour the batter by ¼ cupfuls onto griddle; cook until bubbles on top begin to pop and bottoms are golden brown. Turn; cook until second side is golden brown.

3 pancakes: 360 cal., 15g fat (8g sat. fat), 126mg chol., 817mg sod., 45g carb. (10g sugars, 1g fiber), 10g pro.

THE BEST EVER PANCAKES

BLUEBERRY FRENCH TOAST

Sit down to hot-off-the-griddle stuffed French toast and fresh blueberry sauce in as little as a half hour. The bread is toasted to a golden brown, and the delectable filling features cream cheese mixed with blueberry preserves and maple syrup. The fast sauce is out of this world!

—*Taste of Home* Test Kitchen

- -

Takes: 30 min.
Makes: 8 servings (1¾ cups sauce)

- 1 pkg. (8 oz.) cream cheese, softened
- ¼ cup maple syrup, divided
- 2 Tbsp. blueberry preserves
- 16 slices French bread (½ in. thick)
- 2 large eggs
- 1 cup 2% milk
- 2 Tbsp. all-purpose flour
- 2 tsp. vanilla extract
- ¼ tsp. salt
- SAUCE
- 1 cup sugar
- 1 cup cold water
- 2 Tbsp. cornstarch
- 1 cup fresh or frozen blueberries
- 1 Tbsp. butter

1. Beat the cream cheese, 2 Tbsp. syrup and preserves in a small bowl. Spread over 8 slices of bread; top with remaining bread.
2. Whisk the eggs, milk, flour, vanilla, salt and remaining syrup in a shallow bowl. Dip both sides of sandwiches into egg mixture. Cook on a greased hot griddle until golden brown on both sides.
3. Combine the sugar, water and cornstarch until smooth in a small saucepan. Bring to a boil over medium heat; cook and stir for 3 minutes or until thickened. Stir in the blueberries; bring to a boil. Reduce heat and simmer for 8-10 minutes or until berries burst. Remove from heat; stir in butter. Serve with French toast.

1 serving: 354 cal., 13g fat (7g sat. fat), 62mg chol., 304mg sod., 55g carb. (38g sugars, 1g fiber), 6g pro.

BUTTERMILK PECAN WAFFLES

I like cooking with buttermilk. These nutty, golden waffles are my husband's favorite breakfast, so we enjoy them often. They're as easy to prepare as regular waffles, but their unique taste makes them exceptional.
—Edna Hoffman, Hebron, IN

Takes: 25 min.
Makes: 7 waffles (about 8 in. each)

- 2   cups all-purpose flour
- 1   Tbsp. baking powder
- 1   tsp. baking soda
- ½   tsp. salt
- 4   large eggs, room temperature
- 2   cups buttermilk
- ½   cup butter, melted
- 3   Tbsp. chopped pecans

1. In a large bowl, combine the flour, baking powder, baking soda and salt; set aside.
2. In a large bowl, beat eggs until light. Add buttermilk; mix well. Add dry ingredients and beat until batter is smooth. Stir in butter.
3. Pour about ¾ cup batter onto a lightly greased preheated waffle iron. Sprinkle with some chopped pecans. Bake according to the manufacturer's directions until golden brown. Repeat with the remaining batter and pecans.
1 waffle: 337 cal., 19g fat (10g sat. fat), 159mg chol., 762mg sod., 31g carb. (4g sugars, 1g fiber), 10g pro.

TEST KITCHEN TIP

No buttermilk? No problem! For each cup of buttermilk, you can use 1 Tbsp. white vinegar or lemon juice plus enough milk to measure 1 cup. Stir, then let stand for 5 minutes. You can also use 1 cup of plain yogurt or 1¾ tsp. cream of tartar plus 1 cup milk.

GREEN CHILE
BRUNCH BAKE

GREEN CHILE BRUNCH BAKE

Here's an easy make-ahead dish. It's filling, perfect for a crowd, and helps busy cooks get a hearty meal on the table.
—Trista Thinnes, Fort Worth, TX

Prep: 30 min. + chilling • **Bake:** 45 min.
Makes: 8 servings

- 1   lb. bulk pork sausage
- 10   cups cubed day-old French bread
- 2   cups shredded sharp cheddar cheese
- 1   can (4 oz.) mushroom stems and pieces, drained
- 5   green onions, chopped
- 6   large eggs
- 2¾   cups half-and-half cream
- 1   can (4 oz.) chopped green chiles, drained
- 1½   tsp. Worcestershire sauce
- ½   tsp. salt
- ¼   tsp. ground mustard
- ¼   tsp. paprika
- ¼   tsp. pepper
- ⅛ to ¼   tsp. hot pepper sauce

1. In a large skillet, cook the sausage over medium heat until no longer pink, breaking into crumbles, 5-7 minutes; drain and set aside. Place bread cubes in a greased 13x9-in. baking dish. Top with cheddar cheese, mushrooms, green onions and cooked sausage.
2. In a large bowl, whisk the remaining ingredients. Pour over layers. Refrigerate, covered, overnight.
3. Preheat oven to 350°. Remove strata from refrigerator while oven heats. Bake, uncovered, until a knife inserted near the center comes out clean, 45-50 minutes. Let stand 5-10 minutes before cutting.
1 piece: 503 cal., 34g fat (16g sat. fat), 239mg chol., 1052mg sod., 22g carb. (5g sugars, 1g fiber), 24g pro.

TASTE OF HOME

TEST KITCHEN

RECIPE OF THE YEAR

★ ★ ★ ★ ★

BUTTERMILK PECAN WAFFLES

ULTIMATE FRUITY GRANOLA

ULTIMATE FRUITY GRANOLA

Honey, maple syrup and vanilla coat this wonderfully crunchy treat that's fantastic no matter how you serve it—on its own, with cold milk or in a yogurt parfait.
—Sarah Vasques, Milford, NH

Prep: 15 min. • **Bake:** 20 min. + cooling
Makes: 9 cups

- 5 cups old-fashioned oats
- 1 cup sliced almonds
- ½ cup sunflower kernels
- ½ cup ground flaxseed
- ½ cup packed brown sugar
- ¼ cup maple syrup
- ¼ cup honey
- 2 Tbsp. canola oil
- ½ tsp. salt
- ½ tsp. ground cinnamon
- 1 tsp. vanilla extract
- ½ cup dried cranberries
- ½ cup dried banana chips
- ½ cup dried apricots, halved

1. In a large bowl, combine the oats, almonds, sunflower kernels and flax. In a small saucepan, combine the brown sugar, maple syrup, honey, oil, salt and cinnamon. Cook and stir over medium heat until brown sugar is dissolved and the mixture is heated through, 2-3 minutes. Remove from the heat; stir in vanilla. Pour over oat mixture and toss to coat.

2. Transfer to a 15x10x1-in. baking pan coated with cooking spray. Bake at 350° for 20-25 minutes or until golden brown, stirring every 8 minutes. Cool completely on a wire rack. Stir in dried fruits. Store granola in an airtight container.

½ cup: 253 cal., 10g fat (2g sat. fat), 0 chol., 86mg sod., 38g carb. (18g sugars, 5g fiber), 6g pro.

TEST KITCHEN TIP
Granola typically has healthy whole grains and nuts, but be aware of added sugar and sweetened dried fruit, too. Eat this calorie-dense cereal in relatively small portion sizes.

PRESSURE-COOKER RHUBARB COMPOTE WITH YOGURT

My grandma Dot made rhubarb compote and always had some in the freezer when I came to visit. This breakfast is a tribute to her. No two batches of rhubarb are exactly alike, so make sure to taste your compote before you chill it. It should be tart, but sometimes it needs a little extra sugar.
—Michael Hoffman, Brooklyn, NY

- -

Prep: 10 min. + chilling
Cook: 5 min. + releasing • **Makes:** 6 servings

- 2 **cups finely chopped fresh rhubarb**
- ⅓ **cup water**
- ¼ **cup sugar**
- 3 **cups reduced-fat plain Greek yogurt**
- 2 **Tbsp. honey**
- ¾ **cup sliced almonds, toasted**

1. Place rhubarb, water and sugar in a 6-qt. electric pressure cooker. Lock lid; close the pressure-release valve. Adjust to pressure-cook on high 3 minutes. Let pressure release naturally for 10 minutes; quick-release any remaining pressure. Transfer to a bowl; cool slightly. Refrigerate until cold.
2. In a small bowl, whisk yogurt and honey until blended. Spoon into serving dishes. Top with compote; sprinkle with almonds.
½ cup yogurt with about 2 Tbsp. compote and 2 Tbsp. almonds: 216 cal., 8g fat (2g sat. fat), 7mg chol., 49mg sod., 23g carb. (20g sugars, 2g fiber), 14g pro. **Diabetic exchanges:** 1 starch, 1 reduced-fat milk, 1 fat.

UPSIDE-DOWN BACON PANCAKE

Make a big impression when you present one family-size bacon pancake. The brown sugar adds sweetness that complements the salty bacon. If you can fit more bacon in the skillet and want to add more, go for it.
—Mindie Hilton, Susanville, CA

- -

Takes: 30 min. • **Makes:** 6 servings

- 6 **bacon strips, coarsely chopped**
- ¼ **cup packed brown sugar**
- 2 **cups complete buttermilk pancake mix**
- 1½ **cups water**
  Optional: Maple syrup and butter

1. In a large cast-iron or other ovenproof skillet, cook bacon over medium heat until crisp. Remove bacon to paper towels with a slotted spoon. Remove drippings, reserving 2 Tbsp.. Return bacon to pan with reserved drippings; sprinkle with brown sugar.
2. In a small bowl, combine pancake mix and water just until moistened. Pour into pan.
3. Bake at 350° until a toothpick inserted in the center comes out clean, 18-20 minutes. Cool for 10 minutes before inverting onto a serving plate. Serve warm, with maple syrup and butter if desired.
1 slice: 265 cal., 9g fat (3g sat. fat), 12mg chol., 802mg sod., 41g carb. (13g sugars, 1g fiber), 6g pro.

UPSIDE-DOWN
BACON PANCAKE

CHILES RELLENOS QUICHE

Wake up with a smoky kick of roasted green chiles. I keep the ingredients for this recipe on hand so I can whip up a tasty breakfast on demand.
—Linda Miritello, Mesa, AZ

- -

Prep: 25 min. • **Bake:** 35 min.
Makes: 6 servings

	Pastry for single-crust pie
2	Tbsp. cornmeal
1½	cups shredded Monterey Jack cheese
1	cup shredded cheddar cheese
1	can (4 oz.) chopped green chiles
3	large eggs
¾	cup sour cream
1	Tbsp. minced fresh cilantro
2	to 4 drops hot pepper sauce, optional

1. In a pie plate, line unpricked crust with a double thickness of heavy-duty foil. Bake at 450° for 8 minutes. Remove foil; bake for 5 minutes longer. Cool on a wire rack. Reduce heat to 350°.
2. Sprinkle cornmeal over bottom of crust. In a small bowl, combine cheeses; set aside ½ cup for topping. Add chiles to remaining cheese mixture; sprinkle into crust.
3. In a small bowl, whisk the eggs, sour cream, cilantro and hot pepper sauce if desired. Pour into crust; sprinkle with reserved cheese mixture.
4. Bake until a knife inserted in the center comes out clean, 35-40 minutes. Let stand for 5 minutes before cutting.
Freeze option: Cover and freeze unbaked quiche. To use, remove quiche from the freezer 30 minutes before baking (do not thaw). Preheat oven to 350°. Place on a baking sheet; cover edge loosely with foil. Bake quiche as directed, increasing time as necessary for a knife inserted in the center to come out clean.
1 slice: 444 cal., 31g fat (18g sat. fat), 178mg chol., 520mg sod., 23g carb. (3g sugars, 1g fiber), 17g pro.

GINGERBREAD-SPICED SYRUP

Here's a wonderful treat for the fall season. Stir a tablespoon into coffee, tea or cider. Drizzle it over pancakes, hot cereal or yogurt. Or use it as a glaze for chicken or pork chops. The possibilities are endless!
—Darlene Brenden, Salem, OR

- -

Prep: 20 min. • **Cook:** 30 min. + cooling
Makes: 2 cups

2	cinnamon sticks (3 in.), broken into pieces
16	whole cloves
3	Tbsp. coarsely chopped fresh gingerroot
1	tsp. whole allspice
1	tsp. whole peppercorns
2	cups sugar
2	cups water
2	Tbsp. honey
1	tsp. ground nutmeg

1. Place the first 5 ingredients on a double thickness of cheesecloth; bring up corners of cloth and tie with string to form a bag.
2. In a large saucepan, combine the sugar, water, honey, nutmeg and spice bag; bring to a boil. Reduce heat; simmer, uncovered, for 30-45 minutes or until the syrup reaches desired consistency.
3. Remove from the heat; cool to room temperature. Discard spice bag; transfer syrup to airtight containers. Store in the refrigerator for up to 1 month.
2 Tbsp.: 108 cal., 0 fat (0 sat. fat), 0 chol., 0 sod., 28g carb. (27g sugars, 0 fiber), 0 pro.

CHILES RELLENOS QUICHE

HAM & EGG POCKETS

Refrigerated crescent roll dough makes these savory breakfast pockets a snap to prepare. They taste great, too!
—*Taste of Home* Test Kitchen

Takes: 20 min. • **Makes:** 2 servings

1	large egg
2	tsp. 2% milk
2	tsp. butter
1	oz. thinly sliced deli ham, chopped
2	Tbsp. shredded cheddar cheese
1	tube (4 oz.) refrigerated crescent rolls

1. Preheat oven to 375°. In a small bowl, combine egg and milk. In a small skillet heat butter until hot. Add egg mixture; cook and stir over medium heat until egg is completely set. Remove from heat. Fold in ham and cheese.

2. On a greased baking sheet, separate crescent dough into 2 rectangles. Seal perforations; spoon half of the filling down the center of each rectangle. Fold in ends and sides; pinch to seal. Bake until golden brown, 10-14 minutes.

1 sandwich: 345 cal., 22g fat (8g sat. fat), 132mg chol., 756mg sod., 23g carb. (5g sugars, 0 fiber), 12g pro.

ALMOND-CHAI GRANOLA

Whether you snack on it by the handful or eat it with milk or yogurt, you'll be happy that you found this granola recipe.
—Rachel Preus, Marshall, MI

Prep: 20 min. • **Bake:** 1¼ hours + cooling
Makes: 8 cups

2	chai tea bags
¼	cup boiling water
3	cups quick-cooking oats
2	cups almonds, coarsely chopped
1	cup sweetened shredded coconut
½	cup honey
¼	cup olive oil
⅓	cup sugar
2	tsp. vanilla extract
¾	tsp. salt
¾	tsp. ground cinnamon
¾	tsp. ground nutmeg
¼	tsp. ground cardamom

1. Preheat oven to 250°. Steep chai tea bags in boiling water 5 minutes. Meanwhile, combine the oats, almonds and coconut. Discard tea bags; stir remaining ingredients into tea. Pour tea mixture over oat mixture; mix well to coat.

2. Spread evenly in a greased 15x10-in. rimmed pan. Bake until golden brown, stirring every 20 minutes, about 1¼ hours. Cool completely without stirring; store in an airtight container.

½ cup: 272 cal., 16g fat (3g sat. fat), 0 chol., 130mg sod., 29g carb. (16g sugars, 4g fiber), 6g pro. **Diabetic exchanges:** 3 fat, 2 starch.

ALMOND-CHAI GRANOLA

SOUTHWEST
SAUSAGE BAKE

SOUTHWEST SAUSAGE BAKE

This layered tortilla dish is not only tasty, but a timesaver, too, because it's made the night before. Serve with muffins and fruit.
—Barbara Waddel, Lincoln, NE

- -

Prep: 15 min. + chilling
Bake: 1 hour + standing • **Makes:** 12 servings

- 6 flour tortillas (10 in.), cut into ½-in. strips
- 4 cans (4 oz. each) chopped green chiles, drained
- 1 lb. bulk pork sausage, cooked and drained
- 2 cups shredded Monterey Jack cheese
- 10 large eggs, lightly beaten
- ½ cup 2% milk
- ½ tsp. each salt, garlic salt, onion salt, pepper and ground cumin Paprika
- 2 medium tomatoes, sliced Sour cream and salsa

1. In a greased 13x9-in. baking dish, layer half of the tortilla strips, chiles, sausage and cheese. Repeat layers.
2. In a bowl, whisk the eggs, milk and salt, garlic salt, onion salt, pepper and ground cumin; pour over cheese. Sprinkle with paprika. Cover and refrigerate overnight.
3. Remove from the refrigerator 30 minutes before baking. Bake, uncovered, at 350° for 50 minutes. Arrange tomato slices over the top. Bake 10-15 minutes longer or until a knife inserted in the center comes out clean. Let stand for 10 minutes before cutting. Serve with sour cream and salsa.
1 piece: 329 cal., 19g fat (8g sat. fat), 209mg chol., 701mg sod., 19g carb. (2g sugars, 3g fiber), 16g pro.

> When I first tasted this hearty breakfast bake in the Test Kitchen, I knew it would become a staple in my house. I've made it more times than I can count. It travels well, too, for brunch contributions.

—MARK HAGEN, EXECUTIVE EDITOR

TOAD IN THE HOLE BACON SANDWICH

TOAD IN THE HOLE BACON SANDWICH

Switch up the cheese—pepper jack gives a nice kick—or use sliced kielbasa, ham or sausage in place of the bacon in this versatile grilled cheese sandwich.
—Kallee Krong-McCreery, Escondido, CA

- -

Takes: 15 min. • **Makes:** 1 serving

- 2 slices sourdough bread
- 1 Tbsp. mayonnaise
- 1 large egg
- 1 slice cheddar cheese
- 2 cooked bacon strips

1. Using a biscuit cutter or round cookie cutter, cut out center of 1 slice of bread (discard center or save for another use). Spread mayonnaise on 1 side of bread slices. In a large skillet coated with cooking spray, lightly toast cutout slice, mayonnaise side down, over medium-low heat. Flip slice; crack an egg into center. Add remaining bread slice mayonnaise side down, to skillet; layer with cheese and bacon.
2. Cook, covered, until egg white is set, yolk is soft-set and cheese begins to melt. If needed, flip slice with egg to finish cooking. To assemble sandwich, use solid slice as bottom and cutout slice as top.
1 sandwich: 610 cal., 34g fat (11g sat. fat), 240mg chol., 1220mg sod., 46g carb. (4g sugars, 2g fiber), 30g pro.

SAVORY APPLE-CHICKEN SAUSAGE

These sausages taste incredible, make an elegant brunch dish and are healthier than their ground pork counterpart. The recipe is versatile, as it can be doubled or tripled for a crowd, and the sausage freezes well either cooked or raw.
—Angela Buchanan, Longmont, CO

- -

Takes: 25 min. • **Makes:** 8 patties

- 1 large tart apple, peeled and diced
- 2 tsp. poultry seasoning
- 1 tsp. salt
- ¼ tsp. pepper
- 1 lb. ground chicken

1. In a large bowl, combine the first 4 ingredients. Crumble chicken over the mixture and mix well. Shape into eight 3-in. patties.

2. In a large, greased cast-iron or other heavy skillet, cook patties over medium heat until no longer pink, 5-6 minutes on each side. Drain if necessary.

1 sausage patty: 92 cal., 5g fat (1g sat. fat), 38mg chol., 328mg sod., 4g carb. (3g sugars, 1g fiber), 9g pro. **Diabetic exchanges:** 1 medium-fat meat.

PUFF PANCAKE WITH BOURBON PEACHES

PUFF PANCAKE WITH BOURBON PEACHES

I think I could easily make this breakfast every weekend when we are smack dab in the middle of peach season.
—James Schend, Deputy Editor

- -

Prep: 20 min. • **Cook:** 20 min.
Makes: 6 servings

- 1 Tbsp. butter
- 3 large eggs, room temperature, lightly beaten
- ½ cup 2% milk
- 1 tsp. vanilla extract
- ⅛ tsp. salt
- ½ cup all-purpose flour
- 1 cup water
- 4 Tbsp. bourbon or peach nectar, divided
- 2 Tbsp. honey
- 2 Tbsp. peach preserves
- 3 cups sliced peeled peaches (about 5 medium) or frozen unsweetened sliced peaches

1. Preheat oven to 400°. Place butter in a 9-in. deep-dish pie plate; heat in oven until butter is melted, 2-3 minutes. Meanwhile, in a small bowl, whisk eggs, milk, vanilla and salt until blended; gradually whisk in the flour. Remove pie plate from oven; tilt carefully to coat the bottom and sides with butter. Immediately pour in egg mixture. Bake until puffed and browned, 18-22 minutes.

2. Meanwhile, in a large saucepan, combine water, 3 Tbsp. bourbon, honey and peach preserves. Bring to a boil; reduce heat. Add peaches; cook and stir for 3-4 minutes or until tender. Remove peaches to a bowl; set aside. Bring sauce mixture to a boil; cook and stir until reduced to ½ cup. Remove from heat; stir in peaches and the remaining 1 Tbsp. bourbon.

3. Remove pancake from oven. Serve immediately with warm peach sauce.

1 serving: 192 cal., 5g fat (2g sat. fat), 100mg chol., 110mg sod., 27g carb. (17g sugars, 1g fiber), 6g pro.

VEGGIE-PACKED STRATA

Folks are always eager to try this deliciously different casserole featuring eggs, veggies and cheese. Baked in a springform pan, the colorful strata catches attention no matter where it's served.
—Jennifer Unsell, Vance, AL

- -

Prep: 25 min.
Bake: 1 hour 20 min. + standing
Makes: 8 servings

- 2 medium sweet red peppers, julienned
- 1 medium sweet yellow pepper, julienned
- 1 large red onion, sliced
- 3 Tbsp. olive oil, divided
- 3 garlic cloves, minced
- 2 medium yellow summer squash, thinly sliced
- 2 medium zucchini, thinly sliced
- ½ lb. fresh mushrooms, sliced
- 1 pkg. (8 oz.) cream cheese, softened
- ¼ cup heavy whipping cream
- 2 tsp. salt
- 1 tsp. pepper
- 6 large eggs, room temperature
- 8 slices bread, cut into ½-in. cubes (about 6 cups), divided
- 2 cups shredded Swiss cheese

1. In a large skillet, saute peppers and onion in 1 Tbsp. oil until tender. Add garlic; cook 1 minute longer. Drain; pat dry and set aside. In the same skillet, saute the yellow squash, zucchini and mushrooms in the remaining 2 Tbsp. oil until tender. Drain; pat dry and set aside.

2. Preheat oven to 325°. In a large bowl, beat cream cheese, cream, salt and pepper until smooth. Beat in eggs. Stir in vegetables, half of the bread cubes and Swiss cheese. Arrange the remaining bread cubes in a greased 10-in. springform pan. Place on a baking sheet. Pour egg mixture into pan.

3. Bake the strata, uncovered, until set and a thermometer reads 160°, 80-95 minutes. Let stand for 10-15 minutes before serving. Run a knife around the edge of pan to loosen; remove sides. Cut into wedges.

1 piece: 453 cal., 31g fat (15g sat. fat), 202mg chol., 938mg sod., 26g carb. (8g sugars, 3g fiber), 19g pro.

BREAKFAST IN A PAN

Try this easy one-pan dish for breakfast or brunch. It also works well with bacon or sausage instead of ham. I sometimes saute chopped peppers and onions until tender and whisk them in with the eggs for added flavor and color.
—Andrea Bolden, Unionville, TN

- -

Prep: 15 min. • **Bake:** 25 min.
Makes: 6 servings

- 1 tube (8 oz.) refrigerated crescent rolls
- 2 cups cubed fully cooked ham
- 2 cups frozen shredded hash brown potatoes, thawed
- 5 large eggs
- ½ cup 2% milk
- ½ tsp. pepper
- ⅛ tsp. salt
- 2 cups shredded cheddar cheese

1. Preheat oven to 350°. Unroll crescent dough into a long rectangle; press the perforations to seal. Press onto bottom of a greased 13x9-in. baking pan. Top with ham and potatoes.

2. In a large bowl, whisk eggs, milk, pepper and salt until blended; pour over potatoes. Sprinkle with cheese. Bake until set and cheese is melted, 25-30 minutes.

1 piece: 434 cal., 26g fat (9g sat. fat), 222mg chol., 1216mg sod., 23g carb. (6g sugars, 0 fiber), 28g pro.

VEGGIE-PACKED STRATA

MUSHROOM &
LEEK PIE

MIXED BERRY FRENCH TOAST BAKE

I love this recipe! It's perfect for fuss-free holiday breakfasts or serving company. It's scrumptious and so easy to put together the night before.
—Amy Berry, Poland, ME

- -

Prep: 20 min. + chilling • **Bake:** 45 min.
Makes: 8 servings

> 6 large eggs
> 1¾ cups fat-free milk
> 1 tsp. sugar
> 1 tsp. ground cinnamon
> 1 tsp. vanilla extract
> ¼ tsp. salt
> 1 loaf (1 lb.) French bread, cubed
> 1 pkg. (12 oz.) frozen unsweetened mixed berries
> 2 Tbsp. cold butter
> ⅓ cup packed brown sugar
>   Optional: Confectioners' sugar and maple syrup

1. Whisk together first 6 ingredients. Place bread cubes in a 13x9-in. or 3-qt. baking dish coated with cooking spray. Pour the egg mixture over top. Refrigerate, covered, 8 hours or overnight.
2. Preheat oven to 350°. Remove berries from freezer and French toast from the refrigerator and let stand while oven heats. Bake, covered, 30 minutes.
3. In a small bowl, cut butter into brown sugar until crumbly. Top French toast with berries; sprinkle with brown sugar mixture. Bake, uncovered, until a knife inserted in the center comes out clean, 15-20 minutes. If desired, dust with confectioners' sugar and serve with syrup.

1 serving: 310 cal., 8g fat (3g sat. fat), 148mg chol., 517mg sod., 46g carb. (17g sugars, 3g fiber), 13g pro.

MUSHROOM & LEEK PIE

We live in the Pacific Northwest and often forage for the mushrooms we use in this pie. We like chanterelle, but baby portobello or oyster mushrooms are delicious, too.
—Vickie Woods, Salem, OR

- -

Prep: 30 min. + chilling • **Bake:** 30 min.
Makes: 8 servings

>   Pastry for single-crust pie
> 12 oz. fresh chanterelle, baby portobello or oyster mushrooms, or a combination of mushrooms
> 3 Tbsp. butter, divided
> 1 medium leek (white portion only), halved and sliced
> ½ tsp. salt
> ¼ tsp. pepper
> 1 cup shredded cheddar cheese
> 4 large eggs
> 3 Tbsp. heavy whipping cream
>   Minced fresh parsley, optional

1. Preheat oven to 375°. On a lightly floured surface, roll dough to a ⅛-in.-thick circle; transfer to a 9-in. pie plate. Trim crust to ½ in. beyond rim of plate; flute edge. Refrigerate while preparing filling.
2. Wipe the mushrooms clean with a damp tea towel. Trim the stems; quarter or slice large mushrooms.
3. In a large skillet, heat 1 Tbsp. butter over medium-high heat. Add leek; cook and stir 2-3 minutes or until tender. Remove from the pan.
4. In same pan, heat remaining butter over medium-high heat. Add mushrooms; cook 4-6 minutes or until tender and liquid has evaporated. Stir in leek, salt and pepper. Cool slightly.
5. Sprinkle ½ cup cheese onto bottom of crust. Top with mushroom mixture; sprinkle with remaining cheese. In a large bowl, whisk eggs and cream until blended; pour over top.
6. Bake on a lower oven rack 30-35 minutes or until a knife inserted in the center comes out clean. If desired, sprinkle with parsley before serving.
Pastry for single-crust pie: Combine 1¼ cups all-purpose flour and ¼ tsp. salt; cut in ½ cup cold butter until crumbly. Gradually add 3-5 Tbsp. ice water, tossing with a fork until dough holds together when pressed. Cover and refrigerate 1 hour.
1 piece: 338 cal., 25g fat (15g sat. fat), 157mg chol., 470mg sod., 18g carb. (2g sugars, 1g fiber), 10g pro.

MIXED BERRY
FRENCH TOAST BAKE

EGG BURRITOS

EGG BURRITOS

Zap one of these frozen burritos in the microwave and you'll stave off hunger all morning. This recipe is my family's favorite combo, but I sometimes use breakfast sausage instead of bacon.

—Audra Niederman, Aberdeen, SD

Takes: 25 min. • **Makes:** 10 burritos

- 12 **bacon strips, chopped**
- 12 **large eggs**
- ½ **tsp. salt**
- ¼ **tsp. pepper**
- 10 **flour tortillas (8 in.), warmed**
- 1½ **cups shredded cheddar cheese**
- 4 **green onions, thinly sliced**

1. In a large cast-iron or other heavy skillet, cook the bacon until crisp; drain on paper towels. Remove all but 1-2 Tbsp. drippings from pan.

2. Whisk together eggs, salt and pepper. Heat skillet over medium heat; pour in egg mixture. Cook and stir until the eggs are thickened and no liquid egg remains; remove from heat.

3. Spoon about ¼ cup egg mixture onto center of each tortilla; sprinkle with cheese, bacon and green onions. Roll into burritos.

Freeze option: Cool eggs before making burritos. Individually wrap burritos in paper towels and foil; freeze in an airtight container. To use, remove foil; place paper towel-wrapped burrito on a microwave-safe plate. Microwave on high until heated through, turning once. Let stand 15 seconds.

1 burrito: 376 cal., 20g fat (8g sat. fat), 251mg chol., 726mg sod., 29g carb. (0 sugars, 2g fiber), 19g pro.

TEST KITCHEN TIP
Breakfast burritos are a smart choice to start the day because they include a good amount of protein. To make these healthier, use whole wheat tortillas, skip the bacon, reduce the cheese and add more vegetables.

PEACHES & CREAM WAFFLE DIPPERS

I've made these for many brunches using strawberries and blueberries, but peaches are my favorite. We love dipping the waffle strips into the dreamy whipped cream.
—Bonnie Geavaras, Chandler, AZ

Prep: 30 min. • **Bake:** 5 min./batch
Makes: 6 servings (2 cups sauce)

- 1 cup all-purpose flour
- 1 Tbsp. sugar
- 1 tsp. baking powder
- ¼ tsp. salt
- 2 large eggs, separated
- 1 cup 2% milk
- 2 Tbsp. butter, melted
- ¼ tsp. vanilla extract
- 1¼ cups chopped frozen peaches, thawed, divided
- 2 cups sweetened whipped cream or whipped topping
- ¾ cup peach yogurt
   Optional: Toasted pecans and ground cinnamon

1. In a large bowl, whisk flour, sugar, baking powder and salt. In another bowl, whisk egg yolks, milk, butter and vanilla until blended. Add to the dry ingredients; stir just until moistened. Stir in 1 cup peaches.
2. In a small bowl, beat the egg whites until stiff but not dry. Fold into batter. Bake in a preheated waffle maker according to manufacturer's directions until golden brown. Cut waffles into 1-in. strips.
3. In a small bowl, fold whipped cream into yogurt. Serve with waffles. Sprinkle with remaining peaches and, if desired, pecans and cinnamon.
8 waffle strips with ⅓ cup sauce: 341 cal., 21g fat (13g sat. fat), 122mg chol., 279mg sod., 30g carb. (14g sugars, 1g fiber), 8g pro.

HEARTY BREAKFAST EGG BAKE

I fix this casserole in advance when I host overnight guests, so I have more time to spend with them. Then, I simply add some toast or biscuits and fresh fruit for a meal that everyone loves. It also reheats well.
—Pamela Norris, Fenton, MO

Prep: 10 min. + chilling
Bake: 45 min. + standing • **Makes:** 8 servings

- 1½ lbs. bulk pork sausage
- 3 cups frozen shredded hash brown potatoes, thawed
- 2 cups shredded cheddar cheese
- 8 large eggs, lightly beaten
- 1 can (10¾ oz.) condensed cream of mushroom soup, undiluted
- ¾ cup evaporated milk

1. Crumble sausage into a large skillet. Cook over medium heat until no longer pink; drain. Transfer to a greased 13x9-in. baking dish. Sprinkle with hash browns and cheese.
2. In a large bowl, whisk the remaining ingredients; pour over the top. Cover and refrigerate overnight.
3. Remove from the refrigerator 30 minutes before baking. Bake, uncovered, at 350° for 45-50 minutes or until a knife inserted in the center comes out clean. Let casserole stand for 10 minutes before cutting.
1 piece: 427 cal., 32g fat (15g sat. fat), 281mg chol., 887mg sod., 12g carb. (4g sugars, 1g fiber), 21g pro.

PEACHES & CREAM WAFFLE DIPPERS

SHIITAKE & MANCHEGO SCRAMBLE

This savory breakfast dish takes everyday scrambled eggs up a few notches. The rich flavor is so satisfying in the morning, and it's even better served with buttery toasted Italian bread.

—Thomas Faglon, Somerset, NJ

- -

Takes: 25 min. • **Makes:** 8 servings

- 2 Tbsp. extra virgin olive oil, divided
- ½ cup diced onion
- ½ cup diced sweet red pepper
- 2 cups thinly sliced fresh shiitake mushrooms (about 4 oz.)
- 1 tsp. prepared horseradish
- 8 large eggs, beaten
- 1 cup heavy whipping cream
- 1 cup shredded Manchego cheese
- 1 tsp. kosher salt
- 1 tsp. coarsely ground pepper

1. In a large nonstick skillet, heat 1 Tbsp. olive oil over medium heat. Add onion and red pepper; cook and stir until crisp-tender, 2-3 minutes. Add mushrooms; cook and stir until tender, 3-4 minutes. Stir in horseradish; cook 2 minutes more.

2. In a small bowl, whisk together remaining ingredients and remaining olive oil. Pour into skillet; cook and stir until eggs are thickened and no liquid egg remains.

1 serving: 274 cal., 24g fat (12g sat. fat), 234mg chol., 405mg sod., 4g carb. (2g sugars, 1g fiber), 11g pro.

SCRAMBLED EGG HASH BROWN CUPS

These cuties pack all of your favorite breakfast foods—eggs, hash browns and bacon—in one single serving-sized cup. Grab one and get mingling.

—Talon DiMare, Bullhead City, AZ

- -

Prep: 10 min. • **Bake:** 25 min.
Makes: 1 dozen

- 1 pkg. (20 oz.) refrigerated Southwest-style shredded hash brown potatoes
- 6 large eggs
- ½ cup 2% milk
- ⅛ tsp. salt
- 1 Tbsp. butter
- 10 thick-sliced bacon strips, cooked and crumbled
- 1¼ cups shredded cheddar-Monterey Jack cheese, divided

1. Preheat oven to 400°. Divide potatoes among 12 greased muffin cups; press onto bottoms and up sides to form cups. Bake 18-20 minutes or until light golden brown.
2. Meanwhile, in a small bowl, whisk eggs, milk and salt. In a large nonstick skillet, heat butter over medium heat. Pour in the egg mixture; cook and stir until the eggs are thickened and no liquid egg remains. Stir in bacon and ¾ cup cheese. Spoon into cups; sprinkle with remaining ½ cup cheese.
3. Bake 3-5 minutes or until cheese is melted. Cool 5 minutes before removing from pan.
1 hash brown cup: 180 cal., 10g fat (5g sat. fat), 113mg chol., 487mg sod., 11g carb. (1g sugars, 1g fiber), 10g pro.

SHIITAKE & MANCHEGO SCRAMBLE

MOM'S POTATO PANCAKES

Old-fashioned potato pancakes are fluffy inside and crispy outside. Mom got this recipe from Grandma, so we've enjoyed it for years.
—Dianne Esposite, New Middletown, OH

Takes: 30 min. • **Makes:** 6 servings

- 4 cups shredded peeled potatoes (about 4 large potatoes)
- 1 large egg, lightly beaten
- 3 Tbsp. all-purpose flour
- 1 Tbsp. grated onion
- 1 tsp. salt
- ¼ tsp. pepper
  Oil for frying
  Optional: Chopped parsley, applesauce and sour cream

1. Rinse shredded potatoes in cold water; drain well, squeezing to remove excess water. Place in a large bowl. Stir in egg, flour, onion, salt and pepper.
2. In a large nonstick skillet, heat ¼ in. oil over medium heat. Working in batches, drop potato mixture by ⅓ cupfuls into oil; press to flatten slightly. Fry both sides until golden brown; drain on paper towels. Serve immediately. If desired, sprinkle with parsley and top with applesauce and sour cream.
2 pancakes: 171 cal., 7g fat (1g sat. fat), 31mg chol., 411mg sod., 24g carb. (1g sugars, 2g fiber), 3g pro.

BUTTERMILK
BUCKWHEAT PANCAKES

BUTTERMILK BUCKWHEAT PANCAKES

This flapjack recipe uses buckwheat flour instead of the wheat-based variety. The light and tender pancakes offer a nutty flavor and hearty texture.
—*Taste of Home* Test Kitchen

Takes: 25 min. • **Makes:** 8 pancakes

- 1 cup buckwheat flour
- 2 Tbsp. brown sugar
- 1 tsp. baking powder
- ½ tsp. baking soda
- ½ tsp. salt
- ⅛ tsp. ground cinnamon
- ⅛ tsp. ground nutmeg
- ⅛ tsp. ground cloves
- 1 large egg
- 1 cup buttermilk
- 1 Tbsp. butter, melted
  Optional: Maple syrup and additional butter

1. Combine first 8 ingredients. Whisk the egg, buttermilk and butter; stir into dry ingredients just until moistened.
2. Preheat a lightly greased griddle over medium heat. Pour batter by ¼ cupfuls onto griddle; turn when bubbles on top begin to pop. Cook until second side is golden brown. If desired, serve pancakes with maple syrup and additional butter.
2 pancakes: 195 cal., 6g fat (3g sat. fat), 63mg chol., 667mg sod., 31g carb. (11g sugars, 3g fiber), 7g pro. **Diabetic exchanges:** 2 starch, 1 fat.

HONEY BAGELS
PAGE 77

Breads, Biscuits & More

Anyone who's ever worked in a test kitchen or bakery can attest to the heavenly aroma of freshly baked bread floating through the halls. You can experience all the divine smells, tastes and textures in the comfort of your own kitchen when you give one of these baked beauties a try. Tender and delicate, drizzled with icing, or boasting a blend of herbs or seasonings, these make the perfect companion to any meal.

FLUFFY
BISCUITS

FLUFFY BISCUITS

If you're looking for a flaky basic biscuit, this recipe is the best. These golden brown rolls bake up tall, light and tender. Their mild flavor is even better when the warm biscuits are spread with butter or jam.
—Nancy Horsburgh, Everett, ON

- -

Takes: 30 min. • **Makes:** about 8 biscuits

```
2   cups all-purpose flour
4   tsp. baking powder
1   Tbsp. sugar
½   tsp. salt
½   cup shortening
1   large egg, room temperature
⅔   cup 2% milk
```

1. Preheat oven to 400°. In a bowl, whisk together the first 4 ingredients. Cut in the shortening until the mixture resembles coarse crumbs. Whisk together egg and milk. Add to the dry ingredients; stir just until moistened.

2. On a well-floured surface, knead dough gently 8-10 times. Roll to ½-in. thickness; cut with a floured 2½-in. biscuit cutter. Place on a lightly greased baking sheet.

3. Bake until golden brown, 10-12 minutes. Serve warm.

1 biscuit: 249 cal., 13g fat (4g sat. fat), 25mg chol., 407mg sod., 26g carb. (3g sugars, 1g fiber), 5g pro.

Italian Biscuits: Add 1 tsp. Italian seasoning to the flour mixture.

TEST KITCHEN TIP
Help that dough rise straight and tall. Dip your biscuit cutter in flour, then push it straight down into the dough and pull straight back up. Avoid twisting the cutter. Dip it in flour after each use to prevent sticking.

GOLDEN SWEET
ONION CORNBREAD

GOLDEN SWEET ONION CORNBREAD

Put your cast-iron skillet to a new use when you bake up this hearty cornbread inside it.
—*Taste of Home* Test Kitchen

- -

Prep: 35 min. • **Bake:** 20 min. + standing
Makes: 8 servings

```
2    Tbsp. butter
1    large sweet onion, halved
     and thinly sliced
4    tsp. chopped seeded
     jalapeno pepper
½    tsp. chili powder, divided
2    Tbsp. brown sugar, divided
1½   cups all-purpose flour
1    cup yellow cornmeal
3    Tbsp. sugar
2    tsp. baking powder
½    tsp. kosher salt
½    tsp. baking soda
1¼   cups buttermilk
2    large eggs, room temperature,
     lightly beaten
¼    cup butter, melted
¾    cup shredded cheddar cheese
1    can (4 oz.) chopped green chiles
```
CRANBERRY BUTTER
```
½    cup whole-berry cranberry sauce
½    tsp. grated lime zest
½    cup butter, softened
```

1. In a 10-in. cast-iron skillet, melt 2 Tbsp. butter; tilt to coat bottom and sides. Add the onion, jalapeno and ¼ tsp. chili powder; cook over medium-low heat until onion is lightly browned and tender. Stir in 1 Tbsp. brown sugar until dissolved; set aside.

2. In a large mixing bowl, combine the flour, cornmeal, sugar, baking powder, salt, baking soda, and remaining chili powder and brown sugar. In a small bowl, whisk the buttermilk, eggs and melted butter. Stir into the dry ingredients just until moistened. Fold in the cheese and chiles.

3. Pour over onion mixture in skillet. Bake at 425° for 20-25 minutes or until golden brown. Meanwhile, in a small saucepan, cook cranberry sauce and lime zest over low heat until heated through. Cool completely.

4. Let cornbread stand for 10 minutes. Invert cornbread onto a serving platter; cut into wedges. Pour cranberry mixture over softened butter; serve with cornbread.

Note: Wear disposable gloves when cutting hot peppers; the oils can burn skin. Avoid touching your face.

1 slice with 1 Tbsp. butter and 1 Tbsp. cranberry mixture: 468 cal., 25g fat (16g sat. fat), 118mg chol., 626mg sod., 52g carb. (17g sugars, 3g fiber), 10g pro.

BACON-APPLE CIDER BISCUITS

The sweet and salty flavors of apple and bacon make these special biscuits from our Test Kitchen stand out. Be prepared to make more—they go fast!
—*Taste of Home* Test Kitchen

- -

Prep: 20 min. • **Bake:** 15 min.
Makes: 8 biscuits

- 2 **cups all-purpose flour**
- 2 **tsp. baking powder**
- 2 **tsp. brown sugar**
- ½ **tsp. salt**
- ¼ **tsp. baking soda**
- ¼ **tsp. apple pie spice**
- 8 **Tbsp. cold butter, cubed, divided**
- 5 **bacon strips, cooked and crumbled**
- ¾ **cup apple cider or juice**
- ⅛ **tsp. ground cinnamon**

1. In a large bowl, combine the first 6 ingredients. Cut in 7 Tbsp. butter until mixture resembles coarse crumbs. Add bacon. Stir in cider just until combined.
2. Turn onto a lightly floured surface; knead 8-10 times. Roll into a 10x6-in. rectangle. Melt remaining butter; brush over dough. Sprinkle with cinnamon.
3. Cut into 8 rectangles. Place 1 in. apart on an ungreased baking sheet. Bake at 450° for 12-15 minutes or until golden brown. Serve warm.
1 biscuit: 251 cal., 13g fat (8g sat. fat), 34mg chol., 462mg sod., 28g carb. (4g sugars, 1g fiber), 5g pro.

PINA COLADA ZUCCHINI BREAD

PINA COLADA ZUCCHINI BREAD

My husband encouraged me to enter this recipe at the Pennsylvania Farm Show—and I won first place! You will love the cakelike texture and tropical flavors.
—Sharon Rydbom, Tipton, PA

- -

Prep: 25 min. • **Bake:** 45 min. + cooling
Makes: 3 loaves (12 slices each)

- 4 **cups all-purpose flour**
- 3 **cups sugar**
- 2 **tsp. baking powder**
- 1½ **tsp. salt**
- 1 **tsp. baking soda**
- 4 **large eggs, room temperature**
- 1½ **cups canola oil**
- 1 **tsp. each coconut, rum and vanilla extracts**
- 3 **cups shredded zucchini**
- 1 **cup canned crushed pineapple, drained**
- ½ **cup chopped walnuts or chopped pecans**

1. Line the bottoms of 3 greased and floured 8x4-in. loaf pans with waxed paper and grease the paper; set aside.
2. In a large bowl, combine the flour, sugar, baking powder, salt and baking soda. In another bowl, whisk the eggs, oil and extracts. Stir into dry ingredients just until moistened. Fold in the zucchini, pineapple and walnuts.
3. Transfer to prepared pans. Bake at 350° for 45-55 minutes or until a toothpick inserted in the center comes out clean. Cool for 10 minutes before removing from pans to wire racks. Gently remove waxed paper.
1 slice: 225 cal., 11g fat (1g sat. fat), 24mg chol., 165mg sod., 29g carb. (18g sugars, 1g fiber), 3g pro.

HAM BISCUITS

Our Test Kitchen pros made ordinary biscuits even heartier by stirring in ground ham. These hand-held goodies are great fresh from the oven.
—*Taste of Home* Test Kitchen

Prep: 30 min. • **Bake:** 15 min.
Makes: 10 biscuits

- 1 cup cubed fully cooked ham
- 1 cup all-purpose flour
- 1 tsp. baking powder
- ¼ tsp. baking soda
- ¼ tsp. each onion powder, garlic powder and ground mustard
- 3 Tbsp. shortening
- 1 tsp. minced chives
- 6 Tbsp. buttermilk
- 1 Tbsp. butter, melted

1. In a food processor, process ham until ground; set aside. In a large bowl, combine the flour, baking powder, baking soda, onion powder, garlic powder and mustard. Cut in shortening until mixture is crumbly. Fold in ham and chives. Add buttermilk; stir just until the dough clings together.

2. Turn onto a lightly floured surface; knead gently 10-12 times. Roll the dough to ½-in. thickness. Cut with a floured 2½-in. biscuit cutter. Place in a large ungreased cast-iron or other ovenproof skillet. Bake at 450° until golden brown, 13-15 minutes. Brush with butter. Serve warm.

1 biscuit: 116 cal., 6g fat (2g sat. fat), 11mg chol., 272mg sod., 10g carb. (1g sugars, 0 fiber), 4g pro.

HERB-HAPPY GARLIC BREAD

You'll love the fresh garlic and herbs in this recipe. The mild goat cheese that's sprinkled on top makes it extra rich and wonderful.
—*Taste of Home* Test Kitchen

Takes: 15 min. • **Makes:** 12 servings

- ½ cup butter, softened
- ¼ cup grated Romano cheese
- 2 Tbsp. minced fresh basil or 2 tsp. dried basil
- 1 Tbsp. minced fresh parsley
- 3 garlic cloves, minced
- 1 French bread baguette
- 4 oz. crumbled goat cheese

1. In a small bowl, mix the first 5 ingredients until blended. Cut baguette crosswise in half; cut each piece lengthwise in half. Spread the cut sides with butter mixture. Place on an ungreased baking sheet.

2. Bake, uncovered, at 425° until lightly toasted, 7-9 minutes. Sprinkle with goat cheese; bake until goat cheese is softened, 1-2 minutes longer. Cut into slices.

1 slice: 169 cal., 11g fat (7g sat. fat), 35mg chol., 307mg sod., 14g carb. (0 sugars, 1g fiber), 5g pro.

HAM BISCUITS

STRAWBERRIES &
CREAM BREAD

JALAPENO CORNBREAD FILLED WITH BLUEBERRY QUICK JAM

Fresh jalapenos and blueberry quick jam make the perfect blend of sweet and spicy in this special cornbread. After your first piece, you'll go back for a second!
—Colleen Delawder, Herndon, VA

- -

Prep: 20 min. + chilling
Bake: 30 min. + cooling • **Makes:** 12 servings

- 2 cups fresh blueberries
- 1 cup sugar
- 1 Tbsp. cider vinegar
- ¼ tsp. kosher salt

CORNBREAD

- ½ cup 2% milk
- 1 Tbsp. lemon juice
- 1½ cups all-purpose flour
- ½ cup yellow cornmeal
- ½ cup sugar
- 3 tsp. baking powder
- ½ tsp. kosher salt
- 2 Tbsp. unsalted butter
- 1 Tbsp. honey
- 2 large eggs, room temperature
- ⅓ cup canola oil
- 2 jalapeno peppers, seeded and minced

1. In a large heavy saucepan, combine the blueberries, sugar, vinegar and kosher salt. Bring to a boil over high heat. Cook, stirring constantly, 5 minutes. Cool completely. Refrigerate, covered, overnight.
2. For cornbread, preheat oven to 350°. Combine milk and lemon juice; let stand briefly. In another bowl, whisk the next 5 ingredients. In a small bowl, microwave butter and honey on high for 30 seconds; cool slightly. Whisk eggs and oil into milk mixture (mixture may appear curdled). Add butter mixture; whisk until well combined. Add flour mixture; whisk just until combined. Fold in jalapenos.
3. Pour 2 cups batter into a well-buttered 10-in. fluted tube pan. Spoon half to three-fourths of blueberry quick jam over batter. Cover with remaining batter. Bake until a toothpick inserted in center comes out clean, 30-35 minutes. Cool 10 minutes; invert onto a cake plate or serving platter. Drizzle with remaining blueberry quick jam.
1 slice: 289 cal., 10g fat (2g sat. fat), 37mg chol., 258mg sod., 48g carb. (30g sugars, 1g fiber), 4g pro.

STRAWBERRIES & CREAM BREAD

My husband and I look forward to this bread every summer during strawberry-picking season. Since only fresh berries will do, I'd like to try it with other berries that are in season year-round so we can enjoy it more often. I hope you love it, too!
—Suzanne Randall, Dexter, ME

- -

Prep: 15 min. • **Bake:** 65 min. + cooling
Makes: 1 loaf (12 slices)

- ½ cup butter, softened
- ¾ cup sugar
- 2 large eggs, room temperature
- ½ cup sour cream
- 1 tsp. vanilla extract
- 1¾ cups all-purpose flour
- ½ tsp. baking powder
- ½ tsp. baking soda
- ½ tsp. salt
- ¼ tsp. ground cinnamon
- ¾ cup chopped fresh strawberries
- ¾ cup chopped walnuts, toasted, divided

1. Preheat the oven to 350°. In a large bowl, cream butter and sugar until light and fluffy. Beat in eggs. Add the sour cream and vanilla; mix well.
2. In another bowl, whisk the flour, baking powder, baking soda, salt and cinnamon; gradually stir into creamed mixture just until moistened. Fold in the strawberries and ½ cup nuts.
3. Pour into a greased 8x4-in. loaf pan. Sprinkle with remaining nuts. Bake until a toothpick inserted in center comes out clean, 65-70 minutes. Cool bread in pan for 10 minutes before removing to a wire rack to cool completely.
1 slice: 199 cal., 11g fat (5g sat. fat), 47mg chol., 196mg sod., 21g carb. (10g sugars, 1g fiber), 4g pro.

TASTE OF HOME
TEST KITCHEN
RECIPE OF THE YEAR
★ ★ ★ ★

**JALAPENO CORNBREAD FILLED
WITH BLUEBERRY QUICK JAM**

LEMON
BLUEBERRY
BISCUITS

LEMON BLUEBERRY BISCUITS

Lemon and blueberries make such a fresh and flavorful combination in all kinds of baked goods, especially these delightful drop biscuits.
—*Taste of Home* Test Kitchen

Prep: 30 min. • **Bake:** 15 min.
Makes: 1 dozen

- 2 cups all-purpose flour
- ½ cup sugar
- 2 tsp. baking powder
- ½ tsp. baking soda
- ¼ tsp. salt
- 1 cup lemon yogurt
- 1 large egg, room temperature
- ¼ cup butter, melted
- 1 tsp. grated lemon zest
- 1 cup fresh or frozen blueberries

GLAZE

- ½ cup confectioners' sugar
- 1 Tbsp. lemon juice
- ½ tsp. grated lemon zest

1. Preheat the oven to 400°. In a large bowl, whisk the first 5 ingredients. In another bowl, whisk yogurt, egg, melted butter and lemon zest until blended. Add to flour mixture; stir just until moistened. Fold in blueberries.
2. Drop by ⅓ cupfuls 1 in. apart onto a greased baking sheet. Bake 15-18 minutes or until light brown.
3. In a small bowl, combine glaze ingredients; stir until smooth. Drizzle over warm biscuits
Note: If using frozen blueberries, use without thawing to avoid discoloring the dough.
1 biscuit: 193 cal., 5g fat (3g sat. fat), 29mg chol., 223mg sod., 35g carb. (18g sugars, 1g fiber), 4g pro.

SWISS-ONION BREAD RING

With the ease of refrigerated bread dough, this cheesy bread has delicious down-home goodness. You'll find it crisp and golden on the outside, rich and buttery inside.
—Judi Messina, Coeur d'Alene, ID

Prep: 10 min. • **Bake:** 25 min.
Makes: 1 loaf (12 servings)

2½ tsp. poppy seeds, divided
2   tubes (11 oz. each)
     refrigerated French bread
1   cup shredded Swiss cheese
¾   cup sliced green onions
6   Tbsp. butter, melted

1. Sprinkle ½ tsp. poppy seeds in a greased 10-in. fluted tube pan. Cut the dough into forty 1-in. pieces; place half in prepared pan. Sprinkle with half of the cheese and onions. Top with 1 tsp. poppy seeds; drizzle with half of the butter. Repeat layers.
2. Bake at 375° for 30-35 minutes or until golden brown. Immediately invert onto a wire rack. Serve warm.
1 piece: 152 cal., 9g fat (6g sat. fat), 24mg chol., 246mg sod., 12g carb. (2g sugars, 1g fiber), 5g pro.

MOM'S ITALIAN BREAD

My mom used to bake at least four of these tender loaves at once, and they never lasted long. It's great toasted, too.
—Linda Harrington, Windham, NH

Prep: 30 min. + rising
Bake: 20 min.
Makes: 2 loaves (12 slices each)

1   pkg. (¼ oz.) active dry yeast
2   cups warm water (110° to 115°)
1   tsp. sugar
2   tsp. salt
5½   cups all-purpose flour

1. In a large bowl, dissolve yeast in warm water. Add the sugar, salt and 3 cups flour. Beat on medium speed for 3 minutes. Stir in remaining flour to form a soft dough.
2. Turn onto a floured surface; knead until smooth and elastic, about 6-8 minutes. Place in a greased bowl, turning once to grease the top. Cover and let rise in a warm place until doubled, about 1 hour.
3. Punch dough down. Turn onto a floured surface; divide in half. Shape each portion into a loaf. Place each loaf seam side down on a greased baking sheet. Cover and let rise until doubled, about 30 minutes.
4. Meanwhile, preheat oven to 400°. With a sharp knife, make four shallow slashes across top of each loaf. Bake 20-25 minutes or until golden brown. Remove from pans to wire racks to cool.
1 slice: 106 cal., 0 fat (0 sat. fat), 0 chol., 197mg sod., 22g carb. (1g sugars, 1g fiber), 3g pro. **Diabetic exchanges:** 1½ starch.

TEST KITCHEN TIP
To ensure a light texture, be sure to take the time to knead well. After kneading the first few minutes, press your thumb into the dough. If the indent stays, you're done. If not, knead a few more minutes.

MOM'S ITALIAN BREAD

ICEBOX BUTTERHORNS

If you like a roll that melts in your mouth, try my mom's recipe. She had a way with the dough, giving it just the right touch to turn out beautiful buttery rolls every time.
—Judy Clark, Elkhart, IN

Prep: 15 min. + chilling • **Bake:** 15 min.
Makes: 2 dozen

2   pkg. (¼ oz. each) active dry yeast
¼   cup warm water (110° to 115°)
2   cups warm 2% milk (110° to 115°)
¾   cup butter, melted
½   cup sugar
1   large egg, room temperature
1   tsp. salt
6½ cups all-purpose flour
    Additional melted butter

1. In a small bowl, dissolve yeast in warm water. In a large bowl, combine the milk, butter, sugar, egg, salt, yeast mixture and 3 cups flour; beat on medium speed until smooth. Stir in enough remaining flour to form a soft dough (dough will be sticky).
2. Do not knead. Place in a greased bowl, turning once to grease the top. Cover and refrigerate overnight.
3. Punch down the dough. Turn onto a lightly floured surface; divide in half. Roll each into a 12-in. circle; cut each into 12 wedges. Roll up wedges from the wide ends. Place 2 in. apart on greased baking sheets, point side down. Cover with kitchen towels; let rise in a warm place until doubled, about 1 hour.
4. Bake at 350° for 15-20 minutes or until golden brown. Immediately brush with additional melted butter. Remove from pans to wire racks to cool.
1 roll: 206 cal., 7g fat (4g sat. fat), 27mg chol., 170mg sod., 31g carb. (6g sugars, 1g fiber), 5g pro.

BAKER'S DOZEN YEAST ROLLS

A yummy honey-garlic topping turns these easy dinner rolls into something special.
—*Taste of Home* Test Kitchen

Prep: 25 min. + rising
Bake: 15 min. • **Makes:** 13 rolls

2   to 2½ cups all-purpose flour
2   Tbsp. sugar
1   pkg. (¼ oz.) quick-rise yeast
½   tsp. salt
¾   cup warm water (120° to 130°)
2   Tbsp. plus 4 tsp. butter, melted, divided
¾   cup shredded sharp cheddar cheese
2   tsp. honey
⅛   tsp. garlic salt

1. In a large bowl, combine 1½ cups flour, sugar, yeast and salt. Add water and 2 Tbsp. butter; beat on medium speed for 3 minutes or until smooth. Stir in cheese and enough remaining flour to form a soft dough.
2. Turn onto a lightly floured surface; knead until smooth and elastic, about 4-6 minutes. Cover and let rest for 10 minutes. Divide into 13 pieces. Shape each into a ball. Place in a greased 9-in. round baking pan. Cover and let rise in a warm place until doubled, about 30 minutes.
3. Preheat oven to 375°. Bake the rolls for 11-14 minutes or until lightly browned. Combine honey, garlic salt and remaining butter; brush over rolls. Remove from pan to wire rack.
1 roll: 131 cal., 5g fat (3g sat. fat), 15mg chol., 169mg sod., 18g carb. (3g sugars, 1g fiber), 4g pro. **Diabetic exchanges:** 1 starch, 1 fat.

ICEBOX
BUTTERHORNS

GARLIC-HERB BRAID

Savory flavors of rosemary, dill, garlic and basil blend beautifully in this homey loaf. Get ready for oohs and aahs when you bring this impressive braid to the table!
—*Taste of Home* Test Kitchen

Prep: 20 min. + rising
Bake: 20 min.
Makes: 1 loaf (16 slices)

    4   to 4½ cups all-purpose flour
    3   Tbsp. sugar
    2   pkg. (¼ oz. each) quick-rise yeast
    2   tsp. dried basil
  1¾   tsp. dill weed
  1½   tsp. salt
    ¾   tsp. garlic powder
    ¾   tsp. dried rosemary, crushed
    ¾   cup 2% milk
    ½   cup water
    ¼   cup butter, cubed
    1   large egg, room temperature
    1   Tbsp. butter, melted

1. In a large bowl, combine 1½ cups flour, sugar, yeast and seasonings. In a small saucepan, heat the milk, water and cubed butter to 120°-130°. Add to dry ingredients; beat just until moistened. Add egg; beat until smooth. Stir in enough remaining flour to form a soft dough.
2. Turn onto a floured surface; knead until smooth and elastic, 4-6 minutes. Cover and let rest for 10 minutes.
3. Divide dough into thirds. Shape each into a 15-in. rope. Place ropes on a greased baking sheet, and braid; pinch ends to seal and tuck under. Cover and let rise until doubled, about 25 minutes.
4. Bake at 375° for 20-25 minutes or until golden brown. Brush with melted butter. Remove from pan to a wire rack to cool.
Freeze option: Securely wrap and freeze cooled loaf in heavy-duty foil. To use, thaw at room temperature.
1 slice: 169 cal., 5g fat (3g sat. fat), 24mg chol., 257mg sod., 27g carb. (3g sugars, 1g fiber), 4g pro. **Diabetic exchanges:** 1½ starch, 1 fat.

CRUNCHY BREADSTICKS

CRUNCHY BREADSTICKS

These thin, crisp breadsticks add a bit of elegance to dinner. Each bite is perfectly seasoned with fragrant thyme and a bit of coarse salt.
—*Taste of Home* Test Kitchen

Prep: 20 min. • **Bake:** 20 min.
Makes: 16 breadsticks

    2   cups all-purpose flour
  1½   tsp. baking powder
    ½   tsp. salt
    3   Tbsp. shortening
    ½   to ¾ cup ice water
    1   Tbsp. olive oil
    ¼   tsp. coarse salt
    ¼   tsp. dried thyme

1. In a food processor, combine the flour, baking powder, salt and shortening; cover and process until mixture resembles coarse crumbs. While processing, gradually add water until dough forms a ball.
2. Transfer to a floured surface. Roll dough into a 10x8-in. rectangle. Cut into sixteen 10x½-in. strips. Twist each strip 4 times and place on baking sheets. Brush with oil. Combine coarse salt and thyme; sprinkle over breadsticks.
3. Bake at 350° until golden brown and crisp, 18-20 minutes. Cool on a wire rack.
1 breadstick: 78 cal., 2g fat (1g sat. fat), 0 chol., 156mg sod., 12g carb. (0 sugars, 0 fiber), 2g pro.

HONEY BAGELS

Who has time to make from-scratch bagels? You do, with this easy recipe! The chewy golden bagels offer a hint of honey and will win over even the pickiest eaters.
—*Taste of Home* Test Kitchen

- -

Prep: 1 hour + standing
Bake: 20 min. • **Makes:** 1 dozen

- 1 Tbsp. active dry yeast
- 1¼ cups warm water (110° to 115°)
- 3 Tbsp. canola oil
- 3 Tbsp. sugar
- 3 Tbsp. plus ¼ cup honey, divided
- 1 tsp. brown sugar
- 1½ tsp. salt
- 1 large egg, room temperature
- 4 to 5 cups bread flour
- 1 Tbsp. dried minced onion
- 1 Tbsp. sesame seeds
- 1 Tbsp. poppy seeds

1. In a large bowl, dissolve yeast in warm water. Add the oil, sugar, 3 Tbsp. honey, brown sugar, salt and egg; mix well. Stir in enough flour to form a soft dough.
2. Turn onto a floured surface; knead until a smooth, firm dough forms, 8-10 minutes. Cover and let rest for 10 minutes.
3. Punch dough down. Shape into 12 balls. Push thumb through centers to form a 1½-in. hole. Stretch and shape dough to form an even ring. Place on a floured surface. Cover and let rest for 10 minutes; flatten bagels slightly.
4. In a large saucepan or Dutch oven, bring 8 cups water and remaining honey to a boil. Drop bagels, one at a time, into boiling water. Cook bagels for 45 seconds; turn and cook 45 seconds longer. Remove bagels with a slotted spoon; drain on paper towel and sprinkle with minced onion, sesame seeds and poppy seeds.
5. Place bagels 2 in. apart on baking sheets lined with parchment. Bake bagels at 425° for 12 minutes. Turn and bake until golden brown, about 5 minutes longer.
1 bagel: 265 cal., 5g fat (1g sat. fat), 16mg chol., 303mg sod., 48g carb. (14g sugars, 2g fiber), 7g pro.

CRANBERRY ORANGE SCONES

CRANBERRY ORANGE SCONES

Moist and scrumptious, these scones come out perfect every time. I savor the chewy dried cranberries and sweet orange glaze. The orange butter takes them over the top.
—Karen McBride, Indianapolis, IN

- -

Prep: 20 min. • **Bake:** 15 min.
Makes: 10 scones

- 2 cups all-purpose flour
- 10 tsp. sugar, divided
- 1 Tbsp. grated orange zest
- 2 tsp. baking powder
- ½ tsp. salt
- ¼ tsp. baking soda
- ⅓ cup cold butter
- 1 cup dried cranberries
- ¼ cup orange juice
- ¼ cup half-and-half cream
- 1 large egg, room temperature
- 1 Tbsp. 2% milk

GLAZE (OPTIONAL)
- ½ cup confectioners' sugar
- 1 Tbsp. orange juice
ORANGE BUTTER
- ½ cup butter, softened
- 2 to 3 Tbsp. orange marmalade

1. In a large bowl, combine the flour, 7 tsp. sugar, orange zest, baking powder, salt and baking soda. Cut in butter until the mixture resembles coarse crumbs; set aside. In a small bowl, combine the cranberries, orange juice, cream and egg. Add to flour mixture and stir until a soft dough forms.
2. On a floured surface, gently knead dough 6-8 times. Pat dough into an 8-in. circle. Cut into 10 wedges. Separate wedges and place on a greased baking sheet. Brush with milk; sprinkle with remaining sugar.
3. Bake at 400° 12-15 minutes or until lightly browned. Remove to a wire rack.
4. Combine glaze ingredients if desired; drizzle over scones. Combine orange butter ingredients; serve with warm scones.
1 scone: 331 cal., 17g fat (10g sat. fat), 65mg chol., 396mg sod., 43g carb. (22g sugars, 1g fiber), 4g pro.

BANANA-CHIP NUT BREAD

No one should have to forgo banana bread, even those on a gluten-restrictive diet. This gluten-free version from our Test Kitchen is so delicious, it will be a winner for all. The chocolate chips and chopped walnuts are a nice complement to the mild banana flavor.
—*Taste of Home* Test Kitchen

Prep: 20 min. • **Bake:** 30 min. + cooling
Makes: 1 mini loaf (6 slices)

- 1 Tbsp. plus 1½ tsp. butter, softened
- 1 Tbsp. plus 1½ tsp. brown sugar
- 2 Tbsp. beaten egg, room temperature
- 1 medium ripe banana
- 1½ tsp. buttermilk
- ⅓ cup white rice flour
- ⅓ cup tapioca flour
- 1½ tsp. mashed potato flakes
- ¾ tsp. baking powder
- ⅛ tsp. baking soda
- ⅛ tsp. salt
- 2 Tbsp. chopped walnuts
- 2 Tbsp. semisweet chocolate chips

1. In a small bowl, cream butter and brown sugar. Add egg; mix well. In a small bowl, mash banana with buttermilk. Combine the flours, potato flakes, baking powder, baking soda and salt; add to the creamed mixture alternately with banana mixture just until moistened. Fold in chopped walnuts and chocolate chips.

2. Pour into a 5¾x3x2-in. loaf pan coated with cooking spray. Bake at 350° until a toothpick inserted in the center comes out clean, 30-35 minutes. Cool for 10 minutes before removing from pan to a wire rack.

Note: Read all ingredient labels for possible gluten content prior to use. Ingredient formulas can change, and production facilities vary among brands. If you're concerned that your brand may contain gluten, contact the company.

1 slice: 147 cal., 6g fat (3g sat. fat), 29mg chol., 165mg sod., 23g carb. (9g sugars, 1g fiber), 2g pro.

APPLE STREUSEL MUFFINS

APPLE STREUSEL MUFFINS

These muffins remind us of coffee cake, and my husband and kids love them as a quick breakfast or snack on the run. The sweet drizzle of glaze makes them pretty enough for company.
—Dulcy Grace, Roaring Spring, PA

Prep: 20 min. • **Bake:** 15 min.
Makes: 1 dozen

- 2 cups all-purpose flour
- 1 cup sugar
- 1 tsp. baking powder
- ½ tsp. baking soda
- ½ tsp. salt
- 2 large eggs, room temperature
- ½ cup butter, melted
- 1¼ tsp. vanilla extract
- 1½ cups peeled chopped tart apples

STREUSEL TOPPING
- ⅓ cup packed brown sugar
- 1 Tbsp. all-purpose flour
- ⅛ tsp. ground cinnamon
- 1 Tbsp. cold butter

GLAZE
- ¾ cup confectioners' sugar
- 2 to 3 tsp. 2% milk
- 1 tsp. butter, melted
- ⅛ tsp. vanilla extract
    Dash salt

1. Preheat oven to 375°. Whisk together the first 5 ingredients. In another bowl, whisk together eggs, melted butter and vanilla; add to flour mixture, stirring just until moistened (batter will be stiff). Fold in apples.

2. Fill 12 greased or paper-lined muffin cups three-fourths full. For topping, mix brown sugar, flour and cinnamon; cut in butter until crumbly. Sprinkle over batter.

3. Bake until a toothpick inserted in center comes out clean, 15-20 minutes. Cool for 5 minutes before removing from pan to a wire rack to cool. Mix glaze ingredients; drizzle over tops.

1 muffin: 295 cal., 10g fat (6g sat. fat), 55mg chol., 398mg sod., 49g carb. (32g sugars, 1g fiber), 3g pro.

GOLDEN HONEY PAN ROLLS

A cousin in North Carolina gave me the recipe for these delicious honey-glazed rolls. Using my bread machine to make the dough saves me about two hours compared to the traditional method. The rich buttery taste of these rolls is so popular with family and friends that I usually make two batches so I have enough!
—Sara Wing, Philadelphia, PA

- -

Prep: 35 min. + rising • **Bake:** 20 min.
Makes: 2 dozen

- 1 cup warm 2% milk (70° to 80°)
- 1 large egg, room temperature
- 1 large egg yolk, room temperature
- ½ cup canola oil
- 2 Tbsp. honey
- 1½ tsp. salt
- 3½ cups bread flour
- 2¼ tsp. active dry yeast

GLAZE
- ⅓ cup sugar
- 2 Tbsp. butter, melted
- 1 Tbsp. honey
- 1 large egg white
- Additional honey, optional

1. In bread machine pan, place the first 8 ingredients in the order suggested by the manufacturer. Select the dough setting (check dough after 5 minutes of mixing; add 1 to 2 Tbsp. of water or flour if needed.)

2. When cycle is completed, turn dough onto a lightly floured surface. Punch down; cover and let rest for 10 minutes. Divide into 24 pieces; shape each piece into a ball. Place 12 balls each in 2 greased 8-in. square baking pans. Cover and let rise in a warm place until doubled, about 30 minutes.

3. For glaze, combine the sugar, butter, honey and egg white; drizzle over dough. Bake at 350° 20-25 minutes or until golden brown. Brush rolls with additional honey if desired.

Note: We recommend you do not use a bread machine's time-delay feature for this recipe. If you don't have a bread machine, you can make this the traditional method. Dissolve yeast in warm milk. In another bowl, combine egg, egg yolk, oil, honey, salt, yeast mixture and 2 cups flour; beat on medium speed until smooth. Stir in enough remaining flour to form a soft dough (dough will be sticky). Turn onto a floured surface; knead until smooth and elastic, 6-8 minutes. Place in a greased bowl, turning once to grease top. Cover and let rise in a warm place until doubled, about 1 hour. Punch down dough; cover and let rest for 10 minutes. Turn onto a lightly floured surface. Divide and shape into 24 balls; place 12 each in 2 greased 8x8-in. baking pans. Cover and let rise in a warm place until doubled, about 30 minutes. Preheat oven to 350° glaze and bake as directed.

1 roll: 139 cal., 6g fat (2g sat. fat), 22mg chol., 168mg sod., 18g carb. (5g sugars, 1g fiber), 3g pro.

GARLIC LOAF

This golden loaf has garlicky goodness in every bite. People go wild over its savory flavor. Try serving it with an herb-infused or lightly salted olive oil for dunking.
—*Taste of Home* Test Kitchen

- -

Prep: 15 min. + rising • **Bake:** 20 min.
Makes: 1 loaf (24 pieces)

- 2 loaves (1 lb. each) frozen bread dough or 24 frozen unbaked white dinner rolls, thawed
- ½ cup finely chopped sweet onion
- ½ cup butter, melted
- 2 garlic cloves, minced
- 1 tsp. dried parsley flakes
- ¼ tsp. salt
- Herb-seasoned olive oil, optional

1. Divide dough into 24 pieces. In a small bowl, combine the onion, butter, garlic, parsley and salt. Dip each piece of dough into butter mixture; place in a 10-in. fluted tube pan coated with cooking spray. Cover and let rise in a warm place until doubled, about 1 hour.

2. Bake at 375° for 20-25 minutes or until golden brown. Serve warm, with seasoned olive oil if desired.

1 piece: 141 cal., 5g fat (2g sat. fat), 10mg chol., 263mg sod., 19g carb. (2g sugars, 2g fiber), 4g pro.

GOLDEN HONEY PAN ROLLS

BASIC HOMEMADE
BREAD

IRISH SODA BREAD

This traditional Irish soda bread can be made with an assortment of mix-ins such as dried fruit and nuts, but I like it with a handful of raisins. It's the perfect change-of-pace item to bring to a get-together.
—Gloria Warczak, Cedarburg, WI

- -

Prep: 15 min. • **Bake:** 30 min.
Makes: 8 servings

```
2   cups all-purpose flour
2   Tbsp. brown sugar
1   tsp. baking powder
1   tsp. baking soda
½   tsp. salt
3   Tbsp. cold butter, cubed
2   large eggs, room
    temperature, divided use
¾   cup buttermilk
⅓   cup raisins
```

1. Preheat oven to 375°. Whisk together the first 5 ingredients. Cut in butter until mixture resembles coarse crumbs. In another bowl, whisk together 1 egg and buttermilk. Add to flour mixture; stir just until moistened. Stir in raisins.
2. Turn onto a lightly floured surface; knead gently 6-8 times. Shape into a 6½-in. round loaf; place on a greased baking sheet. Using a sharp knife, make a shallow cross in top of loaf. Whisk remaining egg; brush over top.
3. Bake until golden brown, 30-35 minutes. Remove from baking sheet to a wire rack. Serve warm.
1 piece: 210 cal., 6g fat (3g sat. fat), 59mg chol., 463mg sod., 33g carb. (8g sugars, 1g fiber), 6g pro.
Caraway Irish Soda Bread: Add 1 to 2 Tbsp. caraway seeds to the dry ingredients.

DID YOU KNOW?

Irish soda bread—sometimes shortened to soda bread—is a quick bread that uses sodium bicarbonate, or baking soda, as a leavening agent instead of yeast. The chemical reaction between the baking soda and buttermilk in this recipe produces carbon dioxide which causes it to rise.

BASIC HOMEMADE BREAD

If you've never made homemade bread before, start with this easy recipe. It bakes up two deliciously golden brown loaves, and you will love the pleasant aroma wafting through the kitchen.
—Sandra Anderson, New York, NY

- -

Prep: 20 min. + rising
Bake: 30 min.
Makes: 2 loaves (16 slices each)

```
1    pkg. (¼ oz.) active dry yeast
2¼   cups warm water (110° to 115°)
3    Tbsp. sugar plus ½ tsp. sugar
1    Tbsp. salt
2    Tbsp. canola oil
6¼   to 6¾ cups bread flour
```

1. In a large bowl, dissolve yeast and ½ tsp. sugar in warm water; let stand until bubbles form on surface. Whisk together remaining 3 Tbsp. sugar, salt, and 3 cups flour. Stir oil into yeast mixture; pour into flour mixture and beat until smooth. Stir in enough of the remaining flour, ½ cup at a time, to form a soft dough.
2. Turn onto a floured surface; knead until smooth and elastic, 8-10 minutes. Place in a greased bowl, turning once to grease the top. Cover and let rise in a warm place until doubled, 1½-2 hours.
3. Punch dough down. Turn onto a lightly floured surface; divide dough in half. Shape each into a loaf. Place in 2 greased 9x5-in. loaf pans. Cover and let rise until doubled, 1-1½ hours.
4. Bake at 375° for 30-35 minutes or until golden brown and bread sounds hollow when tapped or has reached an internal temperature of 200°. Remove loaves from pans to wire racks to cool.
1 slice: 102 cal., 1g fat (0 sat. fat), 0 chol., 222mg sod., 20g carb. (1g sugars, 1g fiber), 3g pro.

IRISH SODA
BREAD

EVERYTHING BREAD

Move over, bagels. Here a braided loaf gets the same flavorful treatment of seasonings. I love to make bread from scratch and this has become one of my favorites to serve with any meal, casual or formal.
—Traci Wynne, Denver, PA

- -

Prep: 45 min. + rising • **Bake:** 25 min.
Makes: 1 loaf (25 slices)

- 1   pkg. (¼ oz.) active dry yeast
- ¾   cup warm water (110° to 115°)
- 1   cup warm 2% milk (110° to 115°)
- ¼   cup butter, softened
- 2   Tbsp. sugar
- 1   large egg yolk, room temperature
- 1½   tsp. salt
- 4   to 4½ cups all-purpose flour
- 1   large egg white
- 2   tsp. water
- 1   tsp. coarse sea salt or kosher salt
- 1   tsp. dried minced onion
- 1   tsp. each sesame, caraway and poppy seeds

1. In a large bowl, dissolve yeast in warm water. Add milk, butter, sugar, egg yolk, salt and 2 cups flour. Beat on medium speed for 3 minutes. Stir in enough remaining flour to form a firm dough.
2. Turn onto a floured surface; knead until smooth and elastic, 6-8 minutes. Place the dough in a greased bowl, turning once to grease the top. Cover and let rise until doubled, about 1 hour.
3. Punch dough down. Turn onto a lightly floured surface; divide dough into thirds. Shape each into a 20-in. rope. Place ropes on a large greased baking sheet and braid; pinch ends to seal and tuck under. Cover and let rise until doubled, about 45 minutes.
4. Preheat oven to 375°. Combine egg white and water; brush over dough. Combine salt, onion and seeds; sprinkle over bread. Bake for 22-28 minutes or until golden brown. Remove from pan to a wire rack to cool.
1 slice: 102 cal., 2g fat (1g sat. fat), 14mg chol., 237mg sod., 17g carb. (2g sugars, 1g fiber), 3g pro. **Diabetic exchanges:** 1 starch, ½ fat.

EVERYTHING BREAD

HONEY CORNBREAD

It's a pleasure to serve this moist cornbread to family and guests. Honey gives it a slightly sweet taste. Most people find it's difficult to eat just one piece.
—Adeline Piscitelli, Sayreville, NJ

- -

Takes: 30 min. • **Makes:** 9 servings

- 1   cup all-purpose flour
- 1   cup yellow cornmeal
- ¼   cup sugar
- 3   tsp. baking powder
- ½   tsp. salt
- 2   large eggs, room temperature
- 1   cup heavy whipping cream
- ¼   cup canola oil
- ¼   cup honey

1. In a bowl, combine flour, cornmeal, sugar, baking powder and salt. In a small bowl, beat the eggs. Add cream, oil and honey; beat well. Stir into the dry ingredients just until moistened. Pour into a greased 9-in. square baking pan.

2. Bake at 400° for 20-25 minutes or until a toothpick inserted in the center comes out clean. Serve warm.

1 piece: 318 cal., 17g fat (7g sat. fat), 83mg chol., 290mg sod., 37g carb. (14g sugars, 2g fiber), 5g pro.

CAN'T-EAT-JUST-ONE CINNAMON ROLLS

My cinnamon rolls vanish quickly. One time I dropped off a dozen rolls for my brothers, and they emptied the pan in 10 minutes.
—Regina Farmwald, West Farmington, OH

- -

Prep: 1 hour + rising
Bake: 20 min. • **Makes:** 2 dozen

- 1   pkg. (¼ oz.) active dry yeast
- 1   Tbsp. sugar
- ¼   cup warm water (110° to 115°)
- 1   cup 2% milk
- ⅓   cup instant vanilla pudding mix (half of a 3.4-oz. pkg.)
- 1   large egg, room temperature
- ¼   cup butter, melted
- 1   tsp. salt
- 3   to 3½ cups all-purpose flour

FILLING
- ¾   cup sugar
- 1   Tbsp. ground cinnamon
- ¼   cup butter, melted

FROSTING
- ½   cup butter, softened
- 2   tsp. vanilla extract
- 1   tsp. water
- 1½   to 1¾ cups confectioners' sugar

1. In a small bowl, dissolve yeast and 1 Tbsp. sugar in warm water. In a large bowl, beat milk and pudding mix on low speed 1 minute. Let stand 1 minute or until soft-set. Add egg, melted butter, salt, yeast mixture and 2 cups flour; beat on medium until smooth. Stir in enough remaining flour to form a soft dough (dough will be sticky).

2. Turn dough onto a floured surface; knead until smooth and elastic, 6-8 minutes. Place in a greased bowl, turning once to grease the top. Cover and let rise in a warm place until doubled, about 1 hour.

3. For filling, in a small bowl, mix sugar and cinnamon. Punch down dough; divide in half. Turn 1 portion of the dough onto a lightly floured surface; roll into an 18x10-in. rectangle. Brush with half of the melted butter to within ¼ in. of edges; sprinkle with half of the sugar mixture. Roll up jelly-roll style, starting with a long side; pinch seam to seal. Cut into 12 slices. Repeat with the remaining dough and filling ingredients.

4. Place all slices in a greased 13x9-in. baking pan, cut side down. Cover with a kitchen towel; let rise in a warm place until almost doubled, about 45 minutes. Preheat oven to 350°.

5. Bake 20-25 minutes or until golden brown. Cool in pan on a wire rack.

6. For frosting, in a small bowl, beat butter until creamy. Beat in vanilla extract, water and enough confectioners' sugar to reach desired consistency. Spread over warm rolls. Serve warm.

1 cinnamon roll: 199 cal., 8g fat (5g sat. fat), 29mg chol., 187mg sod., 29g carb. (16g sugars, 1g fiber), 2g pro.

CAN'T-EAT-JUST-ONE CINNAMON ROLLS

THE BEST CHICKEN &
DUMPLINGS, PAGE 107

Soups, Salads & Sandwiches

We know what it's like to be stuck in a noon meeting and suddenly feel that familiar grumble in your tummy. But if you're tired of the same boring PB&J sandwich, microwaved frozen meal or overpriced delivery food, look no further. From hot soups and hearty sandwiches to garden-fresh salads, these recipes make it easy to break out of the lunch (or dinner) rut. Some even make great potluck contributions or an impressive first course to a special meal.

HEARTY ASIAN
LETTUCE SALAD

HEARTY ASIAN LETTUCE SALAD

It might sound too good to be true, but this meatless version of your favorite restaurant salad packs 13 grams of protein per serving. Even better, it's bursting with juicy flavor.
—*Taste of Home* Test Kitchen

Takes: 20 min. • **Makes:** 2 servings

- 1 cup ready-to-serve brown rice
- 1 cup frozen shelled edamame
- 3 cups spring mix salad greens
- ¼ cup reduced-fat sesame ginger salad dressing
- 1 medium navel orange, peeled and sectioned
- 4 radishes, sliced
- 2 Tbsp. sliced almonds, toasted

1. Prepare rice and edamame according to package directions.
2. In a large bowl, combine the salad greens, rice and edamame. Drizzle with salad dressing and toss to coat. Divide salad mixture between 2 plates; top with orange segments, radishes and almonds.
1 serving: 329 cal., 10g fat (1g sat. fat), 0 chol., 430mg sod., 44g carb. (12g sugars, 7g fiber), 13g pro.

TEST KITCHEN TIP
This is a perfect cold-weather main dish salad when gardens are still under a layer of frost. For a heartier version, add sauteed shrimp or shredded rotisserie chicken.

EASY CHICKEN CORN CHOWDER

EASY CHICKEN CORN CHOWDER

I play around with the ingredients in my pantry instead of running to the store when I haven't planned dinner. This chowder was a happy—and tasty—experiment!
—Barbara Banski, Fenton, MI

Takes: 30 min. • **Makes:** 4 servings (1½ qt.)

- 2 Tbsp. butter
- 1 small onion, finely chopped
- 1 celery rib, finely chopped
- 1 small sweet red pepper, finely chopped
- 2 cans (14¾ oz. each) cream-style corn
- 1½ cups chopped cooked chicken
- 1 can (12 oz.) reduced-fat evaporated milk
- 1 tsp. chicken bouillon granules
- ½ tsp. pepper
- 8 bacon strips, cooked and crumbled

1. In a large saucepan, heat butter over medium-high heat. Add onion, celery and red pepper; cook and stir 6-8 minutes or until tender.
2. Stir in corn, chicken, milk, bouillon and pepper; heat through, stirring occasionally (do not boil). Top servings with bacon.
1½ cups: 474 cal., 18g fat (7g sat. fat), 94mg chol., 1252mg sod., 51g carb. (18g sugars, 3g fiber), 31g pro.

CHERRY TOMATO CORN SALAD

Brighten up a picnic lunch or backyard barbecue with this cheerful, fresh-tasting salad. If you use want to use corn straight off the cob, saute the corn for 5 minutes in a skillet before adding to the salad.
—*Taste of Home* Test Kitchen

Takes: 15 min. • **Makes:** 6 servings

- ¼ cup minced fresh basil
- 3 Tbsp. olive oil
- 2 tsp. lime juice
- 1 tsp. sugar
- ½ tsp. salt
- ¼ tsp. pepper
- 2 cups frozen corn, thawed
- 2 cups cherry tomatoes, halved
- 1 cup chopped seeded peeled cucumber

1. In a jar with a tight-fitting lid, combine the basil, oil, lime juice, sugar, salt and pepper; shake well.

2. In a large bowl, combine the corn, tomatoes and cucumber. Drizzle with dressing; toss to coat. Refrigerate salad until serving.

⅔ cup: 125 cal., 7g fat (1g sat. fat), 0 chol., 302mg sod., 15g carb. (3g sugars, 2g fiber), 2g pro.

SESAME ALMOND SLAW

SESAME ALMOND SLAW

Crunchy veggies and noodles are coated in a tangy dressing in this pleasant slaw.
—*Taste of Home* Test Kitchen

Takes: 20 min. • **Makes:** 2 servings

- 1 pkg. (3 oz.) ramen noodles
- ¾ cup shredded cabbage
- ¾ cup shredded romaine
- 2 Tbsp. sliced green onion
- 2 tsp. slivered almonds, toasted
- 2 tsp. sesame seeds, toasted
- 1 Tbsp. rice vinegar
- 1½ tsp. sugar
- 1½ tsp. canola oil
- 1 tsp. water
- ½ tsp. sesame oil
- ¼ tsp. reduced-sodium soy sauce
  - Dash salt
  - Dash pepper

1. Split the ramen noodles in half (save the seasoning and half of the noodles for another use). Break apart the remaining noodles; place in a bowl. Add the cabbage, romaine, onion, almonds and sesame seeds.

2. For dressing, in a jar with a tight-fitting lid, combine the vinegar, sugar, canola oil, water, sesame oil, soy sauce, salt and pepper; shake well. Add dressing to salad and toss to coat. Serve immediately.

1 cup: 187 cal., 10g fat (3g sat. fat), 0 chol., 193mg sod., 20g carb. (4g sugars, 2g fiber), 4g pro. **Diabetic exchanges:** 1½ fat, 1 starch, 1 vegetable.

CHEESEBURGER SOUP

A local restaurant serves a similar soup but wouldn't share its recipe with me. So I developed my own, modifying a recipe for potato soup. I was pleased at the way this all-American soup turned out.

—Joanie Shawhan, Madison, WI

Prep: 45 min. • **Cook:** 10 min.
Makes: 8 servings (2 qt.)

- ½ lb. ground beef
- 4 Tbsp. butter, divided
- ¾ cup chopped onion
- ¾ cup shredded carrots
- ¾ cup diced celery
- 1 tsp. dried basil
- 1 tsp. dried parsley flakes
- 1¾ lbs. (about 4 cups) cubed peeled potatoes
- 3 cups chicken broth
- ¼ cup all-purpose flour
- 2 to 4 cups shredded Velveeta
- 1½ cups whole milk
- ¾ tsp. salt
- ¼ to ½ tsp. pepper
- ¼ cup sour cream

1. In a large saucepan over medium heat, cook and crumble beef until no longer pink; drain and set aside. In same saucepan, melt 1 Tbsp. butter over medium heat. Saute the onion, carrots, celery, basil and parsley until vegetables are tender, about 10 minutes. Add potatoes, ground beef and broth; bring to a boil. Reduce heat; simmer, covered, until potatoes are tender, 10-12 minutes.
2. Meanwhile, in a small skillet, melt the remaining butter. Add flour; cook and stir until bubbly, 3-5 minutes. Add to soup; bring to a boil. Cook and stir 2 minutes. Reduce heat to low. Stir in cheese, milk, salt and pepper; cook until cheese melts. Remove from heat; blend in sour cream.

1 cup: 450 cal., 27g fat (15g sat. fat), 100mg chol., 1421mg sod., 33g carb. (8g sugars, 3g fiber), 19g pro.

LOBSTER ROLLS

Mayonnaise infused with dill and lemon lends refreshing flavor to these super sandwiches. Try pan-toasting the buns in butter for something special.

—*Taste of Home* Test Kitchen

Takes: 30 min. • **Makes:** 8 sandwiches

- 1 cup chopped celery
- ⅓ cup mayonnaise
- 2 Tbsp. lemon juice
- ½ tsp. dill weed
- 5 cups cubed cooked lobster meat (about 4 small lobsters)
- 8 hoagie rolls, split and toasted

In a large bowl, combine the celery, mayonnaise, lemon juice and dill weed. Gently stir in lobster. Serve on rolls.

1 sandwich: 354 cal., 12g fat (2g sat. fat), 133mg chol., 887mg sod., 36g carb. (5g sugars, 1g fiber), 25g pro.

CHEESEBURGER SOUP

TASTE OF HOME
TEST KITCHEN
RECIPE OF THE YEAR
★ ★ ★ ★

PRESSURE-COOKER CLAM CHOWDER

BOK CHOY SALAD

Depending on what I have, I sometimes use only the sunflower kernels or almonds in this salad. The recipe makes a big amount, perfect for cookouts or reunions.
—Stephanie Marchese,
Visual Production Director

- -

Takes: 25 min. • **Makes:** 10 servings

- 1 head bok choy, finely chopped
- 2 bunches green onions, thinly sliced
- 2 pkg. (3 oz. each) ramen noodles, broken
- ¼ cup slivered almonds
- 2 Tbsp. sunflower kernels
- ¼ cup butter

DRESSING

- ⅓ to ½ cup sugar
- ½ cup canola oil
- 2 Tbsp. cider vinegar
- 1 Tbsp. soy sauce

1. In a large bowl, combine bok choy and green onions; set aside. Save seasoning packet from ramen noodles for another use. In a large skillet, saute the noodles, almonds and sunflower kernels in butter for 7 minutes or until browned. Remove from the heat; cool to room temperature. Add to the bok choy mixture.
2. In a jar with a tight fitting lid, combine the dressing ingredients; shake well. Just before serving, drizzle over salad and toss to coat.
¾ cup: 240 cal., 19g fat (5g sat. fat), 12mg chol., 386mg sod., 16g carb. (8g sugars, 2g fiber), 4g pro.

TEST KITCHEN TIP

Select bunches of bok choy with firm white stalks and crisp leaves. Avoid bunches with brown spots on stalks. Store unwashed bok choy in the crisper drawer in the refrigerator for up to 4 days.

PRESSURE-COOKER CLAM CHOWDER

Clam chowder is especially tasty with a sprinkle of fresh thyme, bacon crumbles and crispy oyster crackers on top. If you like it on the thick side, add an extra tablespoon of flour after it's finished cooking.
—*Taste of Home* Test Kitchen

- -

Prep: 20 min. • **Cook:** 25 min.
Makes: 8 servings (2 qt.)

- 4 medium potatoes, peeled and cut into ½-in. cubes (about 5 cups)
- 1 medium onion, chopped
- 2 celery ribs, chopped
- 2 medium carrots, chopped
- 4 garlic cloves, minced
- 1 bottle (8 oz.) clam juice
- 1 cup chicken broth
- 1 tsp. dried thyme
- 1 tsp. salt
- ½ tsp. pepper
- 2 cans (6½ oz. each) minced clams, undrained
- 1 cup heavy whipping cream
- 2 Tbsp. all-purpose flour
- 4 bacon strips, cooked and crumbled
   Optional: Oyster crackers and fresh thyme

1. Place first 10 ingredients in a 6-qt. electric pressure cooker. Drain and reserve liquid from minced clams; add reserved liquid to pressure cooker and set clams aside. Lock lid; close pressure-release valve. Adjust to pressure-cook on high for 15 minutes. Quick-release pressure.
2. Select saute setting and adjust for low heat. Mix flour and cream until smooth; stir into the soup. Cook and stir until slightly thickened, 6-8 minutes. Stir in clams; heat through. Serve with bacon and, if desired, crackers and fresh thyme.
1 cup: 227 cal., 13g fat (7g sat. fat), 56mg chol., 673mg sod., 21g carb. (4g sugars, 2g fiber), 8g pro.

BOK CHOY
SALAD

MEDITERRANEAN SHRIMP SALAD IN A JAR

This Greek salad to go is loaded with so much freshness that it makes any day feel brighter. Just layer it in a jar and pack it up—then serve and enjoy.
—*Taste of Home* Test Kitchen

Prep: 20 min. • **Cook:** 15 min.
Makes: 4 servings

- ¾ cup uncooked orzo pasta
- ¾ cup Greek vinaigrette
- ½ cup minced fresh parsley
- ⅓ cup chopped fresh dill
- ¾ lb. peeled and deveined cooked shrimp (31-40 per lb.)
- 1 can (14 oz.) water-packed quartered artichoke hearts, rinsed and drained
- 1 medium sweet red pepper, chopped
- 1 medium green pepper, chopped
- 1 small red onion, thinly sliced
- ½ cup pitted Greek olives, sliced
- ½ cup crumbled feta cheese
- 8 cups fresh arugula

1. Cook orzo according to the the package directions. Drain; rinse with cold water and drain well. Combine the orzo with Greek vinaigrette and herbs.

2. In each of four 1-qt. wide-mouth canning jars, divide and layer ingredients in the following order: orzo mixture, shrimp, artichokes, red pepper, green pepper, red onion, Greek olives, feta cheese and arugula. Cover and refrigerate until serving. Transfer salads into bowls; toss to combine.

1 serving: 548 cal., 26g fat (5g sat. fat), 137mg chol., 1287mg sod., 47g carb. (5g sugars, 4g fiber), 29g pro.

MEDITERRANEAN SHRIMP
SALAD IN A JAR

TASTE OF HOME
TEST KITCHEN
RECIPE OF THE YEAR
★★★★

AVOCADO TURKEY SALAD

Grape tomatoes and avocado chunks add pretty color and fresh flavor to this salad that's hearty enough for a main dish. If you want to lighten it, use half-and half or milk for the whipping cream. Add a teaspoon at a time until you get the desired consistency.
—*Taste of Home* Test Kitchen

- -

Takes: 15 min. • **Makes:** 6 servings

¼ cup canola oil
2 Tbsp. sour cream
1 Tbsp. heavy whipping cream
¼ tsp. salt
⅛ to ¼ tsp. minced garlic
3 cups torn mixed salad greens
2 cups cubed cooked turkey breast
1 medium ripe avocado, peeled and chopped
1 cup grape tomatoes, halved
   Coarsely ground pepper

In a large mixing bowl, whisk the first 5 ingredients until smooth. Add greens, turkey, avocado and tomatoes; toss to coat. Top with coarse ground pepper. Serve immediately.

1⅓ cups: 225 cal., 17g fat (3g sat. fat), 47mg chol., 141mg sod., 4g carb. (1g sugars, 2g fiber), 16g pro.

BEER-BRAISED PULLED HAM

Buns loaded with ham slow-cooked in beer sauce are irrisistible.
—Ann Sheehy, Lawrence, MA

- -

Prep: 10 min. • **Cook:** 7 hours
Makes: 16 servings

2 bottles (12 oz. each) beer or nonalcoholic beer
¾ cup German or Dijon mustard, divided
½ tsp. coarsely ground pepper
1 fully cooked bone-in ham (about 4 lbs.)
4 fresh rosemary sprigs
16 pretzel hamburger buns, split
   Dill pickle slices, optional

1. In a 5-qt. slow cooker, whisk together beer and ½ cup mustard. Stir in pepper. Add ham and rosemary. Cook, covered, on low until tender, 7-9 hours.

2. Remove ham; cool slightly. Discard the rosemary sprigs. Skim fat. When ham is cool enough to handle, shred meat with 2 forks. Discard bone. Return ham to slow cooker; heat through.

3. Using tongs, place shredded ham on pretzel buns; top with remaining mustard and, if desired, dill pickle slices.

Freeze option: Freeze cooled ham mixture in freezer containers. To use, partially thaw in refrigerator overnight. Heat through in a covered saucepan, stirring gently; add water if necessary.

1 sandwich: 378 cal., 9g fat (1g sat. fat), 50mg chol., 1246mg sod., 48g carb. (4g sugars, 2g fiber), 25g pro.

TEST KITCHEN TIP
You can also place shredded ham on slider buns and top with honey mustard spread.

BEER-BRAISED
PULLED HAM

SOUTHWEST CHICKEN POCKETS

Black beans, convenient chicken strips and chiles star in these loaded pockets. Eat them out of hand (or with a fork if you're feeling civilized). Serve a little salsa on the side for an extra burst of flavor.
—*Taste of Home* Test Kitchen

- -

Prep: 15 min. • **Bake:** 20 min.
Makes: 4 servings

- 1 medium onion, chopped
- 2 tsp. olive oil
- 1 pkg. (9 oz.) ready-to-serve roasted chicken breast strips
- 1 can (15 oz.) black beans, rinsed and drained
- 1 medium tomato, seeded and chopped
- 1 can (4 oz.) chopped green chiles, divided
- 1 sheet frozen puff pastry, thawed
- ¼ cup shredded cheddar cheese
- 1 large egg, beaten
- ½ cup sour cream

1. In a large skillet, saute onion in oil until tender. Remove from the heat; stir in the chicken, beans, tomato and ¼ cup chiles.
2. On a lightly floured surface, roll the puff pastry into a 14-in. square. Cut into 4 squares. Spoon chicken mixture into the center of each square; sprinkle with cheese.
3. Brush egg over edges. Fold dough over filling, forming a triangle; pinch seams to seal. Transfer to a greased baking sheet and brush with remaining egg. Bake at 400° until golden brown, 18-22 minutes.
4. Meanwhile, in a small bowl, combine sour cream and remaining chiles. Serve with pockets.
1 pocket with 2 Tbsp. sauce: 600 cal., 28g fat (9g sat. fat), 88mg chol., 880mg sod., 58g carb. (5g sugars, 10g fiber), 28g pro.

PINEAPPLE-PAPAYA SLAW

This is no ordinary coleslaw! Bursting with flavor from fresh fruit, cilantro and red bell pepper, it just may become your new picnic mainstay. For easier preparation, buy packaged shredded cabbage. If you can't find papaya, substitute mango.
—*Taste of Home* Test Kitchen

- -

Prep: 20 min. + chilling • **Makes:** 8 servings

- ½ cup pineapple juice
- ¼ cup olive oil
- 2 Tbsp. lime juice
- 2 Tbsp. minced fresh cilantro
- ½ tsp. ground cumin
- ¼ tsp. salt
- 6 cups shredded cabbage (about 1 small)
- 1½ cups chopped peeled papaya
- 1½ cups cubed fresh pineapple
- 1 small sweet red pepper, chopped

Whisk together first 6 ingredients. Place the remaining ingredients in a large bowl. Drizzle with dressing; toss to coat. Refrigerate, covered, at least 2 hours. Stir before serving.
1 cup: 112 cal., 7g fat (1g sat. fat), 0 chol., 87mg sod., 13g carb. (7g sugars, 2g fiber), 1g pro. **Diabetic exchanges:** 1½ fat, 1 vegetable, ½ fruit.

TEST KITCHEN TIP
Thanks to the pineapple, papaya, bell pepper and cabbage, this side dish covers more than 75% of the recommended daily value for vitamin C.

PINEAPPLE-PAPAYA SLAW

WINTER
BEET SALAD

VEGETABLE ORZO SOUP

This inviting soup is a perfect way to enjoy a rustic-style dish that's heavy on the veggies but light on the prep work. Hearty broth, protein-rich beans and a handful of orzo help fortify against the cold.
—*Taste of Home* Test Kitchen

- -

Prep: 15 min. • **Cook:** 25 min.
Makes: 6 servings (2 qt.)

- 1   **medium sweet yellow pepper, chopped**
- 1   **medium onion, chopped**
- 2   **tsp. olive oil**
- 3   **garlic cloves, minced**
- 1   **jar (24 oz.) garden-style spaghetti sauce**
- 1   **pkg. (16 oz.) frozen Italian vegetables**
- 1   **can (15 oz.) cannellini beans, rinsed and drained**
- 1   **can (14½ oz.) chicken broth**
- ½   **lb. small red potatoes, quartered**
- 1   **cup water**
- ⅓   **cup uncooked orzo pasta**
- ½   **tsp. dried marjoram**
- ½   **tsp. dried thyme**

Saute the pepper and onion in oil in a Dutch oven until tender. Add garlic; cook 1 minute longer. Stir in the remaining ingredients. Bring to a boil. Reduce heat; cover and simmer for 15-20 minutes or until potatoes and pasta are tender.

1⅓ cups: 254 cal., 4g fat (0 sat. fat), 2mg chol., 841mg sod., 45g carb. (12g sugars, 8g fiber), 8g pro.

WINTER BEET SALAD

Use prepackaged salad greens to save a little time with this recipe. The simple dressing is easy to assemble.
—*Taste of Home* Test Kitchen

- -

Prep: 20 min. • **Bake:** 1 hour + cooling
Makes: 4 servings

- 2   **medium fresh beets**
- 1   **pkg. (5 oz.) mixed salad greens**
- 2   **medium navel oranges, peeled and sliced**
- 1   **small fennel bulb, halved and thinly sliced**
- ¼   **cup chopped hazelnuts, toasted**

DRESSING

- 3   **Tbsp. olive oil**
- 2   **Tbsp. orange juice**
- 1   **Tbsp. balsamic vinegar**
- 2   **tsp. grated orange zest**
- ¼   **tsp. onion powder**

Preheat oven to 425°. Cut slits in beets; place on a baking sheet. Bake until tender, about 1 hour. When cool enough to handle, peel the beets and cut into wedges. Divide greens among salad plates; top with beets, oranges, fennel and hazelnuts. Combine the dressing ingredients in a jar with a tight-fitting lid; shake well. Drizzle over salads.

Note: To toast nuts, bake in a shallow pan in a 350° oven for 5-10 minutes or cook in a skillet over low heat until nuts are lightly browned, stirring occasionally.

1 serving: 213 cal., 15g fat (2g sat. fat), 0 chol., 80mg sod., 21g carb. (12g sugars, 6g fiber), 4g pro. **Diabetic exchanges:** 3 fat, 2 vegetable, ½ starch.

COMFORTING
CHICKEN NOODLE SOUP

TASTE OF HOME
TEST
KITCHEN
RECIPE OF THE YEAR
★★★★

COMFORTING CHICKEN NOODLE SOUP

A good friend made us this rich, comforting soup after the birth of our son. It was such a help to have dinner taken care of until I was back on my feet. It's so simple to fix, I now give a pot of it (along with the recipe) to other new mothers.
—Joanna Sargent, Sandy, UT

- -

Takes: 25 min. • **Makes:** 12 servings (3 qt.)

- 2 qt. water
- 8 tsp. chicken bouillon granules
- 6½ cups uncooked wide egg noodles
- 2 cans (10¾ oz. each) condensed cream of chicken soup, undiluted
- 3 cups cubed cooked chicken
- 1 cup sour cream
   Minced fresh parsley

1. In a large saucepan, bring water and bouillon to a boil. Add the noodles; cook, uncovered, until tender, about 10 minutes. Do not drain. Add the soup and chicken; heat through.
2. Remove from the heat; stir in the sour cream. Sprinkle with minced parsley.
1 cup: 218 cal., 9g fat (4g sat. fat), 67mg chol., 980mg sod., 18g carb. (2g sugars, 1g fiber), 15g pro.

> Here's my favorite recipe! It's so creamy and filling, and it's actually easy to prepare. I'm in love with it.
> —LAURIE DIXON, DIGITAL EDITOR

COBB SALAD

COBB SALAD

Made on the fly by Hollywood restaurateur Bob Cobb in 1937, the Cobb salad now is a world-famous American dish. Here's a fresh take, with all the original appeal and an extra-special presentation.
—*Taste of Home* Test Kitchen

- -

Takes: 40 min.
Makes: 6 servings (1¼ cups dressing)

- ¼ cup red wine vinegar
- 2 tsp. salt
- 1 tsp. lemon juice
- 1 small garlic clove, minced
- ¾ tsp. coarsely ground pepper
- ¾ tsp. Worcestershire sauce
- ¼ tsp. sugar
- ¼ tsp. ground mustard
- ¾ cup canola oil
- ¼ cup olive oil

SALAD
- 6½ cups torn romaine
- 2½ cups torn curly endive
- 1 bunch watercress (4 oz.), trimmed, divided
- 2 cooked chicken breasts, chopped
- 2 medium tomatoes, seeded and chopped
- 1 medium ripe avocado, peeled and chopped
- 3 hard-boiled large eggs, chopped
- ½ cup crumbled blue or Roquefort cheese
- 6 bacon strips, cooked and crumbled
- 2 Tbsp. minced fresh chives

1. In a blender, combine first 8 ingredients. While processing, gradually add canola and olive oils in a steady stream.
2. In a large bowl, combine the romaine, endive and half of the watercress; toss lightly. Transfer to a serving platter. Arrange the chicken, tomatoes, avocado, eggs, cheese and bacon over the greens; sprinkle with chives. Top the with remaining watercress. Cover and chill until serving.
3. To serve, drizzle 1 cup dressing over salad. Serve with remaining dressing if desired.
1 serving: 575 cal., 52g fat (8g sat. fat), 147mg chol., 1171mg sod., 10g carb. (3g sugars, 5g fiber), 20g pro.

TURKEY RANCH WRAPS

Here's a cool idea that's ready to gobble up in no time. It's a terrific use for deli turkey. Just add lettuce, tomato, green pepper, shredded cheese and ranch dressing for a flavorful blend.
—*Taste of Home* Test Kitchen

Takes: 10 min. • **Makes:** 4 servings

8	thin slices cooked turkey
4	flour tortillas (6 in.), room temperature
1	large tomato, thinly sliced
1	medium green pepper, cut into thin strips
1	cup shredded lettuce
1	cup shredded cheddar cheese
⅓	cup ranch salad dressing

Place 2 slices of turkey on each tortilla. Layer with tomato, green pepper, lettuce and cheese. Drizzle with salad dressing. Roll up tightly.
1 serving: 403 cal., 25g fat (9g sat. fat), 76mg chol., 601mg sod., 19g carb. (3g sugars, 1g fiber), 26g pro.

DID YOU KNOW?
Turkey can help you ward off a cold; it's packed with selenium, an immune-boosting mineral.

SHAVED BRUSSELS SPROUT SALAD

TASTE OF HOME
TEST KITCHEN
RECIPE OF THE YEAR
★ ★ ★ ★ ★

SHAVED BRUSSELS SPROUT SALAD

The first time my friends tasted my new side dish, they said it was phenomenal. The longer you let it chill in the fridge, the more tender the sprouts will become.
—Nick Iverson, Denver, CO

Prep: 20 min. + chilling • **Makes:** 6 servings

1	Tbsp. cider vinegar
1	Tbsp. Dijon mustard
2	tsp. honey
1	small garlic clove, minced
2	Tbsp. olive oil
1	lb. Brussels sprouts, halved and thinly sliced
1	small red onion, halved and thinly sliced
⅓	cup dried cherries, chopped
⅓	cup chopped pecans, toasted

1. Whisk together the first 4 ingredients; gradually whisk in oil until blended.
2. Place Brussels sprouts, onion and dried cherries in a large bowl; toss with dressing. Refrigerate, covered, at least 1 hour. Stir in pecans just before serving.
Note: To toast nuts, bake in a shallow pan in a 350° oven for 5-10 minutes or cook in a skillet over low heat until the nuts lightly browned, stirring occasionally.
¾ cup: 156 cal., 9g fat (1g sat. fat), 0 chol., 79mg sod., 18g carb. (10g sugars, 4g fiber), 3g pro. **Diabetic exchanges:** 2 fat, 1 vegetable, ½ starch.

HEARTY BREADED FISH SANDWICHES

Fishing for a burger alternative? Consider it caught. A hint of cayenne is cooled by a creamy yogurt and mayo sauce in this fish sandwich that will put your local drive-thru to shame.
—*Taste of Home* Test Kitchen

- -

Takes: 30 min. • **Makes:** 4 sandwiches

- ½ cup dry bread crumbs
- ½ tsp. garlic powder
- ½ tsp. cayenne pepper
- ½ tsp. dried parsley flakes
- 4 cod fillets (6 oz. each)
- 4 whole wheat hamburger buns, split
- ¼ cup plain yogurt
- ¼ cup fat-free mayonnaise
- 2 tsp. lemon juice
- 2 tsp. sweet pickle relish
- ¼ tsp. dried minced onion
- 4 lettuce leaves
- 4 slices tomato
- 4 slices sweet onion

1. In a shallow bowl, combine the bread crumbs, garlic powder, cayenne and parsley. Coat fillets with bread crumb mixture.
2. On lightly oiled grill rack, grill the cod, covered, over medium heat or broil 4 in. from the heat for 4-5 minutes on each side or until fish flakes easily with a fork. Grill the buns over medium heat for 30-60 seconds or until toasted.
3. Meanwhile, in a small bowl, combine the yogurt, mayonnaise, lemon juice, relish and minced onion; spread over bun bottoms. Top with cod, lettuce, tomato and onion; replace bun tops.

1 sandwich: 292 cal., 4g fat (1g sat. fat), 68mg chol., 483mg sod., 32g carb. (7g sugars, 4g fiber), 32g pro. **Diabetic exchanges:** 5 lean meat, 2 starch.

Salsa Fish Sandwiches: Follow method as directed but replace plain yogurt with salsa and omit lemon juice, relish and dried minced onion. Top sandwiches with sliced tomato and fresh cilantro.

Slaw-Topped Fish Sandwiches: Follow the method as directed but omit relish, substitute the red wine vinegar for lemon juice and stir 1½ cups coleslaw mix into the mayonnaise mixture. Omit lettuce, tomato and onion and top cod with slaw mixture.

SCALLOP & SHRIMP CHOWDER

Shrimp and scallops make a rich and cheesy chowder feel extra special. Crispy bacon makes a yummy classic garnish.
—*Taste of Home* Test Kitchen

- -

Prep: 15 min. • **Cook:** 20 min.
Makes: 6 servings

- 6 bacon strips, chopped
- 2 celery ribs, finely chopped
- ½ cup chopped sweet orange pepper
- 1 small onion, finely chopped
- 2 garlic cloves, minced
- ¼ cup all-purpose flour
- 1 can (14½ oz.) chicken broth
- 2 cups 2% milk
- 2 medium red potatoes, cubed
- 1 tsp. seafood seasoning
- ¼ tsp. salt
- ½ lb. uncooked medium shrimp, peeled and deveined
- ½ lb. bay scallops
- 1½ cups shredded cheddar cheese

1. In a large saucepan, cook the bacon over medium heat until crisp. Remove to paper towels with a slotted spoon; drain, reserving 2 Tbsp. drippings.
2. In the drippings, saute the celery, orange pepper and onion until crisp-tender. Add the garlic; cook 1 minute longer. Stir in the flour until blended; gradually add broth and milk. Bring to a boil; cook and stir for 1 minute or until thickened.
3. Add the potatoes, seafood seasoning and salt; return to a boil. Reduce heat; cover and simmer for 10-15 minutes or until potatoes are tender.
4. Add shrimp and scallops; cook and stir for 3-4 minutes or until shrimp turn pink and scallops are opaque. Stir in cheese until melted. Garnish each serving with bacon.

1 cup: 309 cal., 14g fat (8g sat. fat), 104mg chol., 981mg sod., 19g carb. (6g sugars, 1g fiber), 26g pro.

HEARTY BREADED FISH SANDWICHES

**TEXAS BLACK
BEAN SOUP**

PEAR WALDORF PITAS

Here's a guaranteed table brightener for a shower, luncheon or party. Just stand back and watch these sandwiches vanish. For an eye-catching presentation, I tuck each one into a colorful folded napkin.
—Roxann Parker, Dover, DE

- -

Prep: 20 min. + chilling
Makes: 20 mini pitas halves

- 2   medium ripe pears, diced
- ½   cup thinly sliced celery
- ½   cup halved seedless red grapes
- 2   Tbsp. finely chopped walnuts
- 2   Tbsp. lemon yogurt
- 2   Tbsp. mayonnaise
- ⅛   tsp. poppy seeds
- 20 miniature pita pocket halves
      Lettuce leaves

1. In a large bowl, combine the pears, celery, grapes and walnuts. In another bowl, whisk yogurt, mayonnaise and poppy seeds. Add to pear mixture; toss to coat. Refrigerate for 1 hour or overnight.
2. Line pita halves with lettuce; fill each with 2 Tbsp. pear mixture.
1 pita half: 67 cal., 2g fat (0 sat. fat), 0 chol., 86mg sod., 12g carb. (3g sugars, 1g fiber), 2g pro. **Diabetic exchanges:** 1 starch.

TEXAS BLACK BEAN SOUP

This hearty meatless stew made with convenient canned items is perfect for spicing up a family gathering on a cool day. It tastes like it's made with love, and yet it requires so little time and attention.
—Pamela Scott, Garland, TX

- -

Prep: 5 min. • **Cook:** 4 hours
Makes: 10 servings (2½ qt.)

- 2   cans (15 oz. each) black beans, rinsed and drained
- 1   can (14½ oz.) stewed tomatoes or Mexican stewed tomatoes, cut up
- 1   can (14½ oz.) diced tomatoes or diced tomatoes with green chilies
- 1   can (14½ oz.) chicken broth
- 1   can (11 oz.) Mexicorn, drained
- 2   cans (4 oz. each) chopped green chiles
- 4   green onions, thinly sliced
- 2   to 3 Tbsp. chili powder
- 1   tsp. ground cumin
- ½   tsp. dried minced garlic

In a 3-qt. slow cooker, combine all the ingredients. Cover and cook on high 4-6 hours or until heated through.
1 cup: 91 cal., 0 fat (0 sat. fat), 0 chol., 609mg sod., 19g carb. (6g sugars, 4g fiber), 4g pro.

PEAR
WALDORF
PITAS

SHRIMP GAZPACHO

Here's a refreshing twist on the classic chilled tomato soup. Our recipe features shrimp, lime and plenty of avocado.
—*Taste of Home* Test Kitchen

Prep: 15 min. + chilling
Makes: 12 servings (3 qt.)

6 cups spicy hot V8 juice
2 cups cold water
½ cup lime juice
½ cup minced fresh cilantro
½ tsp. salt
¼ to ½ tsp. hot pepper sauce
1 lb. peeled and deveined cooked shrimp (31-40 per lb.), tails removed
1 medium cucumber, seeded and diced
2 medium tomatoes, seeded and chopped
2 medium ripe avocados, peeled and chopped

SHRIMP
GAZPACHO

In a large nonreactive bowl, mix the first 6 ingredients. Gently stir in remaining ingredients. Refrigerate, covered, 1 hour before serving.

Note: This recipe is best served the same day it's made.

1 cup: 112 cal., 4g fat (1g sat. fat), 57mg chol., 399mg sod., 9g carb. (5g sugars, 3g fiber), 10g pro. **Diabetic exchanges:** 1 lean meat, 2 vegetable, 1 fat.

OLD-FASHIONED TURKEY NOODLE SOUP

Make the most of leftover turkey with a delicious homemade soup. Roasting the turkey bones, garlic and vegetables adds a rich flavor without added fat. Brimming with noodles, this is cozy comfort in a bowl!
—*Taste of Home* Test Kitchen

- -

Prep: 3½ hours + chilling • **Cook:** 45 min.
Makes: 10 servings (3¾ qt.)

BROTH
- 1 leftover turkey carcass (from a 12- to 14-lb. turkey)
- 2 cooked turkey wings, meat removed
- 2 cooked turkey drumsticks, meat removed
- 1 turkey neck bone
- 1 medium unpeeled onion, cut into wedges
- 2 small unpeeled carrots, cut into chunks
- 6 to 8 garlic cloves, peeled
- 4 qt. plus 1 cup cold water, divided

SOUP
- 3 qt. water
- 5 cups uncooked egg noodles
- 2 cups diced carrots
- 2 cups diced celery
- 3 cups cubed cooked turkey
- ¼ cup minced fresh parsley
- 2½ tsp. salt
- 2 tsp. dried thyme
- 1 tsp. pepper

1. Place the turkey carcass, bones from the wings and drumsticks, neck bone, onion, carrots and garlic in a 15x10x1-in. baking pan coated with cooking spray. Bake, uncovered, at 400° for 1 hour, turning once.
2. Transfer carcass, bones and vegetables to an 8-qt. stockpot. Add 4 qts. cold water; set aside. Pour remaining cold water into baking pan, stirring to loosen browned bits. Add to pot. Bring to a boil. Reduce heat; cover and simmer for 3-4 hours.
3. Cool slightly. Strain broth; discard bones and vegetables. Set stockpot in an ice-water bath until broth cools, stirring occasionally. Cover and refrigerate overnight.
4. Skim fat from broth. Cover and bring to a boil. Reduce heat to a simmer. Meanwhile, in a Dutch oven, bring 3 qts. water to a boil. Add the egg noodles and carrots; cook for 4 minutes. Add celery; cook 5-7 minutes longer or until noodles and vegetables are tender. Drain; add to simmering broth. Add cubed turkey; heat through. Stir in the fresh parsley, salt, thyme and pepper.

1½ cups: 188 cal., 4g fat (1g sat. fat), 66mg chol., 670mg sod., 17g carb. (2g sugars, 2g fiber), 20g pro. **Diabetic exchanges:** 2 lean meat, 1 starch.

SOUR CREAM CUCUMBERS

For years it's been a tradition at our house to serve this dish with the other Hungarian specialties my mom learned to make from the women at church. It's especially good during the summer when the cucumbers are fresh-picked from the garden.
—Pamela Eaton, Monclova, OH

- -

Prep: 15 min. + chilling • **Makes:** 8 servings

- ½ cup sour cream
- 3 Tbsp. white vinegar
- 1 Tbsp. sugar
  Pepper to taste
- 4 medium cucumbers, peeled if desired and thinly sliced
- 1 small sweet onion, thinly sliced and separated into rings

In a large bowl, whisk sour cream, vinegar, sugar and pepper until blended. Add the sliced cucumbers and onion; toss to coat. Refrigerate, covered, at least 4 hours. Serve with a slotted spoon.

¾ cup: 62 cal., 3g fat (2g sat. fat), 10mg chol., 5mg sod., 7g carb. (5g sugars, 2g fiber), 2g pro. **Diabetic exchanges:** 1 vegetable, ½ fat.

TASTE OF HOME
TEST KITCHEN
RECIPE OF THE YEAR
★ ★ ★ ★ ★

SOUR CREAM CUCUMBERS

MOZZARELLA BEEF ROLL-UPS

The kids will love these pepperoni and beef wraps. They're easy to assemble because each tortilla is simply wrapped around a portion of hearty meat filling with a piece of string cheese.
—*Taste of Home* Test Kitchen

- -

Takes: 30 min. • **Makes:** 6 servings

- 1 lb. ground beef
- 1 medium green pepper, chopped
- ⅓ cup chopped onion
- 1 can (8 oz.) pizza sauce
- 2 oz. sliced pepperoni (about ⅔ cup)
- ½ tsp. dried oregano
- 6 flour tortillas (10 in.), warmed
- 6 pieces string cheese (about 6 oz.)

1. Preheat oven to 350°. In a large skillet, cook and crumble the beef with pepper and onion over medium-high heat until no longer pink, 5-7 minutes; drain. Stir in pizza sauce, pepperoni and oregano.
2. Spoon ½ cup mixture across center of each tortilla; top with a piece of string cheese. Fold bottom and sides of tortilla over filling and roll up.
3. Place on an ungreased baking sheet, seam side down. Bake until heated through, about 10 minutes.

Freeze option: Cool beef mixture before assembly. Individually wrap roll-ups in foil and freeze in a freezer container. To use, partially thaw overnight in refrigerator. Reheat the foil-wrapped roll-ups on a baking sheet in a preheated 350° oven until heated through. To reheat individually, remove foil and rewrap in paper towel; place on a microwave-safe plate. Microwave roll-ups on high until heated through, turning once. Let stand 15 seconds.
1 roll-up: 513 cal., 25g fat (11g sat. fat), 71mg chol., 1064mg sod., 41g carb. (5g sugars, 4g fiber), 30g pro.

CONTEST-WINNING BAVARIAN MEATBALL HOAGIES

I love the convenience of my slow cooker, and these mouthwatering meatballs are just one reason why. They're a crowd-pleaser when served as appetizers—or spooned over crusty rolls and topped with cheese for irresistible sandwiches.
—Peggy Rios, Mechanicsville, VA

- -

Prep: 15 min. • **Cook:** 3 hours
Makes: 12 sandwiches

- 1 pkg. (32 oz.) frozen fully cooked Italian meatballs
- ½ cup chopped onion
- ¼ cup packed brown sugar
- 1 envelope onion soup mix
- 1 can (12 oz.) beer or nonalcoholic beer
- 12 hoagie buns, split
- 3 cups shredded Swiss cheese

1. In a 3-qt. slow cooker, combine meatballs, onion, brown sugar, soup mix and beer. Cook, covered, on low until meatballs are heated through, 3-4 hours.
2. Place 5-6 meatballs on each bun bottom. Sprinkle each sandwich with ¼ cup cheese. Place on baking sheets. Broil 4-6 in. from the heat until cheese is melted, 2-3 minutes. Replace bun tops.
1 sandwich: 643 cal., 36g fat (18g sat. fat), 95mg chol., 1302mg sod., 49g carb. (13g sugars, 4g fiber), 29g pro.

MOZZARELLA BEEF ROLL-UPS

GUACAMOLE TOSSED SALAD

GRILLED TOMATO SANDWICHES

These sandwiches can be assembled in a snap—and are perfect for summer lunches!
—Wendy Stenman, Germantown, WI

Takes: 30 min. • **Makes:** 4 sandwiches

- 8   slices tomato (¾ in. thick)
- ½   tsp. salt, divided
- 6   Tbsp. mayonnaise
- 1   tsp. lemon juice
- 1   garlic clove, minced
- 1   round cheese focaccia bread or focaccia bread of your choice (12 in.), halved lengthwise
- 1   Tbsp. balsamic vinegar
- ¼   tsp. pepper
- 1   cup chopped water-packed artichoke hearts, rinsed and drained
- 3   cups torn romaine or spinach

1. Sprinkle one side of tomato slices with ⅛ tsp. salt. Place salt side down on paper towels for 10 minutes. Repeat with second side. In a small mixing bowl, combine the mayonnaise, lemon juice and garlic; set mixture aside.
2. Place the bread cut side down on a lightly oiled grill rack. Place tomatoes on grill. Grill, covered, over medium heat or broil 4 in. from the heat for 2 minutes or until bread is golden brown.
3. Sprinkle tomatoes with the vinegar, pepper and remaining salt. Spread the mayonnaise mixture over bread. On the bottom half, layer tomatoes, artichokes and romaine; replace bread top. Cut into wedges; serve immediately.
1 sandwich: 495 cal., 21g fat (3g sat. fat), 8mg chol., 1203mg sod., 64g carb. (3g sugars, 4g fiber), 12g pro.

TEST KITCHEN TIP

For best results, the tomatoes must be sliced thick and grilled no more than the 2 minutes specified in the recipe above.

GUACAMOLE TOSSED SALAD

This blend of avocados, tomatoes, red onion and greens gets additional pizzazz from bacon and a slightly spicy vinaigrette.
—Lori Fischer, Chino Hills, CA

Takes: 15 min. • **Makes:** 4 servings

- 2   medium tomatoes, seeded and chopped
- ½   small red onion, sliced and separated into rings
- 6   bacon strips, cooked and crumbled
- ⅓   cup canola oil
- 2   Tbsp. cider vinegar
- 1   tsp. salt
- ¼   tsp. pepper
- ¼   tsp. hot pepper sauce
- 2   large ripe avocados, peeled and cubed
- 4   cups torn salad greens

1. In a large bowl, combine the tomatoes, onion and bacon; set aside.
2. In a small bowl, whisk the oil, vinegar, salt, pepper and hot pepper sauce. Pour over tomato mixture; toss gently. Add avocados.
3. Place greens in a large salad bowl; add avocado mixture and toss to coat.
1 serving: 531 cal., 51g fat (7g sat. fat), 12mg chol., 868mg sod., 17g carb. (3g sugars, 10g fiber), 9g pro.

TASTE OF HOME
TEST KITCHEN
RECIPE OF THE YEAR
★ ★ ★ ★

THE BEST CHICKEN &
DUMPLINGS

THE BEST CHICKEN & DUMPLINGS

Chicken and dumplings harken back to my childhood and chilly days when we devoured those cute little balls of dough swimming in hot, rich broth.
—Erika Monroe-Williams, Scottsdale, AZ

- -

Prep: 25 min. • **Cook:** 1 hour 10 min.
Makes: 8 servings (3 qt.)

- ¾ cup all-purpose flour, divided
- ½ tsp. salt
- ½ tsp. freshly ground pepper
- 1 broiler/fryer chicken (about 3 lbs.), cut up
- 2 Tbsp. canola oil
- 1 large onion, chopped
- 2 medium carrots, chopped
- 2 celery ribs, chopped
- 3 garlic cloves, minced
- 6 cups chicken stock
- ½ cup white wine or apple cider
- 2 tsp. sugar
- 2 bay leaves
- 5 whole peppercorns

DUMPLINGS
- 1⅓ cups all-purpose flour
- 2 tsp. baking powder
- ¾ tsp. salt
- ⅔ cup 2% milk
- 1 Tbsp. butter, melted

SOUP
- ½ cup heavy whipping cream
- 2 tsp. minced fresh parsley
- 2 tsp. minced fresh thyme
  Additional salt and pepper to taste

1. In a shallow bowl, mix ½ cup flour, salt and pepper. Add the chicken, 1 piece at a time, and toss to coat; shake off excess. In a 6-qt. stockpot, heat oil over medium-high heat. Brown the chicken in batches on all sides; remove from pan.
2. Add onion, carrots and celery to same pan; cook and stir 6-8 minutes or until onion is tender. Add garlic; cook and stir 1 minute longer. Stir in ¼ cup flour until blended. Gradually add stock, stirring constantly. Stir in wine, sugar, bay leaves and peppercorns. Return the chicken to pan; bring to a boil. Reduce heat; simmer, covered, until chicken juices run clear, 20-25 minutes.

3. For dumplings, in a bowl, whisk flour, baking powder and salt. In another bowl, whisk milk and melted butter until blended. Add to flour mixture; stir just until moistened (do not overmix). Drop dough by rounded tablespoonfuls onto a parchment-lined baking sheet; set aside.
4. Remove the chicken from stockpot; cool slightly. Discard bay leaves and skim fat from soup. Remove skin and bones from chicken and discard. Using 2 forks, coarsely shred meat into 1- to 1½-in. pieces; return to soup. Cook, covered, on high until mixture reaches a simmer.
5. Drop dumplings on top of simmering soup, a few at a time. Reduce heat to low; cook, covered, 15-18 minutes or until a toothpick inserted in center of dumplings comes out clean (do not lift cover while simmering). Gently stir in cream, parsley and thyme. Season with additional salt and pepper to taste.
1½ cups: 470 cal., 24g fat (8g sat. fat), 104mg chol., 892mg sod., 29g carb. (5g sugars, 2g fiber), 32g pro.

GRANDMA'S SPINACH SALAD

GRANDMA'S SPINACH SALAD

With all its fresh ingredients, this pretty spinach salad was my grandma's favorite. Even my little ones like it (but don't tell them spinach is good for them!).
—Shelley Riebel, Armada, MI

- -

Takes: 20 min. • **Makes:** 8 servings

- ½ cup sugar
- ½ cup canola oil
- ¼ cup white vinegar
- ½ tsp. celery seed
- 10 oz. fresh baby spinach (about 13 cups)
- 1 small red onion, thinly sliced
- ½ lb. sliced fresh mushrooms
- 5 hard-boiled large eggs, sliced
- 8 bacon strips, cooked and crumbled

1. Whisk first 4 ingredients until the sugar is dissolved.
2. In a 13x9-in. dish, layer half of each of the following: spinach, onion, mushrooms and eggs. Repeat layers. Drizzle with dressing; top with bacon.
1¼ cups: 280 cal., 21g fat (3g sat. fat), 125mg chol., 214mg sod., 16g carb. (14g sugars, 1g fiber), 9g pro.

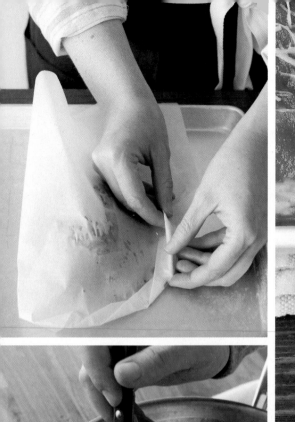

VEGETARIAN
CABBAGE ROLLS
PAGE 127

Fish, Seafood & Meatless

Where's the beef? Not in these dishes—and you'll never miss it! At *Taste of Home*, we have lots of people who have cut down on meat, and you'd better believe they have a wealth of delicious options at their fingertips. These recipes range from light and tasty to hearty and savory, and each provides a perfect, satisfying meal after a busy workday.

CHEESE
MANICOTTI

CHEESE MANICOTTI

This was the first meal I ever cooked for my husband. All these years later, he still enjoys my manicotti!
—Joan Hallford, North Richland Hills, TX

Prep: 25 min. • **Bake:** 1 hour
Makes: 7 servings

- 1 carton (15 oz.) reduced-fat ricotta cheese
- 1 small onion, finely chopped
- 1 large egg, lightly beaten
- 2 Tbsp. minced fresh parsley
- ½ tsp. pepper
- ¼ tsp. salt
- 1 cup shredded part-skim mozzarella cheese, divided
- 1 cup grated Parmesan cheese, divided
- 4 cups marinara sauce
- ½ cup water
- 1 pkg. (8 oz.) manicotti shells

1. Preheat oven to 350°. In a small bowl, mix the first 6 ingredients; stir in ½ cup mozzarella cheese and ½ cup Parmesan cheese. In another bowl, mix the marinara sauce and water; spread ¾ cup sauce onto the bottom of a 13x9-in. baking dish coated with cooking spray. Fill uncooked manicotti shells with the ricotta mixture; arrange over sauce. Top with the remaining sauce.
2. Bake, covered, 50 minutes or until pasta is tender. Sprinkle with the remaining ½ cup mozzarella cheese and ½ cup Parmesan cheese. Bake, uncovered, 10-15 minutes longer or until cheese is melted. If desired, top with additional parsley.

2 stuffed manicotti: 337 cal., 11g fat (5g sat. fat), 59mg chol., 1070mg sod., 41g carb. (12g sugars, 4g fiber), 18g pro. **Diabetic exchanges:** 3 starch, 2 lean meat, ½ fat.

COLORFUL SHRIMP PAD THAI

COLORFUL SHRIMP PAD THAI

Bright fresh veggie flavors, a splash of tart lime juice, the crunch of peanuts and a hint of heat make this healthy and beautiful shrimp stir-fry a real standout.
—*Taste of Home* Test Kitchen

Prep: 30 min. • **Cook:** 15 min.
Makes: 6 servings

- 6 oz. uncooked thick rice noodles
- ¼ cup rice vinegar
- 3 Tbsp. reduced-sodium soy sauce
- 2 Tbsp. sugar
- 2 Tbsp. fish sauce or additional reduced-sodium soy sauce
- 1 Tbsp. lime juice
- 2 tsp. Thai chili sauce
- 1 tsp. sesame oil
- ¼ tsp. crushed red pepper flakes

STIR-FRY
- 1½ lbs. uncooked medium shrimp, peeled and deveined
- 3 tsp. sesame oil, divided
- 2 cups fresh snow peas
- 2 medium carrots, grated
- 2 garlic cloves, minced
- 2 large eggs, lightly beaten
- 2 cups bean sprouts
- 2 green onions, chopped
- ¼ cup minced fresh cilantro
- ¼ cup unsalted dry roasted peanuts, chopped

1. Cook noodles according to the package directions. Meanwhile, in a small bowl, combine vinegar, soy sauce, sugar, fish sauce, lime juice, chili sauce, oil and pepper flakes until blended; set aside.
2. In a large nonstick skillet or wok, stir-fry shrimp in 2 tsp. oil until the shrimp turn pink; remove and keep warm. Stir-fry snow peas and carrots in remaining oil for 1-2 minutes. Add garlic, cook 1 minute longer or until vegetables are crisp-tender. Add eggs; cook and stir until eggs are set.
3. Drain noodles; add to vegetable mixture. Stir the vinegar mixture and add to the skillet. Bring to a boil. Add shrimp, bean sprouts and green onions; heat through. Sprinkle with cilantro and peanuts.

1 cup: 352 cal., 10g fat (2g sat. fat), 208mg chol., 955mg sod., 38g carb. (10g sugars, 4g fiber), 28g pro.

SWEET & SPICY GLAZED SALMON

There's magic here: A glaze of brown sugar, soy sauce, mustard and ginger is baked atop salmon to create a sweet and zesty entree. If you want to reward the family with a little something special, this fits the bill.
—*Taste of Home* Test Kitchen

Takes: 30 min. • **Makes:** 4 servings

- ¼ cup brown sugar
- 3 Tbsp. Dijon mustard
- 2 Tbsp. reduced-sodium soy sauce
- 1 tsp. paprika
- ¼ tsp. ground ginger
- ¼ tsp. sesame oil
- 4 salmon fillets (6 oz. each)
- ½ tsp. pepper
- ¼ tsp. salt

1. Combine the brown sugar, Dijon mustard, soy sauce, paprika, ginger and oil in a small saucepan. Bring to a boil. Cook and stir until brown sugar is dissolved.
2. Place salmon skin side down on a greased broiler pan. Sprinkle with pepper and salt. Broil 6 in. from the heat for 10-15 minutes or until fish flakes easily with a fork; brush with glaze during last 1-2 minutes of cooking.
1 fillet: 337 cal., 16g fat (3g sat. fat), 85mg chol., 795mg sod., 14g carb. (13g sugars, 0 fiber), 29g pro.

CRAB-TOPPED FISH FILLETS

CRAB-TOPPED FISH FILLETS

Elegant but truly no bother, this recipe is perfect for company. Toasting the almonds gives them a little more crunch, which is a delightful way to top the fish fillets.
—Mary Tuthill, Fort Myers Beach, FL

Takes: 30 min. • **Makes:** 4 servings

- 4 sole or cod fillets, or fish fillets of your choice (6 oz. each)
- 1 can (6 oz.) crabmeat, drained and flaked, or 1 cup imitation crabmeat, chopped
- ½ cup grated Parmesan cheese
- ½ cup mayonnaise
- 1 tsp. lemon juice
- ⅓ cup slivered almonds, toasted Paprika, optional

1. Preheat oven to 350°. Place the fillets in a greased 13x9-in. baking dish. Bake, uncovered, until the fish flakes easily with a fork, 18-22 minutes. Meanwhile, in a large bowl, combine the crab, cheese, mayonnaise and lemon juice.
2. Drain cooking juices from baking dish; spoon the crab mixture over the fillets. Broil 4-5 in. from the heat until topping is lightly browned, about 5 minutes. Sprinkle with almonds and, if desired, paprika.
1 fillet: 429 cal., 31g fat (6g sat. fat), 128mg chol., 1063mg sod., 3g carb. (0 sugars, 1g fiber), 33g pro.

VEG JAMBALAYA

This flavorful entree uses convenient canned beans in place of the meat— and never lets you leave hungry!
—Crystal Jo Bruns, Iliff, CO

Prep: 10 min. • **Cook:** 30 min.
Makes: 6 servings

- 1 Tbsp. canola oil
- 1 medium green pepper, chopped
- 1 medium onion, chopped
- 1 celery rib, chopped
- 3 garlic cloves, minced
- 2 cups water
- 1 can (14½ oz.) diced tomatoes, undrained
- 1 can (8 oz.) tomato sauce
- ½ tsp. Italian seasoning
- ¼ tsp. salt
- ¼ tsp. crushed red pepper flakes
- ⅛ tsp. fennel seed, crushed
- 1 cup uncooked long grain rice
- 1 can (16 oz.) butter beans, rinsed and drained
- 1 can (16 oz.) red beans, rinsed and drained

1. In a Dutch oven, heat oil over medium-high heat. Add the green pepper, onion and celery; cook and stir until tender. Add garlic; cook 1 minute longer.
2. Add the water, tomatoes, tomato sauce and seasonings. Bring to a boil; stir in rice. Reduce heat; cover and simmer until liquid is absorbed and rice is tender, 15-18 minutes. Stir in beans; heat through.
1⅓ cups: 281 cal., 3g fat (0 sat. fat), 0 chol., 796mg sod., 56g carb. (6g sugars, 9g fiber), 11g pro.

SESAME SHRIMP & RICE

A handful of convenience items and a flash in the skillet allow you to put a delightfully flavorful, high-quality meal on the table in minutes.
—*Taste of Home* Test Kitchen

Takes: 10 min. • **Makes:** 4 servings

- 1 pkg. (8.8 oz.) ready-to-serve long grain rice
- 1 cup fresh or frozen snow peas, thawed
- 2 green onions, sliced
- 1 tsp. canola oil
- 1 lb. cooked medium shrimp, peeled and deveined
- 1 can (20 oz.) pineapple tidbits, drained
- 1 can (11 oz.) mandarin oranges, drained
- ¼ cup sesame ginger salad dressing
- 2 Tbsp. slivered almonds, toasted

1. Microwave rice according to the package directions.
2. Meanwhile, in a large skillet or wok, stir-fry snow peas and onions in oil for 1 minute. Add shrimp, pineapple, oranges and salad dressing; cook until heated through and vegetables are crisp-tender.
3. Sprinkle with almonds. Serve with rice.
1½ cups: 407 cal., 11g fat (1g sat. fat), 172mg chol., 330mg sod., 49g carb. (24g sugars, 3g fiber), 28g pro.

VEG JAMBALAYA

BROILED PARMESAN TILAPIA

LIGHT & LEMONY SCAMPI

A touch more lemon helped me trim the calories in our favorite shrimp scampi recipe. For those who want to indulge, pass around the Parmesan.
—Ann Sheehy, Lawrence, MA

- -

Prep: 20 min. • **Cook:** 15 min.
Makes: 4 servings

- 1 lb. uncooked shrimp (26-30 per lb.)
- 8 oz. uncooked multigrain angel hair pasta
- 1 Tbsp. butter
- 1 Tbsp. olive oil
- 2 green onions, thinly sliced
- 4 garlic cloves, minced
- ½ cup reduced-sodium chicken broth
- 2 tsp. grated lemon zest
- 3 Tbsp. lemon juice
- ½ tsp. freshly ground pepper
- ¼ tsp. salt
- ¼ tsp. crushed red pepper flakes
- ¼ cup minced fresh parsley
  Grated Parmesan cheese, optional

1. Peel and devein shrimp, removing the tails. Cut each shrimp lengthwise in half. Cook pasta according to package directions.
2. In a large nonstick skillet, heat butter and oil over medium-high heat. Add shrimp, green onions and garlic; cook and stir until the shrimp turn pink, 2-3 minutes. Remove from pan with a slotted spoon.
3. Add broth, lemon zest, lemon juice, pepper, salt and red pepper flakes to the same pan. Bring to a boil; cook until the liquid is slightly reduced, about 1 minute. Return the shrimp to pan; heat through. Remove from heat.
4. Drain pasta; divide among 4 bowls. Top with the shrimp mixture; sprinkle with parsley. If desired, serve with cheese.
1 serving: 378 cal., 10g fat (3g sat. fat), 146mg chol., 405mg sod., 42g carb. (3g sugars, 5g fiber), 29g pro. **Diabetic exchanges:** 3 very lean meat, 2½ starch, 1½ fat.

BROILED PARMESAN TILAPIA

Even picky eaters will find a way to love fish when you plate up this toasty Parmesan-coated entree. I serve it with mashed cauliflower and a green salad for a low-calorie meal everyone can enjoy.
—Trisha Kruse, Eagle, ID

- -

Takes: 20 min. • **Makes:** 6 servings

- 6 tilapia fillets (6 oz. each)
- ¼ cup grated Parmesan cheese
- ¼ cup reduced-fat mayonnaise
- 2 Tbsp. lemon juice
- 1 Tbsp. butter, softened
- 1 garlic clove, minced
- 1 tsp. minced fresh basil or ¼ tsp. dried basil
- ½ tsp. seafood seasoning

1. Place fillets on a broiler pan coated with cooking spray. In a small bowl, combine the remaining ingredients; spread over fillets.
2. Broil 3-4 in. from heat for 10-12 minutes or until the fish flakes easily with a fork.
1 fillet: 207 cal., 8g fat (3g sat. fat), 94mg chol., 260mg sod., 2g carb. (1g sugars, 0 fiber), 33g pro. **Diabetic exchanges:** 5 lean meat, 1 fat.

LIGHT & LEMONY
SCAMPI

LENTIL
TACO CUPS

LENTIL TACO CUPS

My trusty muffin tin never fails to help me put fun and easy hand-held mains on the table for my family on busy weeknights. These festive vegetarian cups are always a hit with my kids; they're so flavorful, nobody misses the meat.
—Shauna Havey, Roy, UT

- -

Prep: 25 min. • **Bake:** 15 min.
Makes: 12 taco cups

- 12 mini flour tortillas, warmed
- 1 can (15 oz.) lentils, drained
- ¾ cup pico de gallo
- ½ cup enchilada sauce
- 2 Tbsp. taco seasoning
- 2 cups shredded Mexican cheese blend, divided

CREMA
- 1 cup sour cream
- ½ cup minced fresh cilantro
- 1 Tbsp. lime juice
- ¼ tsp. sea salt
     Shredded lettuce, sliced ripe olives and chopped tomatoes

1. Preheat oven to 425°. Press warm tortillas into 12 greased muffin cups, pleating sides as needed. In a large bowl, combine the lentils, pico de gallo, enchilada sauce and taco seasoning. Stir in 1½ cups cheese. Divide lentil mixture among the cups. Sprinkle with the remaining cheese.
2. Bake until heated through and cheese is melted, 12-15 minutes. Meanwhile, for the crema, combine sour cream, cilantro, lime juice and sea salt. Serve cups with crema, lettuce, olives and tomatoes.
2 taco cups: 303 cal., 20g fat (11g sat. fat), 43mg chol., 793mg sod., 17g carb. (3g sugars, 5g fiber), 14g pro.

TEST KITCHEN TIP
Skip the ½ cup cheese on top and switch to low-fat Greek yogurt to cut the saturated fat by more than 50 percent.

HERB-CRUMBED SALMON

Often we catch enough of our delicious Northwest salmon to send some to Michigan for my sister to enjoy. This crisp, lemony topping complementing the tender fish is a tasty way to enjoy it.
—Perlene Hoekema, Lynden, WA

- -

Takes: 30 min. • **Makes:** 4 servings

- 1½ cups soft bread crumbs
- 2 Tbsp. minced fresh parsley
- 1 Tbsp. minced fresh thyme or 1 tsp. dried thyme
- 2 garlic cloves, minced
- 1 tsp. grated lemon zest
- ½ tsp. salt
- ¼ tsp. lemon-pepper seasoning
- ¼ tsp. paprika
- 1 Tbsp. butter, melted
- 4 salmon fillets (6 oz. each)

1. Preheat oven to 400°. In a bowl, combine first 8 ingredients. Toss with melted butter.
2. Place the salmon, skin side down, in a 15x10x1-in. baking pan coated with cooking spray. Top with the crumb mixture, patting gently. Bake until topping is golden brown and the fish just begins to flake easily with a fork, 12-15 minutes.
Note: To make soft bread crumbs, tear bread into pieces and place in a food processor or blender. Cover and pulse until crumbs form. One slice of bread yields ½ to ¾ cup crumbs.
1 fillet: 339 cal., 19g fat (5g sat. fat), 93mg chol., 507mg sod., 9g carb. (1g sugars, 1g fiber), 31g pro. **Diabetic exchanges:** 4 lean meat, 1 fat, ½ starch.

HERB-CRUMBED SALMON

THREE-CHEESE PESTO PIZZA

We love the bold flavor of this pizza that's a bit different from the traditional. The pesto, cheese and olive topping makes a delicious statement. Serve it as a main dish, or cut in smaller pieces as a fun appetizer.
—Pat Stevens, Granbury, TX

- -

Takes: 30 min. • **Makes:** 6 servings

- ½ cup chopped red onion
- ½ cup chopped sweet red pepper
- 1 Tbsp. olive oil
- 1 prebaked 12-in. thin pizza crust
- ½ cup prepared pesto sauce
- ½ cup chopped ripe olives
- 1 cup crumbled feta cheese
- 1 cup shredded part-skim mozzarella cheese
- 1 cup shredded Parmesan cheese
- 2 plum tomatoes, thinly sliced

Preheat oven to 400°. In a small skillet, saute the onion and red pepper in oil until tender. Place crust on an ungreased 12-in. pizza pan; spread with pesto. Top with onion mixture, olives, cheeses and tomatoes. Bake until the cheese is melted, 15-20 minutes.

1 piece: 422 cal., 24g fat (8g sat. fat), 32mg chol., 1131mg sod., 31g carb. (4g sugars, 3g fiber), 19g pro.

VEGGIE TACOS

These vegetarian tacos are stuffed with a blend of sauteed cabbage, peppers and black beans that is fresh, filling and delicious. Top with avocado, cheese or a dollop of sour cream.
—*Taste of Home* Test Kitchen

- -

Takes: 30 min. • **Makes:** 8 tacos

- 2 Tbsp. canola oil
- 3 cups shredded cabbage
- 1 medium sweet red pepper, julienned
- 1 medium onion, halved and sliced
- 2 tsp. sugar
- 1 can (15 oz.) black beans, rinsed and drained
- 1 cup salsa
- 1 can (4 oz.) chopped green chiles
- 1 tsp. minced garlic
- 1 tsp. chili powder
- ¼ tsp. ground cumin
- 8 taco shells, warmed
- ½ cup shredded cheddar cheese
- 1 medium ripe avocado, peeled and sliced

1. In a large skillet, heat oil over medium-high heat; saute the cabbage, pepper and onion until crisp-tender, about 5 minutes. Sprinkle with sugar.

2. Stir in the beans, salsa, chiles, garlic, chili powder and cumin; bring to a boil. Reduce heat; simmer, covered, until flavors are blended, about 5 minutes.

3. Serve filling in taco shells. Top with cheese and avocado.

2 tacos: 430 cal., 22g fat (5g sat. fat), 14mg chol., 770mg sod., 47g carb. (8g sugars, 10g fiber), 12g pro.

THREE-CHEESE PESTO PIZZA

STIR-FRY
RICE BOWL

SALMON WITH BROWN SUGAR GLAZE

Need a simple way to serve a whole salmon fillet to a group of friends? This super easy recipe finally made me a fan of the fish!
—Rachel Garcia, Honolulu, HI

- -

Prep: 15 min. • **Bake:** 20 min.
Makes: 8 servings

- 1   Tbsp. brown sugar
- 2   tsp. butter
- 1   tsp. honey
- 1   Tbsp. olive oil
- 1   Tbsp. Dijon mustard
- 1   Tbsp. reduced-sodium soy sauce
- ½   to ¾ tsp. salt
- ¼   tsp. pepper
- 1   salmon fillet (2½ lbs.)

1. Preheat oven to 350°. In a small saucepan over medium heat, cook and stir the brown sugar, butter and honey until melted. Remove from the heat; whisk in the oil, mustard, soy sauce, salt and pepper. Cool for 5 minutes.
2. Place salmon in a large foil-lined baking pan; spoon brown sugar mixture over top. Bake for 20-25 minutes or until the fish flakes easily with a fork.

1 serving: 295 cal., 18g fat (3g sat. fat), 84mg chol., 403mg sod., 3g carb. (2g sugars, 0 fiber), 28g pro.

STIR-FRY RICE BOWL

My version of Korean bibimbap is tasty, pretty and easy to tweak for different spice levels. This dish is traditionally made with beef, but I top mine with a poached egg.
—Devon Delaney, Westport, CT

- -

Takes: 30 min. • **Makes:** 4 servings

- 1   Tbsp. canola oil
- 2   medium carrots, julienned
- 1   medium zucchini, julienned
- ½   cup sliced baby portobello mushrooms
- 1   cup bean sprouts
- 1   cup fresh baby spinach
- 1   Tbsp. water
- 1   Tbsp. reduced-sodium soy sauce
- 1   Tbsp. chili garlic sauce
- 4   large eggs
- 3   cups hot cooked brown rice
- 1   tsp. sesame oil

1. In a large skillet, heat canola oil over medium-high heat. Add carrots, zucchini and mushrooms; cook and stir 3-5 minutes or until carrots are crisp-tender. Add bean sprouts, spinach, water, soy sauce and chili sauce; cook and stir just until the spinach is wilted. Remove from heat; keep warm.
2. Place 2-3 in. of water in a large skillet with high sides. Bring to a boil; adjust heat to maintain a gentle simmer. Break 1 cold egg into a small bowl; holding the bowl close to surface of water, slip egg into water. Repeat with the remaining eggs.
3. Cook, uncovered, 3-5 minutes or until whites are completely set and yolks begin to thicken but are not hard. Using a slotted spoon, lift eggs out of water.
4. Serve rice in bowls; top with vegetables. Drizzle with sesame oil. Top each serving with a poached egg.

1 serving: 305 cal., 11g fat (2g sat. fat), 186mg chol., 364mg sod., 40g carb. (4g sugars, 4g fiber), 12g pro. **Diabetic exchanges:** 2 starch, 1 medium-fat meat, 1 vegetable, 1 fat.

> This is one of my go-to meatless meals on busy nights. Sometimes I swap in red pepper, snow peas or baby bok choy, and I always load it up with extra chili garlic sauce. The poached egg on top makes it seem extra special.
>
> — RACHEL SEIS, SENIOR EDITOR

MUSHROOM BOLOGNESE
WITH WHOLE WHEAT PASTA

MUSHROOM BOLOGNESE WITH WHOLE WHEAT PASTA

A traditional Bolognese sauce is meat-based with everything from pork to pancetta. Skipping the meat, I loaded this pasta dish with baby portobellos and veggies.
—Amber Massey, Argyle, TX

- -

Prep: 10 min. • **Cook:** 35 min.
Makes: 6 servings

- 1   Tbsp. olive oil
- 1   large sweet onion, finely chopped
- 2   medium carrots, finely chopped
- 1   large zucchini, finely chopped
- ½   lb. baby portobello mushrooms, finely chopped
- 3   garlic cloves, minced
- ½   cup dry red wine or reduced-sodium chicken broth
- 1   can (28 oz.) crushed tomatoes, undrained
- 1   can (14½ oz.) diced tomatoes, undrained
- ½   cup grated Parmesan cheese
- ½   tsp. dried oregano
- ½   tsp. pepper
- ⅛   tsp. crushed red pepper flakes
     Dash ground nutmeg
- 4½ cups uncooked whole wheat rigatoni

1. In a 6-qt. stockpot coated with cooking spray, heat oil over medium-high heat. Add onion and carrots; cook and stir until tender. Add zucchini, mushrooms and garlic; cook and stir until tender. Stir in wine; bring to a boil; cook until liquid is almost evaporated.
2. Stir in the crushed and diced tomatoes, cheese and seasonings; bring to a boil. Reduce the heat; simmer, covered, for 25-30 minutes or until slightly thickened.
3. Cook rigatoni according to the package directions; drain. Serve with sauce.

1⅓ cups sauce with 1 cup pasta: 369 cal., 6g fat (2g sat. fat), 6mg chol., 483mg sod., 65g carb. (15g sugars, 12g fiber), 17g pro.

SLOW-COOKER TUNA NOODLE CASSEROLE

SLOW-COOKER TUNA NOODLE CASSEROLE

We tweaked this family-friendly classic to work for the slow cooker. It's easy, wholesome and totally homemade!
—*Taste of Home* Test Kitchen

- -

Prep: 25 min. • **Cook:** 4 hours + standing
Makes: 10 servings

- ¼   cup butter, cubed
- ½   lb. sliced fresh mushrooms
- 1   medium onion, chopped
- 1   medium sweet pepper, chopped
- 1   tsp. salt, divided
- 1   tsp. pepper, divided
- 2   garlic cloves, minced
- ¼   cup all-purpose flour
- 2   cups reduced-sodium chicken broth
- 2   cups half-and-half cream
- 4   cups uncooked egg noodles (about 6 oz.)
- 3   cans (5 oz. each) light tuna in water, drained
- 2   Tbsp. lemon juice
- 2   cups shredded Monterey Jack cheese
- 2   cups frozen peas, thawed
- 2   cups crushed potato chips

1. In a large skillet, melt cubed butter over medium-high heat. Add mushrooms, onion, sweet pepper, ½ tsp. salt and ½ tsp. pepper; cook and stir until tender, 6-8 minutes. Add garlic; cook 1 minute longer. Stir in flour until blended. Gradually whisk in broth. Bring to a boil, stirring constantly; cook and stir until thickened, 1-2 minutes.
2. Transfer to a 5-qt. slow cooker. Stir in cream and noodles. Cook, covered, on low until noodles are tender, 4-5 hours. Meanwhile, in a small bowl, combine tuna, lemon juice and remaining salt and pepper.
3. Remove insert from slow cooker. Stir cheese, tuna mixture and peas into the noodle mixture. Let stand, uncovered, for 20 minutes. Just before serving, sprinkle with potato chips.

1 cup: 393 cal., 21g fat (12g sat. fat), 84mg chol., 752mg sod., 28g carb. (5g sugars, 3g fiber), 22g pro.

TEST KITCHEN TIP

Canned mushrooms also work in this recipe. And you can use frozen mixed peas and carrots for more veggie variety.

TILAPIA WITH SAUTEED SPINACH

You'll love this delicious, restaurant-quality meal fit for guests. Since it's all cooked in the same skillet, cleanup won't be chore at all.
—*Taste of Home* Test Kitchen

Prep: 20 min. • **Cook:** 15 min.
Makes: 4 servings

1	large egg, lightly beaten
½	cup dry bread crumbs
1	tsp. Italian seasoning
¾	tsp. salt, divided
¼	tsp. garlic powder
¼	tsp. paprika
4	tilapia fillets (6 oz. each)
4	Tbsp. olive oil, divided
1	small onion, chopped
1	garlic clove, minced
5	cups fresh baby spinach
⅛	tsp. crushed red pepper flakes
⅛	tsp. pepper
¼	cup chopped walnuts, toasted

1. Place egg in a shallow bowl. In another shallow bowl, combine the bread crumbs, Italian seasoning, ½ tsp. salt, garlic powder and paprika. Dip fillets in egg, then bread crumb mixture.

2. In a large skillet, cook fillets in 3 Tbsp. oil over medium heat for 4-5 minutes on each side or until golden brown and fish flakes easily with a fork. Remove and keep warm.

3. In the same skillet, saute onion in the remaining oil until tender. Add garlic; cook 1 minute longer. Stir in the spinach, pepper flakes, pepper and remaining salt. Cook and stir for 3-4 minutes or until spinach is wilted. Serve with fillets; sprinkle with walnuts.

1 fillet with ¼ cup spinach and 1 Tbsp. walnuts : 362 cal., 21g fat (3g sat. fat), 115mg chol., 446mg sod., 9g carb. (1g sugars, 2g fiber), 37g pro.

REFRIED BEAN TOSTADAS

REFRIED BEAN TOSTADAS

Your family won't miss the meat in these tasty tostadas topped with refried beans, corn, zucchini and salsa.
—*Taste of Home* Test Kitchen

Takes: 30 min. • **Makes:** 6 tostadas

6	flour tortillas (8 in.)
½	lb. sliced fresh mushrooms
1	cup diced zucchini
2	Tbsp. canola oil
1	jar (16 oz.) chunky salsa
1	can (7 oz.) white or shoepeg corn, drained
1	can (16 oz.) vegetarian refried beans, warmed
1½	cups shredded lettuce
1½	cups shredded cheddar cheese
2	medium ripe avocados, peeled and sliced
1½	cups chopped tomatoes
6	Tbsp. sour cream

1. In a large ungreased skillet, cook tortillas for 1-2 minutes on each side or until lightly browned. Remove and set aside.

2. In the same skillet, saute mushrooms and zucchini in oil until crisp-tender. Add salsa and corn; cook for 2-3 minutes or until heated through.

3. Spread warmed refried beans over each tortilla; top with lettuce, the salsa mixture, cheese, avocados, tomatoes and sour cream.

1 tostada: 588 cal., 31g fat (10g sat. fat), 40mg chol., 1250mg sod., 60g carb. (9g sugars, 12g fiber), 19g pro.

TILAPIA WITH GREEN BEANS AMANDINE

Panko bread crumbs give tilapia a light, crispy coating that doesn't overpower the delicate fish. Lemony green beans topped with toasted slivered almonds are the ideal complement to this delightful entree.
—*Taste of Home* Test Kitchen

- -

Prep: 20 min. • **Cook:** 15 min.
Makes: 4 servings

- 4 tilapia fillets (6 oz. each)
- ½ tsp. salt
- 1 large egg
- 1¼ cups panko bread crumbs
- ¾ tsp. dried parsley flakes
- ¾ tsp. dried thyme
- 2 Tbsp. butter
- 1 Tbsp. plus 2 tsp. olive oil, divided
- 1 tsp. cornstarch
- 1 can (14½ oz.) chicken broth
- 4 garlic cloves, minced
- 4 tsp. lemon juice
- ¾ lb. fresh green beans, trimmed
- ¼ cup slivered almonds, toasted

1. Sprinkle fillets with salt. In a shallow bowl, whisk the egg. In another shallow bowl, combine the bread crumbs, parsley and thyme. Dip fillets in egg, then coat with crumb mixture.
2. In a large skillet, cook fillets in butter and 1 Tbsp. oil over medium heat for 5-6 minutes on each side or until golden brown and the fish flakes easily with a fork. Remove and keep warm.
3. In a small bowl, combine the cornstarch, broth, garlic and lemon juice until blended; set aside.
4. In the same skillet, saute beans in the remaining oil until crisp-tender. Stir the cornstarch mixture and pour over beans. Bring to a boil; cook and stir for 1-2 minutes or until slightly thickened. Sprinkle with almonds. Serve with fish.
1 serving: 384 cal., 18g fat (6g sat. fat), 153mg chol., 900mg sod., 18g carb. (3g sugars, 4g fiber), 38g pro.

SHRIMP RISOTTO

This delightful main dish will add elegance to family meals. Instant rice makes it come together quickly for a special dinner any day of the week.
—*Taste of Home* Test Kitchen

- -

Takes: 30 min. • **Makes:** 4 servings

- 1 small onion, chopped
- 2 Tbsp. butter
- 1¾ cups uncooked instant rice
- 2 garlic cloves, minced
- ½ tsp. dried basil
- ¼ tsp. pepper
- 2 cans (14½ oz. each) chicken broth
- 1 lb. peeled and deveined cooked medium shrimp
- 2 cups fresh baby spinach, coarsely chopped
- 1 cup frozen corn, thawed
- 1 plum tomato, chopped
- ¼ cup grated Parmesan cheese
- 2 Tbsp. 2% milk

1. In a large skillet, saute onion in butter until tender. Add the rice, garlic, basil and pepper; cook 2 minutes longer. Stir in 1 can broth. Cook and stir until most of the liquid is absorbed.
2. Add the remaining broth, ½ cup at a time, stirring constantly. Allow the liquid to absorb between additions. Cook until the risotto is creamy and the rice is tender.
3. Add the remaining ingredients; cook and stir until the spinach is wilted and the shrimp are heated through.
1⅓ cups: 420 cal., 10g fat (5g sat. fat), 197mg chol., 1196mg sod., 49g carb. (3g sugars, 3g fiber), 32g pro.

TILAPIA WITH GREEN BEANS AMANDINE

SEAFOOD GUMBO

CHEDDAR-BUTTERNUT SQUASH CLAFOUTIS

I came up with this savory version of the classic French dessert, clafoutis, and shared it for dinner with a salad. My friends loved it, but in the end I could have eaten the whole pan myself while dreaming of being in Paris with every scrumptious bite.
—Joseph Sciascia, San Mateo, CA

Prep: 20 min. • **Cook:** 50 min. + standing
Makes: 6 servings

3	cups cubed peeled butternut squash
2	tsp. olive oil
1	tsp. minced fresh rosemary or ½ tsp. dried rosemary, crushed
1	tsp. minced fresh thyme or ½ tsp. dried thyme
½	tsp. kosher salt
¼	tsp. coarsely ground pepper
4	large eggs
1½	cups 2% milk
½	cup all-purpose flour
¼	tsp. cayenne pepper
2	cups shredded sharp white cheddar cheese
¼	cup grated Parmesan and Romano cheese blend
1	Tbsp. butter
1	Tbsp. minced fresh chives

1. Preheat oven to 400°. Place butternut squash in a 12-in. cast-iron skillet. Drizzle with oil. Sprinkle with rosemary, thyme, salt and pepper; toss to coat. Roast until just tender, 15-20 minutes. Remove from skillet and keep warm.
2. In a large bowl, whisk eggs, milk, flour and cayenne; stir in cheeses.
3. Place butter in the same skillet; place the skillet in oven until butter is melted, 1-2 minutes. Carefully tilt the pan to coat bottom and sides with butter. Pour egg mixture into skillet; top with roasted squash.
4. Bake until puffed and edges are browned, 30-35 minutes. Let stand 15 minutes before cutting. Sprinkle with chives and additional Parmesan and Romano cheese blend.
1 piece: 357 cal., 22g fat (11g sat. fat), 176mg chol., 586mg sod., 22g carb. (5g sugars, 2g fiber), 19g pro.

SEAFOOD GUMBO

Gumbo is one of the dishes that makes Louisiana cuisine so famous. We live across the state line in Texas and can't seem to get enough of this traditional Cajun stew that features okra, shrimp, spicy seasonings and the "holy trinity"—onions, green peppers and celery. This recipe calls for seafood, but you could also use chicken, duck or sausage.
—Ruth Aubey, San Antonio, TX

Prep: 50 min.
Makes: 24 servings (6 qt.)

1	cup all-purpose flour
1	cup canola oil
4	cups chopped onion
2	cups chopped celery
2	cups chopped green pepper
1	cup sliced green onion and tops
4	cups chicken broth
8	cups water
4	cups sliced okra
2	Tbsp. paprika
1	Tbsp. salt
2	tsp. oregano
1	tsp. ground black pepper
6	cups small shrimp, rinsed and drained, or seafood of your choice
1	cup minced fresh parsley
2	Tbsp. Cajun seasoning

1. In a heavy Dutch oven, combine the flour and oil until smooth. Cook over medium-high heat for 5 minutes, stirring constantly. Reduce heat to medium. Cook and stir about 10 minutes longer, or until the mixture is reddish brown.
2. Add the onion, celery, green pepper and green onions; cook and stir for 5 minutes. Add the chicken broth, water, okra, paprika, salt, oregano and pepper. Bring to boil; reduce the heat and simmer, covered, for 10 minutes.
3. Add the shrimp and parsley. Simmer, uncovered, about 5 minutes more or until seafood is done. Remove from heat; stir in Cajun seasoning.
1 cup: 166 cal., 10g fat (1g sat. fat), 96mg chol., 900mg sod., 10g carb. (2g sugars, 2g fiber), 10g pro.

CHEDDAR-BUTTERNUT
SQUASH CLAFOUTIS

SKEWERED GINGER SHRIMP WITH PLUMS

Sweet, simple and sensational, these shrimp skewers boast loads of flavor with just four ingredients. Throw them on the grill for a quick dinner or tasty potluck dish.
—*Taste of Home* Test Kitchen

Takes: 25 min. • **Makes:** 4 servings

- 1 **lb. uncooked large shrimp, peeled and deveined**
- 2 **medium plums or peaches, cut into wedges**
- ½ **cup sesame ginger marinade, divided**
- 1 **green onion, thinly sliced**
  Optional: Sesame seeds and lime wedges

1. In a large bowl, combine shrimp and plums. Drizzle with ¼ cup marinade; toss to coat. Alternately thread shrimp and plums on 4 metal or soaked wooden skewers.
2. On a lightly oiled rack, grill skewers, covered, over medium heat or broil 4 in. from heat until the shrimp turn pink, 6-8 minutes, turning occasionally and basting frequently with the remaining marinade during the last 3 minutes of cooking. Serve with green onion and, if desired, sesame seeds and lime wedges.
1 skewer: 173 cal., 2g fat (0 sat. fat), 138mg chol., 1295mg sod., 19g carb. (15g sugars, 1g fiber), 19g pro.

TEST KITCHEN TIP
Freestone plums can be pitted the same way as a peach, but fixed stone plums require a different approach. Make a vertical cut on 2 sides of the pit; slice the 2 sides into wedges. Then make 2 more cuts on the other 2 sides of the pit, freeing the remaining wedges.

SKEWERED GINGER SHRIMP WITH PLUMS

THAI SCALLOP SAUTE

Just open a bottle of Thai peanut sauce to give this seafood stir-fry some serious authenticity.
—*Taste of Home* Test Kitchen

- -

Prep: 15 min. • **Cook:** 20 min.
Makes: 4 servings

3	tsp. olive oil, divided
1½	lbs. sea scallops
2	cups fresh broccoli florets
2	medium onions, halved and sliced
1	medium zucchini, sliced
4	small carrots, sliced
¼	cup Thai peanut sauce
¼	tsp. salt
	Hot cooked rice
	Lime wedges, optional

1. In a large skillet, heat 1 tsp. oil over medium-high heat. Add half the scallops; stir-fry until firm and opaque. Remove from pan. Repeat with an additional 1 tsp. oil and the remaining scallops.
2. In the same skillet, heat the remaining oil over medium-high heat. Add vegetables; stir-fry until crisp-tender, 7-9 minutes. Stir in peanut sauce and salt. Return scallops to pan; heat through. Serve with rice and, if desired, lime wedges.
1½ cups: 268 cal., 8g fat (1g sat. fat), 41mg chol., 1000mg sod., 24g carb. (10g sugars, 4g fiber), 25g pro.

VEGETARIAN CABBAGE ROLLS

This marvelous meatless entree comes from my 89-year-old grandmother, who cooks a lot with grains, particularly bulgur.
—Michelle Dougherty, Lewiston, ID

- -

Prep: 30 min. • **Bake:** 15 min.
Makes: 8 cabbage rolls

1½	cups chopped fresh mushrooms
1	cup diced zucchini
¾	cup chopped green pepper
¾	cup chopped sweet red pepper
¾	cup vegetable broth
½	cup bulgur
1	tsp. dried basil
½	tsp. dried marjoram
½	tsp. dried thyme
¼	tsp. pepper
1	large head cabbage
6	Tbsp. shredded Parmesan cheese, divided
2	tsp. lemon juice
1	can (8 oz.) tomato sauce
⅛	tsp. hot pepper sauce

1. In a large saucepan, combine the first 10 ingredients. Bring to a boil over medium heat. Reduce heat; cover and simmer for 5 minutes. Remove from the heat; let stand for 5 minutes.
2. Meanwhile, cook cabbage in boiling water just until the leaves the fall off the head. Set aside 8 large leaves for rolls (refrigerate the remaining cabbage for another use). Cut out the thick vein from each leaf, making a V-shape cut. Overlap cut ends before filling.
3. Stir 4 Tbsp. Parmesan cheese and the lemon juice into vegetable mixture. Place a heaping ⅓ cupful of vegetables on each leaf; fold in sides. Starting at an unfolded edge, roll to completely enclose filling.
4. Combine tomato sauce and hot pepper sauce; pour ⅓ cup sauce into a 2-qt. baking dish. Place cabbage rolls in dish; spoon the remaining sauce over top. Cover and bake at 400° for 15 minutes or until heated through. Sprinkle with remaining Parmesan cheese.
2 rolls: 142 cal., 3g fat (1g sat. fat), 5mg chol., 675mg sod., 25g carb. (0 sugars, 6g fiber), 8g pro. **Diabetic exchanges:** 2 vegetable, 1 starch.

VEGETARIAN
CABBAGE ROLLS

SHRIMP TORTELLINI PASTA TOSS

No matter how you toss 'em up, shrimp and thyme play nicely with any spring-fresh vegetable.
—*Taste of Home* Test Kitchen

Takes: 20 min. • **Makes:** 4 servings

- 1 pkg. (9 oz.) refrigerated cheese tortellini
- 1 cup frozen peas
- 3 Tbsp. olive oil, divided
- 1 lb. uncooked shrimp (31-40 per lb.), peeled and deveined
- 2 garlic cloves, minced
- ¼ tsp. salt
- ¼ tsp. dried thyme
- ¼ tsp. pepper

1. Cook tortellini according to the package directions, adding peas during the last 5 minutes of cooking.

2. Meanwhile, in a large nonstick skillet, heat 2 Tbsp. oil over medium-high heat. Add shrimp; cook and stir 2 minutes. Add garlic; cook 1-2 minutes longer or until shrimp turn pink.

3. Drain tortellini mixture; add to the skillet. Stir in salt, thyme, pepper and remaining oil; toss to coat.

1¼ cups: 413 cal., 17g fat (4g sat. fat), 165mg chol., 559mg sod., 36g carb. (4g sugars, 3g fiber), 29g pro. **Diabetic exchanges:** 4 lean meat, 2 starch, 2 fat.

Shrimp Asparagus Fettuccine: Bring 4 qt. water to a boil. Add 9 oz. refrigerated fettuccine and 1 cup cut fresh asparagus. Boil for 2-3 minutes or until pasta is tender. Proceed with recipe as written but replace thyme with ¾ tsp. dried basil.

Soy Shrimp with Rice Noodles: Cook 8.8 oz. thin rice noodles according to the package directions adding 1 cup frozen shelled edamame during the last 4 minutes of cooking. Proceed with recipe as written but replace thyme with ¼ cup reduced-sodium soy sauce and omit salt.

TOMATO TART WITH THREE CHEESES

This quick and easy recipe will delight the pizza lovers in your home. You will be surprised at how quickly it comes together.
—*Taste of Home* Test Kitchen

Takes: 30 min. • **Makes:** 4 servings

- 1 sheet frozen puff pastry, thawed
- ¾ cup shredded part-skim mozzarella cheese
- ¾ cup shredded provolone cheese
- ¼ cup minced fresh basil
- 4 plum tomatoes, thinly sliced
  Salt and pepper to taste
- ¼ cup shredded Parmesan cheese
  Additional minced fresh basil

1. Preheat oven to 400°. Unfold pastry sheet on a lightly floured surface. Roll into a 12-in. square; transfer to a parchment-lined baking sheet. Prick with a fork.

2. Combine mozzarella cheese, provolone cheese and basil; sprinkle over the pastry to within 1 in. of edges. Arrange the tomato slices over the cheese. Season with salt and pepper; sprinkle with Parmesan cheese.

3. Bake for 15-20 minutes or until the pastry is golden brown. Remove tart from baking sheet to a wire rack to cool for 5 minutes. Sprinkle with additional basil. Cut into slices. Serve hot or at room temperature.

1 serving: 461 cal., 27g fat (10g sat. fat), 31mg chol., 575mg sod., 38g carb. (2g sugars, 5g fiber), 18g pro.

SHRIMP TORTELLINI PASTA TOSS

CRISPY FISH & CHIPS

If you're fond of the tender fish and crunchy coating of the traditional British pub classic but you're not fond of deep frying, try this crown jewel made with horseradish, panko and Worcestershire sauce.
—Linda Schend, Kenosha, WI

Takes: 30 min. • **Makes:** 4 servings

- 4 cups frozen steak fries
- 4 salmon fillets (6 oz. each)
- 1 to 2 Tbsp. prepared horseradish
- 1 Tbsp. grated Parmesan cheese
- 1 Tbsp. Worcestershire sauce
- 1 tsp. Dijon mustard
- ¼ tsp. salt
- ½ cup panko bread crumbs
  Cooking spray

1. Preheat oven to 450°. Arrange steak fries in a single layer on a baking sheet. Bake on lowest oven rack for 18-20 minutes or until light golden brown.
2. Meanwhile, place salmon on a foil-lined baking sheet coated with cooking spray. In a small bowl, mix horseradish, cheese, Worcestershire sauce, mustard and salt; stir in panko. Press mixture onto fillets. Spritz tops with cooking spray.
3. Bake the salmon on middle oven rack for 8-10 minutes or until fish just begins to flake easily with a fork. Serve with fries.
1 fillet with ¾ cup fries: 416 cal., 19g fat (4g sat. fat), 86mg chol., 698mg sod., 26g carb. (2g sugars, 2g fiber), 32g pro. **Diabetic exchanges:** 5 lean meat, 1½ starch.

TEST KITCHEN TIP
You can use this technique for practically any fish. It's especially good with a firm white fish, such as cod or haddock—like they serve at British chip shops!

CRISPY FISH & CHIPS

SALMON & FETA
WILTED SPINACH SALAD

SALMON & FETA WILTED SPINACH SALAD

My friend mentioned a Turkish salmon and couscous dish that sounded fantastic, so I started experimenting. I prefer this salad warm, but it's also tasty served cold.
—Jeni Pittard, Statham, GA

Takes: 30 min. • **Makes:** 2 servings

- 1   salmon fillet (8 oz.)
- 2   tsp. lemon juice
- ½   tsp. Greek seasoning
- ½   cup quinoa, rinsed
- 1   cup reduced-sodium chicken broth
- 1   tsp. olive oil
- 4   cups coarsely chopped fresh spinach
- 1   cup grape tomatoes, halved
- ¼   cup crumbled feta cheese
- 2   Tbsp. chopped fresh parsley
- 1   Tbsp. minced fresh oregano
- ⅛   tsp. pepper
     Lemon wedges

1. Preheat oven to 375°. Place salmon on a foil-lined baking sheet, skin side down. Sprinkle with lemon juice and Greek seasoning. Bake until fish begins to flake easily with a fork, 15-18 minutes.
2. In a small saucepan, combine quinoa, broth and oil; bring to a boil. Reduce heat; simmer, covered, until liquid is absorbed and quinoa is tender, 12-15 minutes.
3. Break salmon into 1-in. pieces using a fork. Place spinach, tomatoes, quinoa and salmon in a large bowl. Add cheese, herbs and pepper; toss gently to combine. Serve with lemon wedges.
2 cups: 427 cal., 18g fat (4g sat. fat), 64mg chol., 773mg sod., 34g carb. (3g sugars, 6g fiber), 32g pro.

> I love cooking salmon for myself and this is a great way to enjoy it. The warm salad is so delicious and satisfying. Best of all, it's a healthy dinner I can feel good about. I sometimes double it for meal-planning purposes.
>
> – ANNAMARIE HIGLEY, ASSITANT EDITOR

NEW ORLEANS-STYLE SPICY SHRIMP

NEW ORLEANS-STYLE SPICY SHRIMP

We have family members who attended college in New Orleans. This dish captures their favorite flavors from The Big Easy, with the right touch of spices and heat.
—Susan Seymour, Valatie, NY

Prep: 15 min. • **Bake:** 20 min.
Makes: 12 servings

- 3   medium lemons, sliced
- ⅔   cup butter, cubed
- ½   cup ketchup
- ¼   cup Worcestershire sauce
- 2   Tbsp. seafood seasoning
- 2   Tbsp. chili garlic sauce
- 2   Tbsp. Louisiana-style hot sauce
- 1   Tbsp. Italian salad dressing mix
- 4   lbs. uncooked shell-on shrimp (31-40 per lb.)
- 2   bay leaves
     French bread

1. Preheat the oven to 350°. In a microwave-safe bowl, combine the first 8 ingredients. Microwave, covered, on high for 2-3 minutes or until butter is melted; stir until blended.
2. Divide shrimp and bay leaves between 2 ungreased 13x9-in. baking dishes. Add half the lemon mixture to each dish; toss to combine.
3. Bake, uncovered, for 20-25 minutes or until the shrimp turn pink, stirring halfway. Remove bay leaves. Serve with bread.
1 cup: 242 cal., 12g fat (7g sat. fat), 211mg chol., 940mg sod., 7g carb. (4g sugars, 0 fiber), 25g pro.

SLOW-COOKED
BEEF ENCHILADAS
PAGE 141

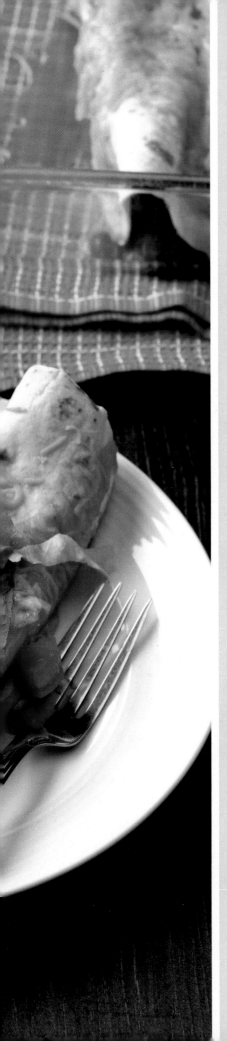

Beef, Chicken & Pork

A hard day's work makes for a hearty appetite, and that's no exception for the staff members at *Taste of Home*. We may be editing and testing recipes during office hours, but that doesn't mean we don't look forward to something comforting and satisfying when we go home. From grilled steaks and pan-roasted chicken to fast fajitas and slow-cooked stews, we turn to these meaty favorites that are sure to become staples at your table, too. Dig in!

CHEESEBURGER
STUFFED PASTA SHELLS

CHEESEBURGER STUFFED PASTA SHELLS

You could call this a comfort food mashup made in heaven. Jumbo stuffed pasta shells are loaded up with cheeseburger goodness in a dish that will soon become a favorite.
—*Taste of Home* Test Kitchen

Prep: 25 min. • **Bake:** 25 min.
Makes: 6 servings

- 18 uncooked jumbo pasta shells
- 1½ lbs. lean ground beef (90% lean)
- 1 medium onion, chopped
- 1 can (8 oz.) tomato sauce
- ½ cup ketchup
- ¼ cup prepared mustard
- ¼ tsp. pepper
- 1½ cups shredded cheddar cheese, divided
  Optional toppings: Shredded lettuce, and chopped pickles and tomatoes

1. Preheat oven to 350°. Cook the pasta according to package directions. Drain and rinse in cold water; drain again.
2. Meanwhile, in a large skillet, cook beef and onion over medium-high heat until beef is no longer pink, 6-8 minutes, breaking beef into crumbles; drain. Stir in the tomato sauce, ketchup, mustard and pepper until blended. Stir in ¾ cup shredded cheese.
3. Spoon about 2 Tbsp. filling into each shell. Place in a greased 11x7-in. baking dish.
4. Bake, covered, until heated through, 12-15 minutes. Sprinkle with remaining cheese; bake, uncovered, until cheese is melted, about 5 minutes. If desired, serve with optional toppings.
Freeze option: Cool unbaked casserole; cover and freeze. To use, partially thaw in the refrigerator overnight. Remove from the refrigerator 30 minutes before baking. Preheat oven to 350°. Cover casserole with foil; bake as directed, increasing the time as necessary to heat through and for a thermometer inserted in center to read 165°. If desired, serve with optional toppings.
3 stuffed shells: 431 cal., 20g fat (9g sat. fat), 99mg chol., 673mg sod., 31g carb. (8g sugars, 2g fiber), 33g pro.

GARLIC RANCH CHICKEN

GARLIC RANCH CHICKEN

Simple ingredients give boneless chicken breasts a tantalizing flavor the whole family will enjoy. Add a fresh green salad to round out the meal.
—*Taste of Home* Test Kitchen

Takes: 30 min. • **Makes:** 4 servings

- 4 boneless skinless chicken breast halves (5 oz. each)
- ¼ cup 2% milk
- ½ tsp. minced garlic
- ¼ cup all-purpose flour
- 1 Tbsp. ranch salad dressing mix
- ⅛ tsp. pepper
- 1 Tbsp. olive oil
- 1 Tbsp. butter

1. Flatten chicken slightly; set aside. In a shallow bowl, combine milk and garlic. In another shallow bowl, combine the flour, salad dressing mix and pepper. Dip chicken in milk mixture, then coat with flour mixture.
2. In a large cast-iron or other heavy skillet, cook chicken in oil and butter over medium heat until no longer pink, 6-8 minutes.
1 chicken breast half: 264 cal., 12g fat (4g sat. fat), 88mg chol., 125mg sod., 7g carb. (1g sugars, 0 fiber), 30g pro.

QUICK TATER TOTS BAKE

I make this dish when I need to get supper on the table and time is tight. If we have unexpected company, I just double the ingredients and use a 13x9-in. pan. I call it my Please Stay Casserole!
—Jean Ferguson, Elverta, CA

- -

Prep: 15 min. • **Bake:** 30 min.
Makes: 4 servings

- ¾ to 1 lb. ground beef or turkey
- 1 small onion, chopped
  Salt and pepper to taste
- 1 pkg. (16 oz.) frozen Tater Tots
- 1 can (10¾ oz.) condensed cream of mushroom soup, undiluted
- ⅔ cup 2% milk or water
- 1 cup shredded cheddar cheese

1. Preheat oven to 350°. In a large skillet, cook beef and onion over medium heat until meat is no longer pink; drain. Season with salt and pepper.
2. Transfer to a greased 2-qt. baking dish. Top with Tater Tots. Combine soup and milk; pour over potatoes. Sprinkle with cheese. Bake, uncovered, 30-40 minutes or until heated through.
1½ cups: 570 cal., 35g fat (12g sat. fat), 87mg chol., 1357mg sod., 37g carb. (5g sugars, 4g fiber), 26g pro.

STEAK SANDWICH KABOBS

STEAK SANDWICH KABOBS

Skewers with seasoned steak, bread and veggies are grilled and topped with cheese for a fantastic meal. Coleslaw, spruced up with chopped walnuts, makes a great sidekick for the kabobs.
—*Taste of Home* Test Kitchen

- -

Takes: 25 min. • **Makes:** 4 servings

- 1 lb. beef top sirloin steak, cut into 1-in. cubes
- 1 tsp. steak seasoning
- 1 medium sweet red pepper, cut into 1-in. chunks
- 6 oz. focaccia bread, cut into 1-in. cubes
- 1 medium onion, cut into 1-in. chunks
- 1 Tbsp. olive oil
- 3 slices provolone cheese, cut into strips
- 2 cups deli coleslaw
- ½ cup chopped walnuts

1. Sprinkle the beef with steak seasoning. Alternately thread the beef, red pepper, bread cubes and onion onto 4 metal or soaked wooden skewers; brush with oil.
2. Grill steak, covered, over medium heat for 8-10 minutes or until the meat reaches desired doneness, turning occasionally. For medium-rare, a thermometer should read 135°; medium, 140°; medium-well, 145°. Top with cheese; grill 1-2 minutes longer or until cheese is melted.
3. In a small bowl, combine coleslaw and walnuts. Serve with kabobs.
1 kabob with ½ cup coleslaw: 597 cal., 33g fat (6g sat. fat), 83mg chol., 729mg sod., 45g carb. (17g sugars, 5g fiber), 32g pro.

SLOW-COOKER COUNTRY CAPTAIN CHICKEN

Supposedly, the recipe for Country Captain Chicken was brought to Georgia in the early 1800s by a British sea captain. Although it's traditional to serve this over rice, it's also delicious with noodles or mashed potatoes.
—Suzanne Banfield, Basking Ridge, NJ

- -

Prep: 20 min. • **Cook:** 3½ hours
Makes: 8 servings

- 1 large onion, chopped
- 1 medium sweet red pepper, chopped
- 2 tsp. minced garlic
- 3 lbs. boneless skinless chicken thighs
- 1 Tbsp. curry powder
- 1 tsp. ground cinnamon
- 1 tsp. ground ginger
- 1 tsp. dried thyme
- 1 Tbsp. packed brown sugar
- ½ cup chicken broth
- ½ cup golden raisins or raisins
- 1 can (14½ oz.) diced tomatoes, undrained
  Hot cooked rice
  Chopped fresh parsley, optional

1. Place onion, pepper and garlic in a 6-qt. slow cooker. Arrange the chicken pieces over the vegetables.
2. Whisk the next 5 ingredients with the chicken broth. Pour over chicken. Cover and cook on high for 1 hour. Add raisins and tomatoes. Reduce heat to low and cook until chicken reaches 165°, about 2½ hours. Serve over rice; if desired, sprinkle with parsley.
1 cup: 298 cal., 13g fat (3g sat. fat), 114mg chol., 159mg sod., 13g carb. (9g sugars, 2g fiber), 32g pro. **Diabetic exchanges:** 4 lean meat, 1 vegetable, ½ starch.

CHILI STEAK & PEPPERS

Bright and flavorful, this sirloin steak makes a delicious dish you'll be proud to serve.
—*Taste of Home* Test Kitchen

- -

Takes: 30 min. • **Makes:** 4 servings

- 2 Tbsp. chili sauce
- 1 Tbsp. lime juice
- 1 tsp. brown sugar
- ½ tsp. crushed red pepper flakes
- ½ tsp. salt, divided
- 1 beef top sirloin steak (1¼ lbs.)
- 1 medium onion, halved and sliced
- 1 medium green pepper, cut into strips
- 1 medium sweet yellow pepper, cut into strips
- 2 tsp. olive oil
- 1 small garlic clove, minced
- ⅛ tsp. pepper
- ¼ cup reduced-fat sour cream
- 1 tsp. prepared horseradish

1. Combine the chili sauce, lime juice, brown sugar, pepper flakes and ¼ tsp. salt; brush over steak. Broil steak 4-6 in. from the heat for 5-7 minutes on each side or until meat reaches desired doneness (for medium-rare, a thermometer should read 135°; medium, 140°; medium-well, 145°).
2. Meanwhile, in a large skillet, saute onion and green and yellow peppers in oil until tender. Add the garlic, pepper and remaining salt; cook 1 minute longer. In a small bowl, combine the sour cream and horseradish. Slice steak and serve with pepper mixture and sauce.
4 oz. cooked beef with ⅓ cup pepper mixture and 1 Tbsp. sauce: 265 cal., 9g fat (3g sat. fat), 62mg chol., 491mg sod., 12g carb. (8g sugars, 2g fiber), 32g pro. **Diabetic exchanges:** 4 lean meat, 1 vegetable, 1 fat.

SLOW-COOKER COUNTRY CAPTAIN CHICKEN

MINI REUBEN
CASSEROLES

PRESSURE-COOKER FABULOUS FAJITAS

When friends ask for a new recipe to try, suggest these flavorful fajitas. It's wonderful to put the beef in the pressure cooker and have a hot, delicious main dish in no time.
—*Taste of Home* Test Kitchen

Prep: 20 min. • **Cook:** 25 min. + releasing
Makes: 8 fajitas

1½	lbs. beef top sirloin steak, cut into thin strips
1½	tsp. ground cumin
½	tsp. seasoned salt
½	tsp. chili powder
¼ to ½	tsp. crushed red pepper flakes
2	Tbsp. canola oil
2	Tbsp. lemon juice
1	garlic clove, minced
½	cup water
1	large sweet red pepper, thinly sliced
1	large onion, thinly sliced
8	flour tortillas (8 in.), warmed

Optional toppings: Sliced avocado and jalapeno peppers, shredded cheddar cheese and chopped tomatoes

1. In a bowl, toss steak with cumin, salt, chili powder and red pepper flakes. Select the saute setting on a 6-qt. electric pressure cooker. Adjust for medium heat; add oil. When oil is hot, brown meat in batches and remove. Add water, lemon juice and garlic to cooker; stir to loosen any browned bits. Press cancel. Return beef to cooker. Lock lid; close pressure-release valve. Adjust to pressure-cook on high for 20 minutes.
2. Allow pressure to naturally release for 10 minutes, then quick-release any remaining pressure. Remove the steak with a slotted spoon; keep warm.
3. Add red pepper and onion to the cooker. Lock lid; close pressure-release valve. Adjust to pressure-cook on high for 5 minutes. Quick-release pressure. Serve vegetables and steak with tortillas and desired toppings.
1 fajita: 314 cal., 11g fat (2g sat. fat), 34mg chol., 374mg sod., 31g carb. (1g sugars, 2g fiber), 23g pro. **Diabetic exchanges:** 3 lean meat, 2 starch, 1 fat.

MINI REUBEN CASSEROLES

If you like Reuben sandwiches, you'll love these creamy individual beef casseroles that boast the same classic flavors.
—*Taste of Home* Test Kitchen

Prep: 20 min. • **Bake:** 20 min.
Makes: 4 servings

1	medium onion, chopped
1	medium green pepper, chopped
2	tsp. olive oil
2	cups cubed cooked beef roast
1	can (14 oz.) sauerkraut, rinsed and well drained
1	can (10¾ oz.) condensed cream of chicken soup, undiluted
1¼	cups shredded Swiss cheese, divided
⅓	cup 2% milk
½	cup Thousand Island salad dressing
2	slices rye bread, cubed
1	Tbsp. butter, melted
½	tsp. onion powder

1. Preheat oven to 350°. In a large skillet, saute onion and pepper in oil until tender. Stir in the meat, sauerkraut, soup, 1 cup Swiss cheese, milk and salad dressing; heat through. Transfer to 4 greased 10-oz. ramekins or custard cups. Place ramekins on a baking sheet.
2. In a small bowl, toss bread cubes with butter and onion powder. Arrange over tops. Bake, uncovered, 15 minutes. Sprinkle with remaining cheese. Bake until the cheese is melted, 5-10 minutes longer.
1 serving: 650 cal., 41g fat (15g sat. fat), 130mg chol., 1782mg sod., 31g carb. (12g sugars, 5g fiber), 37g pro.

PRESSURE-COOKER
FABULOUS FAJITAS

CLASSIC BEEF STEW

CLASSIC BEEF STEW

Here's a good old-fashioned stew with lots of veggies in a rich beef gravy. It's the perfect dish for a blustery winter day.
—Alberta McKay, Bartlesville, OK

Prep: 15 min. • **Bake:** 2½ hours
Makes: 8 servings (2 qt.)

- 2 lbs. beef stew meat, cut into 1-in. cubes
- 1 to 2 Tbsp. canola oil
- 1½ cups chopped onions
- 1 can (14½ oz.) diced tomatoes, undrained
- 1 can (10½ oz.) condensed beef broth, undiluted
- 3 Tbsp. quick-cooking tapioca
- 1 garlic clove, minced
- 1 Tbsp. dried parsley flakes
- 1 tsp. salt
- ¼ tsp. pepper
- 1 bay leaf
- 6 medium carrots, cut into 2-in. pieces
- 3 medium potatoes, peeled and cut into 2-in. pieces
- 1 cup sliced celery (1-in. lengths)

1. In an oven-safe Dutch oven, brown beef in batches in oil; drain. Return all meat to the pan. Add onions, tomatoes, broth, tapioca, garlic, parsley, salt, pepper and bay leaf. Bring to a boil.

2. Cover stew and bake at 350° for 1 hour. Stir in carrots, potatoes and celery. Bake, covered, 1 hour longer or until meat and vegetables are tender. Discard bay leaf.

1 cup: 245 cal., 10g fat (3g sat. fat), 71mg chol., 751mg sod., 14g carb. (6g sugars, 3g fiber), 24g pro.

TEST KITCHEN TIP
To make a fresh garlic clove easy to peel, gently crush it with the flat side of a large knife blade to loosen the peel. If you don't have a large knife, you can crush the garlic with a small can. The peel will come right off.

CHICKEN CHEESE STRATA

You can never go wrong with chicken, broccoli and cheese. The spices in this simple strata offer an extra special taste.
—*Taste of Home* Test Kitchen

Takes: 30 min. • **Makes:** 8 servings

- ¾ lb. boneless skinless chicken breasts, cut into ½-in. cubes
- 4 Tbsp. butter, divided
- 3 cups frozen broccoli florets, thawed
- ½ tsp. onion salt
- ½ tsp. dried thyme
- ½ tsp. dried rosemary, crushed
- ¼ tsp. pepper
- 6 cups cubed French bread
- 2 large eggs
- ¾ cup 2% milk
- ⅔ cup condensed cream of onion soup, undiluted
- 1 cup shredded Colby-Monterey Jack cheese

1. Preheat the oven to 400°. In a 10-in. ovenproof skillet, saute chicken in 2 Tbsp. butter until no longer pink. Add broccoli, onion salt, thyme, rosemary and pepper; heat through. Remove from skillet and keep warm.

2. In same skillet, toast the bread cubes in remaining butter until lightly browned. In a small bowl, combine eggs, milk and soup; pour over bread cubes. Stir in the chicken mixture. Sprinkle with cheese.

3. Bake, uncovered, 15-20 minutes or until a knife inserted in the center comes out clean. Let stand 5 minutes before cutting.

1 piece: 570 cal., 16g fat (8g sat. fat), 108mg chol., 1282mg sod., 77g carb. (6g sugars, 4g fiber), 30g pro.

SLOW-COOKED BEEF ENCHILADAS

Enchiladas get a boost of beefy goodness from slow-cooked roast. When the meat is done, assemble with tortillas and bake. Top with lettuce and tomatoes if desired.
—*Taste of Home* Test Kitchen

Prep: 15 min. • **Cook:** 7¼ hours
Makes: 6 enchiladas

- 1 boneless beef chuck roast (1¾ lbs.)
- 1 envelope taco seasoning
- 1 medium onion, chopped
- 1 cup beef broth
- 2 Tbsp. all-purpose flour
- 1 Tbsp. cold water
- 6 flour tortillas (8 in.)
- 1 can (4 oz.) chopped green chiles
- 1½ cups shredded Mexican cheese blend, divided
- 1 can (10 oz.) enchilada sauce
  Optional: Chopped lettuce and chopped tomatoes

1. Rub roast with taco seasoning. Transfer to a greased 3-qt. slow cooker. Top with onion and broth. Cook, covered, on low 7-8 hours or until meat is tender. Remove roast; cool slightly. Reserve ½ cup cooking juices in a saucepan; discard remaining juices. Skim the fat from reserved juices. Shred the beef with 2 forks; return to slow cooker.

2. In a small bowl, mix flour and cold water until smooth; add to saucepan. Cook and stir 2 minutes or until thickened. Stir into the meat mixture.

3. Preheat oven to 425°. Spoon ½ cup meat mixture off center on each tortilla; top with chiles and 2 Tbsp. shredded cheese. Roll up and place in a greased 13x9-in. baking dish, seam side down. Top with the enchilada sauce; sprinkle with remaining cheese. Bake, uncovered, 15-20 minutes or until the cheese is melted. If desired, top with chopped lettuce and tomatoes.

1 enchilada: 551 cal., 26g fat (11g sat. fat), 111mg chol., 1388mg sod., 40g carb. (3g sugars, 2g fiber), 38g pro.

SLOW-COOKED BEEF ENCHILADAS

FAVORITE COMPANY CASSEROLE

Even my friends who don't eat a lot of broccoli or mushrooms agree this casserole is a winner. It's so easy to throw together, and the leftovers are delicious.

—Suzann Verdun, Lisle, IL

Prep: 15 min. • **Bake:** 45 min.
Makes: 8 servings

- 1 pkg. (6 oz.) wild rice, cooked
- 3 cups frozen chopped broccoli, thawed
- 1½ cups cubed cooked chicken
- 1 cup cubed cooked ham
- 1 cup shredded cheddar cheese
- 1 jar (4½ oz.) sliced mushrooms, drained
- 1 cup mayonnaise
- 1 tsp. prepared mustard
- ½ to 1 tsp. curry powder
- 1 can (10¾ oz.) condensed cream of mushroom soup, undiluted
- ¼ cup grated Parmesan cheese

1. Preheat oven to 350°. In a greased 2-qt. baking dish, layer the first 6 ingredients in order listed. Combine mayonnaise, mustard, curry and soup. Spread over top. Sprinkle with Parmesan cheese.
2. Bake, uncovered, 45-60 minutes or until top is light golden brown.

1 cup: 405 cal., 32g fat (8g sat. fat), 61mg chol., 872mg sod., 11g carb. (1g sugars, 2g fiber), 18g pro.

SQUASH & CHICKEN STEW

We created a satisfying stew that's nutritious, loaded with flavor and family-friendly. Chicken thighs are slowly simmered with stewed tomatoes, butternut squash, green peppers and onion for meal-in-one convenience.

—*Taste of Home* Test Kitchen

Prep: 15 min. • **Cook:** 6 hours
Makes: 5 servings

- 2 lbs. boneless skinless chicken thighs, cut into ½-in. pieces
- 1 can (28 oz.) stewed tomatoes, cut up
- 3 cups cubed peeled butternut squash
- 2 medium green peppers, cut into ½-in. pieces
- 1 small onion, sliced and separated into rings
- 1 cup water
- 1 tsp. salt
- 1 tsp. ground cumin
- ½ tsp. ground coriander
- ½ tsp. pepper
- 2 Tbsp. minced fresh parsley
  Hot cooked couscous, optional

In a 5-qt. slow cooker, combine the first 10 ingredients. Cover and cook on low for 6-7 hours or until chicken is no longer pink. Sprinkle with parsley. Serve with couscous if desired.

1½ cups: 384 cal., 14g fat (4g sat. fat), 121mg chol., 867mg sod., 31g carb. (13g sugars, 7g fiber), 37g pro.

FAVORITE
COMPANY CASSEROLE

FLANK STEAK PINWHEELS

MOSTACCIOLI

Even though we're not Italian, this rich, cheesy pasta dish is a family tradition for holidays and other special occasions. It tastes just like a lasagna without the work of layering the ingredients.
—Nancy Mundhenke, Kinsley, KS

- -

Prep: 15 min. • **Bake:** 45 min.
Makes: 12 servings

- 1 **lb. uncooked mostaccioli**
- 1½ **lbs. bulk Italian sausage**
- 1 **jar (28 oz.) meatless spaghetti sauce**
- 1 **large egg, lightly beaten**
- 1 **carton (15 oz.) ricotta cheese**
- 2 **cups shredded part-skim mozzarella cheese**
- ½ **cup grated Romano cheese**

1. Cook pasta according to the package directions; drain. Crumble sausage into a Dutch oven. Cook over medium heat until no longer pink; drain. Stir in spaghetti sauce and pasta. In a large bowl, combine the egg, ricotta cheese and mozzarella cheese.
2. Spoon half of the pasta mixture into a greased shallow 3-qt. baking dish; layer with cheese mixture and remaining pasta mixture.
3. Cover and bake at 375° for 40 minutes or until a thermometer reads 160°. Uncover; top with Romano cheese. Bake 5 minutes longer or until heated through.
1 cup: 386 cal., 18g fat (9g sat. fat), 74mg chol., 747mg sod., 36g carb. (8g sugars, 2g fiber), 22g pro.

FLANK STEAK PINWHEELS

The secret to these pretty pinwheels lies in their butterfly treatment. Because the steaks are flattened, they don't need marinade. Instead, they're filled with colorful, holiday-appropriate red pepper and green spinach and topped with a flavorful, homemade blue cheese sauce.
—*Taste of Home* Test Kitchen

- -

Prep: 30 min. • **Grill:** 10 min.
Makes: 4 servings

- 8 **bacon strips**
- 1 **beef flank steak (1½ lbs.)**
- 4 **cups fresh baby spinach**
- 1 **jar (7 oz.) roasted sweet red peppers, drained**

CREAM CHEESE SAUCE
- 3 **oz. cream cheese, softened**
- ¼ **cup 2% milk**
- 1 **Tbsp. butter**
- ¼ **tsp. pepper**
- ½ **cup crumbled blue cheese**

1. Place bacon strips on a microwave-safe plate lined with paper towels. Cover with another paper towel; microwave on high for 2-3 minutes or until partially cooked.

2. Meanwhile, cut steak horizontally from a long side to within ½ in. of opposite side. Open meat so it lies flat; cover with plastic wrap. Flatten to ¼-in. thickness. Remove plastic. Place spinach over steak to within 1 in. of edges; top with red peppers.
3. With the grain of the meat going from left to right, roll up jelly-roll style. Wrap bacon strips around beef; secure with toothpicks. Slice beef across the grain into 8 slices.
4. Grill the pinwheels, covered, over medium heat for 5-7 minutes on each side or until the meat reaches desired doneness (for medium-rare, a thermometer should read 135°; medium, 140°; medium-well, 145°). Discard the toothpicks.
5. In a small saucepan, combine the cream cheese, milk, butter and pepper. Cook and stir over low heat just until smooth (do not boil). Stir in blue cheese. Serve with the steak pinwheels.
2 pinwheels: 509 cal., 34g fat (17g sat. fat), 138mg chol., 812mg sod., 5g carb. (3g sugars, 1g fiber), 43g pro.

PAN-ROASTED
CHICKEN & VEGETABLES

PAN-ROASTED CHICKEN & VEGETABLES

This one-dish meal tastes as if it took hours of hands-on time, but the simple ingredients can be prepped in minutes. The rosemary gives it a rich flavor, and the meat juices cook the veggies to perfection. So easy!
—Sherri Melotik, Oak Creek, WI

- -

Prep: 15 min. • **Bake:** 45 min.
Makes: 6 servings

- 2 lbs. red potatoes (about 6 medium), cut into ¾-in. pieces
- 1 large onion, coarsely chopped
- 2 Tbsp. olive oil
- 3 garlic cloves, minced
- 1¼ tsp. salt, divided
- 1 tsp. dried rosemary, crushed, divided
- ¾ tsp. pepper, divided
- ½ tsp. paprika
- 6 bone-in chicken thighs (about 2¼ lbs.), skin removed
- 6 cups fresh baby spinach (about 6 oz.)

1. Preheat oven to 425°. In a large bowl, combine potatoes, onion, oil, garlic, ¾ tsp. salt, ½ tsp. rosemary and ½ tsp. pepper; toss to coat. Transfer to a 15x10x1-in. baking pan coated with cooking spray.
2. In a small bowl, mix paprika and the remaining salt, rosemary and pepper. Sprinkle chicken with paprika mixture; arrange over vegetables. Roast until a thermometer inserted in chicken reads 170°-175° and vegetables are just tender, 35-40 minutes.
3. Remove chicken to a serving platter; keep warm. Top vegetables with spinach. Roast until vegetables are tender and spinach is wilted, 8-10 minutes longer. Stir vegetables to combine; serve with chicken.

1 chicken thigh with 1 cup vegetables: 357 cal., 14g fat (3g sat. fat), 87mg chol., 597mg sod., 28g carb. (3g sugars, 4g fiber), 28g pro.
Diabetic exchanges: 4 lean meat, 1½ starch, 1 vegetable, 1 fat.

This all-in-one meal only takes a few minutes to prep. We love the leftovers, too!

—MARK HAGEN, EXECUTIVE EDITOR

SAUSAGE-STUFFED ACORN SQUASH

SAUSAGE-STUFFED ACORN SQUASH

Acorn squash gets a sweet and savory treatment when stuffed with sausage, onion, spinach and cranberries. Cooking the squash in the microwave makes this cozy main dish quick enough for even your busiest weeknight.
—*Taste of Home* Test Kitchen

- -

Takes: 30 min. • **Makes:** 4 servings

- 2 medium acorn squash
- 1 lb. bulk spicy pork sausage
- ½ cup chopped onion
- 1 cup fresh spinach, finely chopped
- ½ cup dried cranberries
- 1½ cups soft bread crumbs
- 1 large egg
- 2 Tbsp. 2% milk

1. Halve squash lengthwise; discard seeds. Place squash in a microwave-safe dish, cut side down. Microwave, covered, on high until tender, 10-12 minutes.
2. Meanwhile, in a large skillet, cook and crumble sausage with onion over medium heat until no longer pink, 5-7 minutes; drain. Remove from the heat; stir in the spinach, cranberries and bread crumbs. In a small bowl, whisk together egg and milk; add to sausage mixture and toss until moistened.
3. Turn squash; fill with sausage mixture. Microwave, covered, until a thermometer inserted in stuffing reads 165°, 2-3 minutes.
Note: To make soft bread crumbs, tear bread into pieces and place in a food processor or blender. Cover and pulse until crumbs form. One slice of bread yields ½ to ¾ cup crumbs.
1 stuffed squash half: 485 cal., 23g fat (8g sat. fat), 133mg chol., 843mg sod., 49g carb. (18g sugars, 5g fiber), 25g pro.

GOLDEN CHICKEN CORDON BLEU

For an entree that's as elegant as it is easy, try this tender chicken classic. It's a simple recipe that's also special.
—*Taste of Home* Test Kitchen

- -

Prep: 20 min. • **Bake:** 20 min.
Makes: 2 servings

2	boneless skinless chicken breast halves (6 oz. each)
2	slices deli ham (¾ oz. each)
2	slices Swiss cheese (¾ oz. each)
½	cup all-purpose flour
¼	tsp. salt
⅛	tsp. paprika
⅛	tsp. pepper
1	large egg
2	Tbsp. 2% milk
½	cup seasoned bread crumbs
1	Tbsp. canola oil
1	Tbsp. butter, melted

1. Flatten chicken to ¼-in. thickness; top each with a slice of ham and cheese. Roll up and tuck in ends; secure with toothpicks.
2. In a shallow bowl, combine the flour, salt, paprika and pepper. In another bowl, whisk egg and milk. Place bread crumbs in a third bowl. Dip chicken in flour mixture, then egg mixture; roll in crumbs.
3. In a small skillet, brown chicken in oil on all sides. Transfer to an 8-in. square baking dish coated with cooking spray.
4. Bake chicken, uncovered, at 350° until a thermometer reads 170°, for 20-25 minutes. Discard toothpicks; drizzle with butter.
1 serving: 501 cal., 23g fat (9g sat. fat), 172mg chol., 728mg sod., 23g carb. (2g sugars, 1g fiber), 49g pro.

ROASTED KIELBASA & VEGETABLES

ROASTED KIELBASA & VEGETABLES

I love this dish featuring kielbasa and veggies for two reasons. The first is that it's hearty. Second, it's a one-pan meal. To me, that's a win-win dinner!
—Marietta Slater, Justin, TX

- -

Prep: 20 min. • **Bake:** 40 min.
Makes: 6 servings

3	medium sweet potatoes, peeled and cut into 1-in. pieces
1	large sweet onion, cut into 1-in. pieces
4	medium carrots, cut into 1-in. pieces
2	Tbsp. olive oil
1	lb. smoked kielbasa or Polish sausage, halved and cut into 1-in. pieces
1	medium yellow summer squash, cut into 1-in. pieces
1	medium zucchini, cut into 1-in. pieces
¼	tsp. salt
¼	tsp. pepper
	Dijon mustard, optional

1. Preheat oven to 400°. Divide sweet potatoes, onion and carrots between 2 greased 15x10x1-in. baking pans. Drizzle with oil; toss to coat. Roast 25 minutes, stirring occasionally.
2. Add kielbasa, squash and zucchini to pans; sprinkle with salt and pepper. Roast until the vegetables are tender, 15-20 minutes longer. Transfer to a serving bowl; toss to combine. If desired, serve with mustard.
1⅔ cups: 378 cal., 25g fat (8g sat. fat), 51mg chol., 954mg sod., 26g carb. (12g sugars, 4g fiber), 13g pro.

BALSAMIC CHICKEN FETTUCCINE

Skip the marinara sauce and try this elegant twist on fettuccine. Our balsamic-infused entree is a meal in itself.
—*Taste of Home* Test Kitchen

Takes: 25 min. • **Makes:** 5 servings

- 8 oz. uncooked fettuccine
- 1½ lbs. boneless skinless chicken breasts, cut into strips
- 2 Tbsp. plus ½ cup balsamic vinaigrette, divided
- ½ lb. sliced fresh mushrooms
- 1 medium red onion, chopped
- 2 cans (14½ oz. each) diced tomatoes, undrained
- 2 cups frozen broccoli florets
- ½ tsp. Italian seasoning

1. Cook fettuccine according to the package directions. Meanwhile, in a large skillet, saute chicken in 1 Tbsp. vinaigrette until no longer pink. Remove and keep warm.

2. In the same skillet, saute mushrooms and onion in 1 Tbsp. vinaigrette until tender. Add the tomatoes, broccoli, Italian seasoning and remaining vinaigrette; cook 5-6 minutes longer or until heated through.

3. Drain fettuccine. Add fettuccine and chicken to skillet and toss to coat.

1½ cups: 423 cal., 9g fat (2g sat. fat), 75mg chol., 548mg sod., 49g carb. (12g sugars, 6g fiber), 37g pro.

WASABI BEEF FAJITAS

These beef fajitas get an Eastern spin with gingerroot, sesame oil and wasabi, a type of Japanese horseradish. You can find it in the Asian section at your supermarket.
—*Taste of Home* Test Kitchen

Takes: 20 min. • **Makes:** 8 servings

- 2 tsp. cornstarch
- 3 Tbsp. reduced-sodium soy sauce
- 2 tsp. prepared wasabi
- 2 tsp. minced fresh gingerroot
- 1 garlic clove, minced
- 2 Tbsp. sesame oil, divided
- 1 lb. uncooked beef stir-fry strips
- 12 green onions with tops, cut in half lengthwise
- 1 large sweet red pepper, julienned
- 8 flour tortillas (8 in.), warmed
- 1 cup coleslaw mix

1. In a small bowl, mix cornstarch, soy sauce, wasabi, ginger and garlic until blended. In a large skillet, heat 1 Tbsp. oil over medium-high heat. Add beef; stir-fry 4-6 minutes or until no longer pink. Remove from pan.

2. Stir-fry green onions and red pepper in remaining oil 2-3 minutes or until vegetables are crisp-tender.

3. Stir cornstarch mixture and add to pan. Bring to a boil; cook and stir 1-2 minutes or until sauce is thickened. Return beef to pan; heat through. Serve mixture with tortillas and coleslaw mix.

1 fajita: 287 cal., 9g fat (2g sat. fat), 23mg chol., 507mg sod., 32g carb. (2g sugars, 3g fiber), 17g pro. **Diabetic exchanges:** 2 starch, 2 lean meat, ½ fat.

BALSAMIC CHICKEN FETTUCCINE

MEDITERRANEAN
PORK & ORZO

ROOT BEER GLAZED HAM

For a unique spin on traditional glazed ham, try this southern specialty from our Test Kitchen. Our secret ingredient? Root beer!
—*Taste of Home* Test Kitchen

- -

Prep: 15 min. • **Bake:** 2½ hours
Makes: 15 servings

1	bone-in fully cooked spiral-sliced ham (7 to 9 lbs.)
3	cups root beer
¾	cup packed brown sugar
½	cup ketchup
¼	cup white wine vinegar
3	Tbsp. steak sauce
1	Tbsp. Dijon mustard
½	tsp. crushed red pepper flakes
¼	tsp. ground cloves

1. Place ham on a rack in a shallow roasting pan. Score the surface of the ham, making diamond shapes ½ in. deep. Bake at 325° for 2 hours.

2. In a large saucepan, combine remaining ingredients. Bring to a boil; cook until liquid is reduced by half, about 30 minutes.

3. Brush ham with some of the glaze; bake 30-60 minutes longer or until a thermometer reads 140°, brushing occasionally with the remaining glaze.

6 oz. cooked ham: 338 cal., 5g fat (1g sat. fat), 47mg chol., 2097mg sod., 36g carb. (19g sugars, 0 fiber), 38g pro.

MEDITERRANEAN PORK & ORZO

This meal in a bowl is one of my top picks on busy days. It's quick to put together, leaving me more time to relax at the table.
—Mary Relyea, Canastota, NY

- -

Takes: 30 min. • **Makes:** 6 servings

1½	lbs. pork tenderloin
1	tsp. coarsely ground pepper
2	Tbsp. olive oil
3	qt. water
1¼	cups uncooked orzo pasta
¼	tsp. salt
1	pkg. (6 oz.) fresh baby spinach
1	cup grape tomatoes, halved
¾	cup crumbled feta cheese

1. Rub pork with pepper; cut into 1-in. cubes. In a large nonstick skillet, heat the oil over medium heat. Add pork; cook and stir until no longer pink, 8-10 minutes.

2. Meanwhile, in a Dutch oven, bring water to a boil. Stir in orzo and salt; cook, uncovered, 8 minutes. Stir in spinach; cook until orzo is tender and spinach is wilted, 45-60 seconds longer. Drain.

3. Add tomatoes to pork; heat through. Stir in orzo mixture and cheese.

1⅓ cups: 372 cal., 11g fat (4g sat. fat), 71mg chol., 306mg sod., 34g carb. (2g sugars, 3g fiber), 31g pro. **Diabetic exchanges:** 3 lean meat, 2 starch, 1 vegetable, 1 fat.

When I'm craving something Mediterranean, this is the recipe I always turn to. It's also the dish that introduced me to orzo, and I love it to this day.

—SYDNEY WATSON, VISUAL DESIGNER

ROOT BEER
GLAZED HAM

SATURDAY AFTERNOON OVEN POT ROAST

This Saturday afternoon pot roast will be a welcome sight on your weekend dinner table and will leave your house smelling heavenly. If you find that the cooking liquid evaporates too quickly, add more broth to the Dutch oven.

—Colleen Delawder, Herndon, VA

Prep: 40 min. • **Bake:** 3 hours
Makes: 8 servings

- 1 boneless beef chuck roast (2½ lbs.)
- 1 tsp. salt
- ½ tsp. pepper
- 1 Tbsp. olive oil
- 1 Tbsp. butter
- 4 cups sliced sweet onion
- 1 can (6 oz.) tomato paste
- 4 garlic cloves, minced
- 1 tsp. dried thyme
- ½ tsp. celery seed
- ½ cup dry red wine
- 1 carton (32 oz.) reduced-sodium beef broth
- 6 medium carrots, cut into 1½-in. pieces
- ½ lb. medium fresh mushrooms, quartered

1. Preheat oven to 325°. Sprinkle roast with salt and pepper.
2. In a Dutch oven, heat oil and butter over medium-high heat; brown roast on all sides. Remove from pan. Add onion to the same pan; cook and stir over medium heat until tender, 8-10 minutes. Add tomato paste, garlic, thyme and celery seed; cook and stir 1 minute longer.
3. Add wine, stirring to loosen browned bits from pan; stir in broth. Return roast to pan. Arrange carrots and mushrooms around roast; bring to a boil. Bake, covered, until meat is fork-tender, 2½-3 hours. If desired, skim fat and thicken cooking juices for gravy.
4 oz. cooked beef with ½ cup vegetables and ¼ cup gravy: 339 cal., 17g fat (6g sat. fat), 98mg chol., 621mg sod., 14g carb. (7g sugars, 2g fiber), 32g pro.

PEAR PORK CHOPS & CORNBREAD STUFFING

You'll be tempted to eat this stovetop entree straight out of the pan. But save some for your guests—it's sure to wow them at the dinner table.

—*Taste of Home* Test Kitchen

Takes: 30 min. • **Makes:** 4 servings

- 1 pkg. (6 oz.) cornbread stuffing mix
- 4 boneless pork loin chops (6 oz. each)
- ½ tsp. pepper
- ¼ tsp. salt
- 2 Tbsp. butter
- 2 medium pears, chopped
- 1 medium sweet red pepper, chopped
- 2 green onions, thinly sliced

1. Prepare stuffing mix according to package directions. Meanwhile, sprinkle chops with pepper and salt. In a large skillet, brown pork chops in butter. Sprinkle with chopped pears and red pepper.
2. Top with stuffing and onions. Cook, uncovered, over medium heat until a thermometer inserted in pork reads 145°, 8-10 minutes.
1 pork chop with ¾ cup stuffing mixture: 603 cal., 28g fat (14g sat. fat), 127mg chol., 1094mg sod., 47g carb. (14g sugars, 5g fiber), 38g pro.

SATURDAY AFTERNOON
OVEN POT ROAST

GOLDEN
CHICKEN POTPIE

INSIDE-OUT STUFFED CABBAGE

Stuffed cabbage can be time-consuming to make, but this version is table-ready in just 30 minutes and it's got all the classic flavors. Butternut squash is an added bonus.
—*Taste of Home* Test Kitchen

- -

Prep: 10 min. • **Cook:** 25 min.
Makes: 4 servings

- 1   lb. ground beef
- 2   cups cubed peeled butternut squash (about 12 oz.)
- 1   medium green pepper, chopped
- 1   envelope Lipton beefy onion soup mix
- 1   Tbsp. brown sugar
- 1   can (11½ oz.) Spicy Hot V8 juice
- 1   cup water
- 6   cups chopped cabbage (about 1 small head)
- ½   cup uncooked instant brown rice

1. In a Dutch oven, cook and crumble beef with squash and pepper over medium-high heat until no longer pink; drain. Stir in the beefy onion soup mix, brown sugar, V8 juice, water and cabbage; bring to a boil. Reduce heat; simmer, covered, until the cabbage is tender, 8-10 minutes, stirring occasionally.
2. Stir in rice; return to a boil. Simmer, covered, 5 minutes. Remove from heat; let stand, covered, until rice is tender, about 5 minutes.

1½ cups: 382 cal., 15g fat (5g sat. fat), 70mg chol., 841mg sod., 40g carb. (13g sugars, 7g fiber), 25g pro.

GOLDEN CHICKEN POTPIE

The golden crust and creamy sauce make this veggie-packed pie a surefire hit. Mild and comforting, the family favorite has convenient freezer instructions for a night when there's no time for prep.
—*Taste of Home* Test Kitchen

- -

Prep: 20 min. • **Bake:** 35 min.
Makes: 2 potpies (6 servings each)

- 4   cups cubed cooked chicken
- 4   cups frozen cubed hash brown potatoes, thawed
- 1   pkg. (16 oz.) frozen mixed vegetables, thawed and drained
- 1   can (10½ oz.) condensed cream of chicken soup, undiluted
- 1   can (10½ oz.) condensed cream of onion soup, undiluted
- 1   cup whole milk
- 1   cup sour cream
- 2   Tbsp. all-purpose flour
- ½   tsp. salt
- ½   tsp. pepper
- ¼   tsp. garlic powder
- 2   sheets refrigerated pie crust

1. Preheat oven to 400°. Combine the first 11 ingredients. Divide between two 9-in. deep-dish pie plates.
2. Roll out crusts to fit top of each pie. Place over filling; trim, seal and flute the edges. Cut slits in top. Bake potpies until golden brown, 35-40 minutes.

Freeze option: Cover and freeze unbaked pies up to 3 months. To use, remove from freezer 30 minutes before baking (do not thaw). Preheat oven to 425°. Place pie on a baking sheet; cover edges loosely with foil. Bake 30 minutes. Reduce heat to 350°. Remove foil and bake potpies until they are golden brown or until heated through and a thermometer inserted in center reads 165°, 50-55 minutes longer.

1 serving: 415 cal., 19g fat (8g sat. fat), 69mg chol., 706mg sod., 39g carb. (5g sugars, 3g fiber), 20g pro.

SLOW-COOKER SPICY PORK CHILI

Tender pork adds extra heartiness to this slow-cooked chili. Feel free to use pork tenderloin, boneless pork roast or boneless pork chops for the pork in the recipe.
—*Taste of Home* Test Kitchen

- -

Prep: 10 min. • **Cook:** 6 hours
Makes: 6 servings (2½ qt.)

- 2 lbs. boneless pork, cut into ½-in. cubes
- 1 Tbsp. canola oil
- 1 can (28 oz.) crushed tomatoes
- 2 cups frozen corn
- 1 can (15 oz.) black beans, rinsed and drained
- 1 cup chopped onion
- 2 cups beef broth
- 1 can (4 oz.) chopped green chiles
- 1 Tbsp. chili powder
- 1 tsp. minced garlic
- ½ tsp. salt
- ½ tsp. cayenne pepper
- ½ tsp. pepper
- ¼ cup minced fresh cilantro
  Shredded cheddar cheese, optional

1. In a large skillet, cook pork in oil over medium-high heat 5-6 minutes or until browned. Transfer pork and drippings to a 5-qt. slow cooker. Stir in tomatoes, corn, beans, onion, broth, chiles, chili powder, garlic, salt, cayenne and pepper.
2. Cover and cook on low until pork is tender, 6-7 hours. Stir in cilantro. Serve with cheese if desired.
1¾ cups: 395 cal., 12g fat (4g sat. fat), 89mg chol., 1055mg sod., 34g carb. (9g sugars, 8g fiber), 39g pro.

SLOW-COOKER
SPICY PORK CHILI

CHICKEN MOLE CASSEROLE WITH OLIVES

Mole sauce has layers of rich, earthy flavor with mild to moderate heat. The hint of chocolate flavor helps offset the heat without being overpowering, which is why we added spicy chocolate cinnamon cane sugar to this dish originally submitted by Barbara White from Livingston, Texas.
—*Taste of Home* Test Kitchen

Prep: 50 min. • **Bake:** 40 min. + standing
Makes: 8 servings

- 2 large onions, finely chopped, divided
- 3 Tbsp. olive oil
- 3 garlic cloves, minced
- 1 tsp. salt
- 1 tsp. dried oregano
- 1 tsp. ground cumin
- 5 Tbsp. chili powder
- 2 Tbsp. Gustus Vitae spicy chocolate cinnamon cane sugar
- 3 Tbsp. all-purpose flour
- 4½ cups reduced-sodium chicken broth
- 6 cups shredded cooked chicken
- 12 corn tortillas (6 in.), warmed
- 1 cup sliced pimiento-stuffed olives
- 4 cups shredded Monterey Jack cheese

1. In a large saucepan, saute 1 cup onion in oil until tender. Reduce heat to low. Add the garlic, salt, oregano and cumin; cover and cook for 10 minutes. Stir in chili powder, spicy chocolate cinnamon sugar and flour until blended. Gradually stir in broth. Bring to a boil. Cook until mixture is reduced to 3 cups, about 35 minutes.

2. In a large bowl, combine chicken and ½ cup sauce. Spread ½ cup sauce into a greased 13x9-in. baking dish. Layer with half of the tortillas, chicken mixture, remaining onion and olives; top with 1 cup sauce and 2 cups cheese. Repeat layers.

3. Cover and bake at 375° for 30 minutes. Uncover; bake 10-15 minutes longer or until cheese is melted. Let stand for 10 minutes before serving.

1 serving: 622 cal., 35g fat (14g sat. fat), 144mg chol., 1568mg sod., 29g carb. (3g sugars, 6g fiber), 50g pro.

ORANGE-GLAZED HAM

I always thought this delicious ham looked like a sparkling jewel when my mom served it for Easter. The spice rub penetrates every tender slice, and the enticing aroma is only a hint of how good it will taste.
—Ruth Seitz, Columbus Junction, IA

Prep: 10 min. • **Bake:** 2 hours
Makes: 12 servings

- 1 fully cooked bone-in ham (6 to 8 lbs.)
- 1 Tbsp. ground mustard
- 1 tsp. ground allspice
- ¾ cup orange marmalade

1. Place ham on a rack in a shallow roasting pan. Score the surface of the ham, making diamond shapes ½ in. deep. Combine the mustard and allspice; rub over ham.

2. Bake the ham, uncovered, at 325° until a thermometer reads 140°, 2-2¼ hours. Spread top of ham with marmalade during the last hour of baking, basting occasionally.

6 oz. cooked ham: 243 cal., 6g fat (2g sat. fat), 100mg chol., 1203mg sod., 14g carb. (13g sugars, 0 fiber), 34g pro.

CHICKEN MOLE CASSEROLE WITH OLIVES

TACO CORNBREAD CASSEROLE

TACO CORNBREAD CASSEROLE

Here's a beefy cornbread casserole with a Mexican twist. A whole can of green chiles adds a pop of fire, but you can use fewer if you prefer less heat.
—Lisa Paul, Terre Haute, IN

Prep: 25 min. • **Bake:** 1 hour
Makes: 8 servings

- 2 lbs. ground beef
- 2 envelopes taco seasoning
- 2 cans (14½ oz. each) diced tomatoes, drained
- 1 cup water
- 1 cup cooked rice
- 1 can (4 oz.) chopped green chiles
- 2 pkg. (8½ oz. each) cornbread/muffin mix
- 1 can (8¾ oz.) whole kernel corn, drained
- 1 cup sour cream
- 2 cups corn chips
- 2 cups shredded Mexican cheese blend or cheddar cheese, divided
- 1 can (2¼ oz.) sliced ripe olives, drained
  Optional: Shredded lettuce, chopped tomatoes and chopped red onion

1. Preheat oven to 400°. In a Dutch oven, cook beef over medium heat until no longer pink, breaking into crumbles, 8-10 minutes; drain. Stir in taco seasoning. Add tomatoes, water, rice and green chiles; heat through, stirring occasionally.
2. Meanwhile, prepare the cornbread mix according to package directions; stir in the corn. Pour half of the batter into a greased 13x9-in. baking dish. Layer with half of the meat mixture, all the sour cream, half of the corn chips and 1 cup cheese. Top with remaining batter, remaining meat mixture, olives and remaining corn chips.
3. Bake, uncovered, until the cornbread is cooked through, 55-60 minutes. Sprinkle with remaining cheese; bake until melted, 3-5 minutes longer. If desired, serve with lettuce, tomatoes and red onion.
1½ cups: 817 cal., 40g fat (17g sat. fat), 183mg chol., 1982mg sod., 74g carb. (20g sugars, 4g fiber), 36g pro.

THE BEST BEEF STEW

THE BEST BEEF STEW

Our recipe for the best beef stew has tons of flavor, thanks to its blend of herbs and the addition of red wine and balsamic vinegar. It's a comfort classic stepped up a notch.
—James Schend, Deputy Editor

Prep: 30 min. • **Cook:** 2 hours
Makes: 6 servings (2¼ qt.)

- 1½ lbs. beef stew meat, cut into 1-in. cubes
- ½ tsp. salt, divided
- 6 Tbsp. all-purpose flour, divided
- ½ tsp. smoked paprika
- 1 Tbsp. canola oil
- 3 Tbsp. tomato paste
- 2 tsp. herbes de Provence
- 2 garlic cloves, minced
- 2 cups dry red wine
- 2 cups beef broth
- 1½ tsp. minced fresh rosemary, divided
- 2 bay leaves
- 3 cups cubed peeled potatoes
- 3 cups coarsely chopped onions (about 2 large)
- 2 cups sliced carrots
- 2 Tbsp. cold water
- 2 Tbsp. balsamic or red wine vinegar
- 1 cup fresh or frozen peas

1. In a small bowl, toss beef and ¼ tsp. salt. In a large bowl, combine 4 Tbsp. flour and paprika. Add beef, a few pieces at a time, and toss to coat.
2. In a Dutch oven, brown beef in oil over medium heat. Stir in tomato paste, herbes de Provence and garlic; cook until fragrant and color starts to darken slightly. Add red wine; cook until the mixture just comes to a boil. Simmer until reduced by half, about 5 minutes. Stir in broth, 1 tsp. rosemary and bay leaves. Bring to a boil. Reduce the heat; cover and simmer until the meat is almost tender, about 1½ hours.
3. Add potatoes, onions and carrots. Cover; simmer until meat and vegetables are tender, about 30 minutes longer.
4. Discard bay leaves. In a small mixing bowl, combine the remaining ½ tsp. rosemary, remaining ¼ tsp. salt and remaining 2 Tbsp. flour. Add cold water and vinegar; stir until smooth. Stir into stew. Bring to a boil; add the peas. Cook, stirring, until thickened, about 2 minutes. If desired, top with additional fresh rosemary.
1½ cups: 366 cal., 11g fat (3g sat. fat), 71mg chol., 605mg sod., 40g carb. (9g sugars, 6g fiber), 28g pro. **Diabetic exchanges:** 3 lean meat, 2½ starch, ½ fat.

PEPPERONI PENNE CARBONARA

Sun-dried tomatoes and turkey pepperoni lend fantastic flavor to this creamy, hearty pasta dish. It's a great change of pace from everyday spaghetti.
—*Taste of Home* Test Kitchen

Takes: 30 min. • **Makes:** 6 servings

- 3 cups uncooked penne pasta
- 2 cups chopped sun-dried tomatoes (not packed in oil)
- 3 cups boiling water
- ¼ cup butter
- ½ tsp. minced garlic
- 1 cup chopped turkey pepperoni
- 1 cup shredded Parmesan cheese
- 1 cup heavy whipping cream
- 3 Tbsp. minced fresh basil
- ½ tsp. salt
- ¼ tsp. pepper

1. Cook pasta according to the package directions. Meanwhile, soak tomatoes in boiling water for 10 minutes; drain well.
2. In a large skillet, saute the tomatoes in butter for 3 minutes. Add the garlic; cook 1 minute longer.
3. Stir in the turkey pepperoni, Parmesan cheese, cream, basil, salt and pepper. Cook over low heat until heated through. Drain pasta; toss with sauce.
1½ cups: 483 cal., 29g fat (17g sat. fat), 108mg chol., 1245mg sod., 39g carb. (7g sugars, 4g fiber), 19g pro.

GREEK TORTELLINI SKILLET

GREEK TORTELLINI SKILLET

One of our staff members loved this skillet entree so much, she made it for her young daughter, who said "Mmmmm!" after every bite. She declared it a keeper!
—*Taste of Home* Test Kitchen

Takes: 30 min. • **Makes:** 6 servings

- 1 pkg. (19 oz.) frozen cheese tortellini
- 1 lb. ground beef
- 1 medium zucchini, sliced
- 1 small red onion, chopped
- 3 cups marinara or spaghetti sauce
- ½ cup water
- ¼ tsp. pepper
- 2 medium tomatoes, chopped
- ½ cup cubed feta cheese
- ½ cup pitted Greek olives, halved
- 2 Tbsp. minced fresh basil, divided

1. Cook tortellini according to the package directions. Meanwhile, in a large skillet, cook the beef, zucchini and onion over medium heat until meat is no longer pink; drain.
2. Drain tortellini; add to skillet. Stir in the marinara sauce, water and pepper. Bring to a boil. Reduce heat; simmer, uncovered, for 5 minutes. Add tomatoes, cheese, olives and 1 Tbsp. basil. Sprinkle with remaining basil.
1½ cups: 543 cal., 20g fat (8g sat. fat), 89mg chol., 917mg sod., 58g carb. (13g sugars, 6g fiber), 32g pro.

CRUMB-CRUSTED PORK ROAST WITH ROOT VEGETABLES

Our pork roast boasts sweet roasted veggies with a savory herb-crumb coating. It's perfect in fall when you're craving something warm and comforting.
—*Taste of Home* Test Kitchen

- -

Prep: 25 min. • **Bake:** 1 hour + standing
Makes: 8 servings

- 1 boneless pork loin roast (2 to 3 lbs.)
- 4 tsp. honey
- 1 Tbsp. molasses
- 1½ tsp. spicy brown mustard
- 2 tsp. rubbed sage
- 1 tsp. dried thyme
- 1 tsp. dried rosemary, crushed
- ½ cup soft whole wheat bread crumbs
- 2 Tbsp. grated Parmesan cheese
- 1 large rutabaga, peeled and cubed
- 1 large sweet potato, peeled and cubed
- 1 large celery root, peeled and cubed
- 1 large onion, cut into wedges
- 2 Tbsp. canola oil
- ½ tsp. salt
- ¼ tsp. pepper

1. Preheat oven to 350°. Place roast on a rack in a shallow roasting pan coated with cooking spray. In a small bowl, mix honey, molasses and mustard; brush over roast.

2. In a large bowl, mix the sage, thyme and rosemary. In a small bowl, toss bread crumbs with Parmesan cheese and 2 tsp. of the herb mixture; press onto roast.

3. Add the vegetables, oil, salt and pepper to the remaining herb mixture; toss to coat. Arrange vegetables around roast.

4. Roast the pork for 1-1½ hours or until a thermometer reads 145°. Remove from pan; let stand 10 minutes before slicing. Serve with vegetables.

3 oz. cooked pork with ¾ cup vegetables: 302 cal., 10g fat (2g sat. fat), 57mg chol., 313mg sod., 29g carb. (15g sugars, 5g fiber), 25g pro. **Diabetic exchanges:** 3 lean meat, 2 starch, ½ fat.

PIEROGI BEEF SKILLET

Here's a new way to dress up frozen pierogi. Ground beef and vegetables make this dish hearty, thick and delicious.
—*Taste of Home* Test Kitchen

- -

Takes: 25 min. • **Makes:** 4 servings

- 1 lb. ground beef
- ½ cup chopped onion
- ¼ cup all-purpose flour
- ½ tsp. Italian seasoning
- ½ tsp. pepper
- ⅛ tsp. salt
- 1 can (14½ oz.) beef broth
- 1 pkg. (16 oz.) frozen cheese and potato pierogi, thawed
- 2 cups frozen mixed vegetables (about 10 oz.), thawed and drained
- ½ cup shredded cheddar cheese

1. In a large cast-iron or other heavy skillet, cook and crumble beef with onion over medium heat 5-7 minutes or until no longer pink; drain, reserving 3 Tbsp. drippings. Stir in the flour and seasonings until blended. Gradually stir in broth; bring to a boil. Cook and stir until thickened, 1-2 minutes.

2. Stir in pierogi and vegetables. Cook, uncovered, until heated through, about 5 minutes, stirring occasionally. Sprinkle with cheese.

1¾ cups: 654 cal., 31g fat (12g sat. fat), 102mg chol., 1157mg sod., 57g carb. (12g sugars, 7g fiber), 34g pro.

CRUMB-CRUSTED PORK ROAST WITH ROOT VEGETABLES

ZUCCHINI
PIZZA CASSEROLE

THAI CHICKEN THIGHS

Thanks to the slow cooker, a traditional Thai dish with peanut butter, jalapeno peppers and chili sauce becomes incredibly easy to make. If you want to crank up the spice a bit, use more jalapeno peppers.
—*Taste of Home* Test Kitchen

Prep: 25 min. • **Cook:** 5 hours
Makes: 8 servings

8   **bone-in chicken thighs
(about 3 lbs.), skin removed**
½   **cup salsa**
¼   **cup creamy peanut butter**
2   **Tbsp. lemon juice**
2   **Tbsp. reduced-sodium soy sauce**
1   **Tbsp. chopped seeded
jalapeno pepper**
2   **tsp. Thai chili sauce**
1   **garlic clove, minced**
1   **tsp. minced fresh gingerroot**
2   **green onions, sliced**
2   **Tbsp. sesame seeds, toasted
Hot cooked basmati rice, optional**

1. Place chicken in a 3-qt. slow cooker. In a small bowl, combine the salsa, peanut butter, lemon juice, soy sauce, jalapeno, Thai chili sauce, garlic and ginger; pour over chicken.
2. Cover and cook on low until the chicken is tender, 5-6 hours. Sprinkle with green onions and sesame seeds. Serve with rice if desired.
Note: Wear disposable gloves when cutting hot peppers; the oils can burn skin. Avoid touching your face.
1 chicken thigh with ¼ cup sauce: 261 cal., 15g fat (4g sat. fat), 87mg chol., 350mg sod., 5g carb. (2g sugars, 1g fiber), 27g pro.
Diabetic exchanges: 4 lean meat, 1 fat, ½ starch.

ZUCCHINI PIZZA CASSEROLE

My husband has a hearty appetite, our two kids never tire of pizza, and I grow lots of zucchini. So this tasty, tomatoey casserole is absolutely tops with us throughout the year. Once you've tried it, you may even decide to grow zucchini (or more of it)!
—Lynn Bernstetter, White Bear Lake, MN

Prep: 20 min. • **Bake:** 40 min.
Makes: 8 servings

4   **cups shredded unpeeled zucchini**
½   **tsp. salt**
2   **large eggs**
½   **cup grated Parmesan cheese**
2   **cups shredded part-skim
mozzarella cheese, divided**
1   **cup shredded cheddar
cheese, divided**
1   **lb. ground beef**
½   **cup chopped onion**
1   **can (15 oz.) Italian tomato sauce**
1   **medium green or sweet
red pepper, chopped**

1. Preheat oven to 400°. Place zucchini in colander; sprinkle with salt. Let stand 10 minutes, then squeeze out moisture.
2. Combine zucchini with eggs, Parmesan and half of mozzarella and cheddar cheeses. Press into a greased 13x9-in. or 3-qt. baking dish. Bake 20 minutes.

3. Meanwhile, in a large saucepan, cook beef and onion over medium heat, crumbling the beef, until meat is no longer pink; drain. Add tomato sauce; spoon over zucchini mixture. Sprinkle with remaining cheeses; add green pepper. Bake until heated through, about 20 minutes longer.
Freeze option: Cool the baked casserole; cover and freeze. To use, partially thaw in the refrigerator overnight. Remove from refrigerator 30 minutes before baking. Preheat oven to 350°. Unwrap casserole; reheat on a lower oven rack until heated through and a thermometer inserted in center reads 165°.
1 cup: 315 cal., 20g fat (10g sat. fat), 119mg chol., 855mg sod., 10g carb. (4g sugars, 2g fiber), 25g pro.

I've made this easy weeknight dinner more times than I can count. I sometimes swap in ground turkey and top the dish with chopped onions and red pepper flakes.

—CAROLINE STANKO, ASSOCIATE DIGITAL EDITOR

THAI CHICKEN
THIGHS

GARLIC-ROASTED
BRUSSELS SPROUTS
WITH MUSTARD SAUCE
PAGE 168

Side Dishes

A memorable menu just isn't complete without on-the-side sensations that perfectly complement the main course. From speedy weeknight favorites to picnic crowd-pleasers and holiday all-stars, these side dishes rank among our most loved and most requested when we cook for our own families. See for yourself how these superb sidekicks make the perfect dinner a reality!

SWEET POTATO, ORANGE
& PINEAPPLE CRUNCH

SWEET POTATO, ORANGE & PINEAPPLE CRUNCH

I combined my two absolute favorite sweet potato casseroles to create my own version of the holiday classic.
—Lisa Varner, El Paso, TX

- -

Prep: 35 min. • **Bake:** 40 min.
Makes: 12 servings

- 2   lbs. sweet potatoes, peeled and cubed (about 6 cups)
- ¾   cup sugar
- 1   can (8 oz.) crushed pineapple, drained
- 2   large eggs, lightly beaten
- ½   cup sour cream or plain yogurt
- ½   tsp. grated orange zest
- ¼   cup orange juice
- ¼   cup butter, melted
- 1   tsp. vanilla extract

TOPPING

- 1   cup sweetened shredded coconut
- 1   cup chopped pecans
- 1   cup packed brown sugar
- ½   cup all-purpose flour
- ¼   cup butter, melted

1. Preheat oven to 350°. Place the sweet potatoes in a large saucepan; add water to cover. Bring to a boil over high heat. Reduce heat to medium; cook, uncovered, until tender, 10-15 minutes. Drain.
2. Place sweet potatoes in a large bowl; mash potatoes. Stir in sugar, pineapple, eggs, sour cream, orange zest, juice, butter and vanilla; transfer to a greased 13x9-in. baking dish. For topping, in a large bowl, mix coconut, pecans, brown sugar and flour. Add butter; mix until crumbly. Sprinkle over top.
3. Bake, uncovered, until heated through and topping is golden brown, 40-45 minutes.
½ cup: 432 cal., 20g fat (9g sat. fat), 58mg chol., 110mg sod., 62g carb. (45g sugars, 4g fiber), 4g pro.

CAULIFLOWER-BROCCOLI CHEESE BAKE

CAULIFLOWER-BROCCOLI CHEESE BAKE

Here is one of the first dishes my mother taught me—a tasty pairing of broccoli and cauliflower baked in eggs and cheese. Enjoy this as a side dish with dinner or add it to your brunch spread. Feel free to use all broccoli or all cauliflower if you're not a fan of one of them.
—Devin Mulertt, Cedarburg, WI

- -

Prep: 15 min. • **Bake:** 50 min. + standing
Makes: 9 servings

- 2   Tbsp. butter
- 1   small onion, chopped
- 2   Tbsp. all-purpose flour
- ½   cup 2% milk
- 1   pkg. (8 oz.) Velveeta, cubed
- ¼   tsp. salt
- 3   large eggs, lightly beaten
- 2   pkg. (12 oz. each) frozen broccoli-cauliflower blend, thawed

1. Preheat oven to 325°. In a Dutch oven, heat the butter over medium-high heat. Add onion; cook and stir 2-3 minutes or until tender. Stir in flour until blended; gradually whisk in milk. Bring mixture to a boil, stirring constantly; cook and stir 1-2 minutes or until thickened. Stir in cheese and salt until cheese is melted.
2. Remove from heat. Gradually whisk in eggs. Stir in vegetable blend. Transfer to a greased 8-in. square baking dish. Bake, uncovered, until set, 50-60 minutes. Let stand 10 minutes before serving.
1 piece: 170 cal., 11g fat (6g sat. fat), 95mg chol., 461mg sod., 8g carb. (2g sugars, 1g fiber), 8g pro.

SUGAR SNAP PEA STIR-FRY

Fresh ginger, balsamic vinegar, soy sauce and sesame oil provide a nice blend of flavors in this Asian-inspired recipe for fresh sugar snap peas. This quick-to-cook recipe will complement most any spring entree, whether it's ham, lamb, chicken or fish. Best of all, it's easy to double for large crowds.
—*Taste of Home* Test Kitchen

- -

Takes: 20 min. • **Makes:** 6 servings

1	lb. fresh sugar snap peas
2	tsp. canola oil
1	garlic clove, minced
2	tsp. minced fresh gingerroot
1½	tsp. balsamic vinegar
1½	tsp. reduced-sodium soy sauce
1	tsp. sesame oil
	Dash cayenne pepper
1	Tbsp. minced fresh basil
	or 1 tsp. dried basil
2	tsp. sesame seeds, toasted

In a large nonstick skillet or wok, saute the peas in canola oil until crisp-tender. Add the garlic, ginger, vinegar, soy sauce, sesame oil and cayenne; saute 1 minute longer. Add basil; toss to combine. Sprinkle with toasted sesame seeds.

½ cup: 60 cal., 3g fat (0 sat. fat), 0 chol., 59mg sod., 6g carb. (3g sugars, 2g fiber), 3g pro. **Diabetic exchanges:** 1 vegetable, ½ fat.

GREEK-STYLE STUFFED ACORN SQUASH

GREEK-STYLE STUFFED ACORN SQUASH

With a truckload of acorn squash in my pantry, I wanted to make stuffed squash in lots of different ways. A bottle of Greek seasoning got my creativity flowing.
—Teri Lee Rasey, Cadillac, MI

- -

Prep: 45 min. • **Bake:** 30 min.
Makes: 12 servings

3	medium acorn squash, halved and seeds removed
1	cup lentils
2	cups chicken broth
¾	cup uncooked orzo pasta
1	lb. bulk pork sausage
½	cup crumbled feta cheese
2	tsp. Greek seasoning
2	Tbsp. all-purpose flour
1	cup french-fried onions
	Additional crumbled feta cheese, optional

1. Preheat oven to 350°. Place squash, cut side up, on a large baking sheet; roast until they can just be pierced with a fork, about 40 minutes. Remove to a wire rack to cool.

Meanwhile, place lentils in a large saucepan; add water to cover. Bring to a boil. Reduce heat; cook, covered, 20-25 minutes or until tender. Drain. Remove and set aside. In the same saucepan, bring broth to a boil. Add orzo; cook according to package directions for al dente. Drain orzo, reserving broth.

2. In a large skillet, cook sausage, crumbling the meat, until no longer pink, 6-8 minutes; drain. Add lentils and orzo to skillet; remove from heat. Add ½ cup feta cheese and Greek seasoning; mix well.

3. Pour reserved chicken broth back into saucepan. Over medium heat, whisk in the flour until thickened, then pour into the sausage mixture.

4. When cool enough to handle, quarter squash and return to baking sheet. Top with sausage mixture. Bake until the squash are tender, about 30 minutes. Before serving, sprinkle with french-fried onions and, if desired, additional feta.

1 serving: 335 cal., 14g fat (4g sat. fat), 29mg chol., 704mg sod., 41g carb. (5g sugars, 5g fiber), 13g pro.

BEETS IN ORANGE SAUCE

An irresistible orange glaze is just the thing to ensure that your family eats their veggies! The sweet and tangy glaze is simply the perfect complement to the earthy flavor of the beets.
—*Taste of Home* Test Kitchen

- -

Prep: 15 min. • **Cook:** 35 min.
Makes: 8 servings

- 8 whole fresh beets
- ¼ cup sugar
- 2 tsp. cornstarch
  Dash pepper
- 1 cup orange juice
- 1 medium navel orange, halved and sliced, optional
- ½ tsp. grated orange zest

1. Place beets in a large saucepan; cover with water. Bring to a boil. Reduce heat; cover and cook for 25-30 minutes or until tender. Drain and cool slightly. Peel and slice; place in a serving bowl and keep warm.

2. In a small saucepan, combine the sugar, cornstarch and pepper; stir in orange juice until smooth. Bring to a boil; cook and stir for 2 minutes or until thickened. Remove from the heat; stir in orange slices if desired and zest. Pour over beets.

Note: A 15-oz. can of sliced beets may be substituted for the fresh beets. Drain the canned beets and omit the first step of the recipe.

1 cup: 63 cal., 0 fat (0 sat. fat), 0 chol., 39mg sod., 15g carb. (12g sugars, 1g fiber), 1g pro.

NANNY'S PARMESAN MASHED POTATOES

My grandsons rave over these creamy potatoes loaded with Parmesan. That's all the endorsement I need. Sometimes I use golden or red potatoes, with skins on.
—Kallee Krong-McCreery, Escondido, CA

- -

Prep: 20 min. • **Cook:** 20 min.
Makes: 12 servings

- 5 lbs. potatoes, peeled and cut into 1-in. pieces
- ¾ cup butter, softened
- ¾ cup sour cream
- ½ cup grated Parmesan cheese
- 1¼ tsp. garlic salt
- 1 tsp. salt
- ½ tsp. pepper
- ¾ to 1 cup 2% milk, warmed
- 2 Tbsp. minced fresh parsley

1. Place potatoes in a 6-qt. stockpot; add water to cover. Bring to a boil. Reduce heat; cook, uncovered, 10-15 minutes or until tender. Drain potatoes; return to pot and stir over low heat for 1 minute to dry.

2. Coarsely mash potatoes, gradually adding butter, sour cream, cheese, seasonings and enough milk to reach desired consistency. Stir in parsley.

¾ cup: 264 cal., 15g fat (10g sat. fat), 45mg chol., 456mg sod., 27g carb. (3g sugars, 2g fiber), 5g pro.

BEETS IN ORANGE SAUCE

PARMESAN RISOTTO

SLOW-COOKER CHICKPEA TAGINE

While traveling through Morocco, my wife and I fell in love with the complex flavors of the many tagines we tried. Resist the urge to stir, as it will break down the veggies. Feel free to add shredded cooked chicken in the last 10 minutes, or serve with grilled fish.
—Raymond Wyatt, West St. Paul, MN

- -

Prep: 20 min. • **Cook:** 4 hours
Makes: 12 servings

- 1 small butternut squash (about 2 lbs.), peeled and cut into ½-in. cubes
- 2 medium zucchini, cut into ½-in. pieces
- 1 medium sweet red pepper, coarsely chopped
- 1 medium onion, coarsely chopped
- 1 can (15 oz.) chickpeas or garbanzo beans, rinsed and drained
- 12 dried apricots, halved
- 2 Tbsp. olive oil
- 2 garlic cloves, minced
- 2 tsp. paprika
- 1 tsp. ground ginger
- 1 tsp. ground cumin
- ½ tsp. salt
- ¼ tsp. pepper
- ¼ tsp. ground cinnamon
- 1 can (14.5 oz.) crushed tomatoes
- 2 to 3 tsp. harissa chili paste
- 2 tsp. honey
- ¼ cup chopped fresh mint leaves
  Plain Greek yogurt, optional
  Optional: Additional olive oil, honey and fresh mint

1. Place the first 6 ingredients in a 5- or 6-qt. slow cooker.

2. In a skillet, heat oil over medium heat. Add garlic, paprika, ginger, cumin, salt, pepper and cinnamon; cook and stir until fragrant, about 1 minute. Add tomatoes, harissa and honey; bring to a boil. Pour tomato mixture over the vegetables; stir to combine. Cook, covered, on low until vegetables are tender and sauce has thickened, 4-5 hours. Stir in fresh mint.

3. If desired, top with yogurt, and additional mint, olive oil and honey to serve.
¾ cup: 127 cal., 3g fat (0 sat. fat), 0 chol., 224mg sod., 23g carb. (9g sugars, 6g fiber), 4g pro. **Diabetic exchanges:** 1½ starch, ½ fat.

PARMESAN RISOTTO

Risotto is a creamy Italian rice dish. In this version from our Test Kitchen, the rice is briefly sauteed, then slowly cooked in wine and seasonings.
—*Taste of Home* Test Kitchen

- -

Prep: 15 min. • **Cook:** 30 min.
Makes: 12 servings

- 8 cups chicken broth
- ½ cup finely chopped onion
- ¼ cup olive oil
- 3 cups arborio rice
- 2 garlic cloves, minced
- 1 cup dry white wine or water
- ½ cup shredded Parmesan cheese
- ¼ tsp. salt
- ¼ tsp. pepper
- 3 Tbsp. minced fresh parsley

1. In a large saucepan, heat broth and keep warm. In a Dutch oven, saute onion in oil until tender. Add the rice and garlic; cook and stir for 2-3 minutes. Reduce the heat; stir in wine. Cook and stir until all of the liquid is absorbed.

2. Add heated broth, ½ cup at a time, stirring constantly and allowing the liquid to absorb between additions. Cook 20 minutes or just until the risotto is creamy and rice is almost tender. Add remaining ingredients; cook and stir until heated through. Serve immediately.
¾ cup: 260 cal., 6g fat (1g sat. fat), 2mg chol., 728mg sod., 41g carb. (1g sugars, 1g fiber), 6g pro.

Sausage Mushroom Risotto: Reduce olive oil to 2 Tbsp. In a large skillet, cook 1 lb. bulk Italian sausage over medium heat until the meat is no longer pink; drain. Set aside and keep warm. Add onion, oil and ½ lb. quartered fresh mushrooms to skillet and cook until tender. Proceed as directed.

Asparagus Risotto: Trim 1 pound asparagus and cut into 2-in. pieces. Place asparagus in a large saucepan; add ½ in. of water. Bring to a boil. Reduce the heat; cover and simmer for 3 minutes or until crisp-tender. Drain and set aside. After finishing step 1 of recipe, add the asparagus; heat through. Proceed with step 2.

SLOW-COOKER
CHICKPEA TAGINE

GARLIC-ROASTED
BRUSSELS SPROUTS
WITH MUSTARD SAUCE

GARLIC-ROASTED BRUSSELS SPROUTS WITH MUSTARD SAUCE

Don't be afraid to bring out the Brussels sprouts. Mellowed by roasting and tossed with mustard sauce, they may just delight even the most skeptical folks.
—Becky Walch, Orland, CA

- -

Takes: 20 min. • **Makes:** 6 servings

1½	lbs. fresh Brussels sprouts, halved
2	Tbsp. olive oil
3	garlic cloves, minced
½	cup heavy whipping cream
3	Tbsp. Dijon mustard
⅛	tsp. white pepper
	Dash salt

1. Place Brussels sprouts in an ungreased 15x10x1-in. baking pan. Combine oil and garlic; drizzle over sprouts and toss to coat.
2. Bake, uncovered, at 450° until tender, 10-15 minutes, stirring occasionally.
3. Meanwhile, in a small saucepan, combine the cream, mustard, pepper and salt. Bring to a gentle boil; cook until slightly thickened, 1-2 minutes. Spoon over Brussels sprouts.
¾ cup: 167 cal., 12g fat (5g sat. fat), 27mg chol., 241mg sod., 13g carb. (3g sugars, 4g fiber), 4g pro.

TEST KITCHEN TIP
Trim and chop the Brussels sprouts prior to roasting. Cut off any dry or woody stems from their bottoms, then slice in half. Aim for all of the sprouts to be of similar size so they cook evenly.

SWISS CORN CASSEROLE

My mother shared this recipe with me back in the '80s and now it's a Thanksgiving Day mainstay. We freeze locally grown corn during peak season, and I love to use it in this special side dish.
—Wendy Young, Cordova, MD

Prep: 20 min.
Bake: 35 min. + standing
Makes: 8 servings

 4 large eggs
 1 can (12 oz.) evaporated milk
 ½ tsp. salt
 ¼ tsp. pepper
 4 cups frozen corn
  (about 20 oz.), thawed
 3 cups shredded Swiss cheese, divided
 ¼ cup chopped onion
 3 cups soft bread crumbs
 ¼ cup butter, melted

1. Preheat oven to 350°. In a large bowl, whisk together first 4 ingredients; stir in corn, 1½ cups cheese and onion. Transfer to a greased 11x7-in. baking dish.
2. Toss bread crumbs with melted butter; distribute over casserole. Sprinkle with remaining cheese.
3. Bake, uncovered, until golden brown and heated through, 35-45 minutes. Let stand 10 minutes before serving.
Note: To make soft bread crumbs, tear bread into pieces and place in a food processor or blender. Cover and pulse until crumbs form. One slice of bread yields ½ to ¾ cup crumbs.
⅔ cup: 412 cal., 25g fat (14g sat. fat), 161mg chol., 434mg sod., 28g carb. (7g sugars, 2g fiber), 21g pro.

ROASTED PARMESAN CARROTS

Mom always reminded us to eat our carrots because they promote optimal vision. Rich in beta carotene, carrots not only support eye health, but also taste amazing when roasted and tossed with Parmesan.
—*Taste of Home* Test Kitchen

Takes: 25 min. • **Makes:** 4 servings

 1 lb. fresh carrots, peeled
 1 tsp. olive oil
 ½ tsp. kosher salt
 ¼ tsp. freshly ground pepper
 ¼ tsp. dried thyme
 3 Tbsp. grated Parmesan cheese

1. Preheat oven to 450°. Cut the carrots crosswise in half and then lengthwise into ½-in.-thick sticks. Toss the carrots with oil, salt, pepper and thyme; spread evenly in a greased 15x10x1-in. baking pan.
2. Roast until tender and lightly browned, stirring once, 12-15 minutes. Toss with Parmesan cheese.
1 serving: 72 cal., 2g fat (1g sat. fat), 3mg chol., 386mg sod., 11g carb. (5g sugars, 3g fiber), 2g pro. **Diabetic exchanges:** 1 vegetable, ½ fat.

SWISS CORN CASSEROLE

FESTIVE RICE

My mom and I transformed plain rice by adding feta, cranberries, pumpkin seeds and cayenne. We wound up with a sweet and spicy crowd-pleaser.

—Lisa de Perio, Dallas, TX

- -

Prep: 20 min. • **Bake:** 30 min.
Makes: 6 servings

2¼	cups water
¼	cup butter, cubed
1	tsp. salt
1	tsp. white vinegar
½	tsp. garlic powder
1	cup uncooked jasmine rice
¼	cup salted pumpkin seeds or pepitas
2	tsp. brown sugar
¼	to ½ tsp. cayenne pepper
¼	cup crumbled feta cheese
¼	cup chopped fresh mint
¼	cup dried cranberries

1. Preheat oven to 325°. In a small saucepan, bring first 5 ingredients to a boil. Remove from heat. Pour over rice in a greased 8-in. square baking dish. Bake, covered, until all liquid is absorbed, 30-35 minutes.

2. Meanwhile, in a small nonstick skillet over medium-high heat, cook pumpkin seeds, brown sugar and cayenne pepper, stirring constantly until sugar melts and cayenne coats pumpkin seeds, about 4-5 minutes. Remove from the heat; transfer to a plate, spreading out seeds to cool. Sprinkle cooked rice with feta, mint, cranberries and spiced pumpkin seeds.

⅔ cup: 244 cal., 11g fat (6g sat. fat), 23mg chol., 514mg sod., 32g carb. (5g sugars, 1g fiber), 5g pro.

OKTOBERFEST RED CABBAGE

Four generations of our family celebrate Oktoberfest. We love this dish of red cabbage and apples, known as *rotkohl*, for the tart and sweet flavors.

—Diana Likes, Chandler, AZ

- -

Prep: 20 min. • **Cook:** 50 min.
Makes: 6 servings

3	Tbsp. bacon drippings or canola oil
1	small head red cabbage (about 1½ lbs.), shredded
2	medium tart apples, peeled and chopped
1	cup water
¼	cup sugar
¾	tsp. salt
¼	tsp. pepper
⅛	tsp. ground cloves
¼	cup white vinegar

1. In a Dutch oven, heat bacon drippings over medium heat. Add cabbage and apples; cook and stir 2-3 minutes. Stir in water, sugar, salt, pepper and cloves.

2. Bring to a boil. Reduce heat; simmer, covered, 40-45 minutes or until cabbage is tender, stirring occasionally. Stir in vinegar.

¾ cup: 146 cal., 7g fat (3g sat. fat), 6mg chol., 331mg sod., 22g carb. (17g sugars, 3g fiber), 1g pro.

FESTIVE RICE

TASTE OF HOME
TEST KITCHEN
RECIPE OF THE YEAR
★ ★ ★ ★

SIMPLE AU GRATIN
POTATOES

BALSAMIC ZUCCHINI SAUTE

This super fast vegetarian dish is flavorful and only uses a few ingredients, so it's easy to whip up as your entree is cooking.
—Elizabeth Bramkamp, Gig Harbor, WA

- -

Takes: 20 min. • **Makes:** 4 servings

- 1　Tbsp. olive oil
- 3　medium zucchini, cut into thin slices
- ½　cup chopped sweet onion
- ½　tsp. salt
- ½　tsp. dried rosemary, crushed
- ¼　tsp. pepper
- 2　Tbsp. balsamic vinegar
- ⅓　cup crumbled feta cheese

In a large skillet, heat oil over medium-high heat; saute the zucchini and onion until crisp-tender, 6-8 minutes. Stir in seasonings. Add vinegar; cook and stir 2 minutes. Top with cheese.

½ cup: 94 cal., 5g fat (2g sat. fat), 5mg chol., 398mg sod., 9g carb. (6g sugars, 2g fiber), 4g pro. **Diabetic exchanges:** 1 vegetable, 1 fat.

ROASTED ASPARAGUS WITH THYME

This good-for-you springtime side dish is so easy to prepare, yet the simply seasoned spears look appealing enough to serve to guests or take to a carry-in dinner.
—Sharon Leno, Keansburg, NJ

- -

Takes: 20 min. • **Makes:** 12 servings

- 3　lbs. fresh asparagus, trimmed
- 3　Tbsp. olive oil
- 2　tsp. minced fresh thyme
　　or ¾ tsp. dried thyme
- ½　tsp. salt
- ¼　tsp. pepper

1. Place asparagus in a baking pan lined with heavy-duty foil. Drizzle with oil and toss to coat. Sprinkle asparagus with the thyme, salt and pepper.

2. Bake, uncovered, at 425° 10-15 minutes or until crisp-tender.

7 asparagus spears: 55 cal., 4g fat (1g sat. fat), 0 chol., 101mg sod., 4g carb. (0 sugars, 1g fiber), 3g pro. **Diabetic exchanges:** 1 vegetable, ½ fat.

SIMPLE AU GRATIN POTATOES

These cheesy potatoes are always welcome at our dinner table, and they're so simple to make. A perfect complement to ham, this versatile, homey side dish also goes well with pork, chicken and other entrees.
—Cris O'Brien, Virginia Beach, VA

- -

Prep: 20 min. • **Bake:** 1½ hours
Makes: 8 servings

- 3　Tbsp. butter
- 3　Tbsp. all-purpose flour
- 1½　tsp. salt
- ⅛　tsp. pepper
- 2　cups 2% milk
- 1　cup shredded cheddar cheese
- 5　cups thinly sliced peeled potatoes (about 6 medium)
- ½　cup chopped onion
　　Additional pepper, optional

1. Preheat oven to 350°. In a large saucepan, melt butter over low heat. Stir in flour, salt and pepper until smooth. Gradually add milk. Bring to a boil; cook and stir 2 minutes or until thickened. Remove from heat; stir in cheese until melted. Add the potatoes and chopped onion.

2. Transfer to a greased 2-qt. baking dish. Cover and bake 1 hour. Uncover; bake until the potatoes are tender, 30-40 minutes. If desired, top with additional pepper.

¾ cup: 224 cal., 10g fat (7g sat. fat), 35mg chol., 605mg sod., 26g carb. (4g sugars, 2g fiber), 7g pro.

TEST KITCHEN TIP

It's easier to shred cheddar and other sharp cheeses when the block of cheese is cold.

ONION PIE

ONION PIE

My grandmother and mother always make onion pie during the holidays, but it's good any time of year. This is a savory side dish you can serve with almost any meat or main course. It's especially good with roast beef.
—Mary West, Marstons Mills, MA

- -

Prep: 15 min. • **Bake:** 35 min.
Makes: 8 servings

- 6 to 8 medium onions, thinly sliced
- 2 Tbsp. canola oil
- 6 large eggs
- 1 cup soft bread crumbs
- ½ cup grated Parmesan cheese
- ½ cup minced fresh parsley

1. In a large skillet, saute onions in oil until soft but not browned; drain well. In a large bowl, whisk eggs. Stir in the bread crumbs, cheese, parsley and onions.
2. Place in a greased 10-in. pie pan. Bake at 350° for 35-40 minutes or until a knife inserted in the center comes out clean.
1 piece: 170 cal., 9g fat (3g sat. fat), 163mg chol., 176mg sod., 14g carb. (8g sugars, 3g fiber), 9g pro.

GRANDMOTHER'S CORN PUDDING

Corn pudding is a popular side dish on Maryland's eastern shore. My grandmother served this pudding for family reunions and other gatherings.
—Susan Brown Langenstein, Salisbury, MD

- -

Prep: 10 min. • **Bake:** 50 min.
Makes: 9 servings

- 4 large eggs
- 1 cup whole milk
- 1 can (15 oz.) cream-style corn
- ½ cup sugar
- 5 slices day-old bread, crusts removed
- 1 Tbsp. butter, softened

In a bowl, beat eggs and milk. Add corn and sugar; mix well. Cut bread into ½-in. cubes and place in a greased 9-in. square baking dish. Pour egg mixture over bread. Dot with butter. Bake, uncovered, at 350° until a knife inserted in the center comes out clean, 50-60 minutes.
1 serving: 175 cal., 5g fat (2g sat. fat), 102mg chol., 264mg sod., 28g carb. (14g sugars, 1g fiber), 6g pro.

SPICY POTATOES WITH GARLIC AIOLI

SPICY POTATOES WITH GARLIC AIOLI

This is my take on Spanish *patatas bravas*. The potatoes are tossed in a flavorful spice mix and then finished to a crispy golden brown. The garlic aioli takes it over the top for an unconventional potato salad that'll be a hit at any party.
—John Stiver, Bowen Island, BC

- -

Prep: 35 min. • **Bake:** 25 min.
Makes: 10 servings (1¾ cups aioli)

- 3 lbs. medium Yukon Gold potatoes, cut into 1½-in. cubes (about 8 potatoes)
- 2 Tbsp. olive oil
- 2 garlic cloves, minced
- 2 Tbsp. smoked paprika
- 2 tsp. garlic powder
- 1½ tsp. chili powder
- 1½ tsp. ground cumin
- ¼ tsp. salt
- ¼ tsp. crushed red pepper flakes
- ⅛ tsp. pepper

AIOLI
- 1½ cups mayonnaise
- 3 Tbsp. lemon juice
- 3 garlic cloves, minced
- 1 Tbsp. minced fresh chives plus additional for topping
- 1 tsp. red wine vinegar
- ¼ tsp. salt
- ¼ tsp. pepper

1. Preheat oven to 375°. Place potatoes in a Dutch oven; add water to cover. Bring to a boil. Reduce heat; cook, uncovered, until just tender, 8-10 minutes. Drain; pat dry with paper towels. Transfer potatoes to a mixing bowl. Toss potatoes in oil and minced garlic to coat evenly.
2. Combine the paprika, garlic powder, chili powder, cumin, salt, red pepper flakes and pepper; sprinkle over potatoes. Gently toss to coat. Transfer potatoes to 2 greased 15x10x1-in. baking pans, spreading into a single layer. Bake 25 minutes or until crispy, stirring potatoes and rotating pans halfway through cooking.
3. For aioli, combine ingredients until blended. Transfer potatoes to a serving platter; sprinkle with chives. Serve warm with aioli.
¾ cup potatoes with about 3 Tbsp. aioli: 469 cal., 34g fat (5g sat. fat), 3mg chol., 396mg sod., 37g carb. (3g sugars, 4g fiber), 5g pro.

COLCANNON IRISH POTATOES

My mother came from Ireland as a teenager and brought this homey recipe with her. I find that it's a great way to get my family to eat cooked cabbage...hidden in Grandma's comforting potatoes!
—Marie Pagel, Lena, WI

Takes: 30 min. • **Makes:** 10 servings

2½ lbs. potatoes (about 6 medium), peeled and cut into 1-in. pieces
  2 cups chopped cabbage
  1 large onion, chopped
  1 tsp. salt
 ¼ tsp. pepper
 ¼ cup butter, softened
  1 cup 2% milk

1. Place potatoes in a 6-qt. stockpot; add water to cover. Bring to a boil. Reduce heat to medium; cook, covered, until potatoes are almost tender, 8-10 minutes.
2. Add cabbage and onion; cook, covered, until cabbage is tender, 5-7 minutes. Drain; return to pot. Add salt and pepper; mash to desired consistency, gradually adding butter and milk.
¾ cup: 129 cal., 5g fat (3g sat. fat), 14mg chol., 290mg sod., 19g carb. (4g sugars, 2g fiber), 3g pro. **Diabetic exchanges:** 1 starch, 1 fat.

LEMON-PARMESAN
BROILED ASPARAGUS

LEMON-PARMESAN BROILED ASPARAGUS

These special spears are packed with flavor, thanks to the lemon-garlic dressing they're tossed in before roasting. It's a simple, quick side that goes with almost anything!
—Tina Mirilovich, Johnstown, PA

Takes: 15 min. • **Makes:** 4 servings

 ¼ cup mayonnaise
  4 tsp. olive oil
1½ tsp. grated lemon zest
  1 garlic clove, minced
 ½ tsp. seasoned salt
 ½ tsp. pepper
  1 lb. fresh asparagus, trimmed
  2 Tbsp. shredded Parmesan cheese
    Lemon wedges, optional

1. Preheat broiler. In large bowl, combine first 6 ingredients. Add asparagus; toss to coat. Place in a single layer on a wire rack over a foil-lined 15x10x1-in. baking pan.
2. Broil 5-6 in. from heat 5-7 minutes or until tender and lightly browned. Transfer to a serving platter; sprinkle with Parmesan cheese. If desired, serve with lemon wedges.
1 serving: 156 cal., 15g fat (3g sat. fat), 3mg chol., 309mg sod., 3g carb. (1g sugars, 1g fiber), 2g pro. **Diabetic exchanges:** 3 fat, 1 vegetable.

PECAN-CORNBREAD DRESSING

Plenty of pecans and bacon give this stuffing a unique flavor, while using a packaged mix cuts down on the preparation time.
—*Taste of Home* Test Kitchen

Prep: 25 min. • **Bake:** 45 min.
Makes: 10 servings

  3 cups water
  ½ cup butter
  1 pkg. (16 oz.) cornbread stuffing mix
  10 bacon strips, diced
  1 cup chopped celery
  1½ cups chopped green onions
  ½ cup coarsely chopped pecans
  ½ tsp. salt
  ¼ tsp. pepper

1. In a large saucepan, bring water and butter to a boil. Remove from the heat and stir in stuffing mix; cover and set aside.
2. In a large skillet, cook bacon until crisp; remove with a slotted spoon to drain on paper towels. Discard all but 3 Tbsp. of drippings; cook celery in drippings over medium heat for 5 minutes. Add onions and cook 5 minutes or until celery is tender, stirring constantly. Add to the cornbread mixture along with pecans, salt, pepper and bacon; mix well.
3. Transfer to a greased 2-qt. casserole. Cover and bake at 325° for 45 minutes or until heated through.
¾ cup: 404 cal., 26g fat (10g sat. fat), 43mg chol., 1035mg sod., 14g carb. (4g sugars, 3g fiber), 9g pro.

PECAN-CORNBREAD DRESSING

OVEN-DRIED TOMATOES

We owned an organic greenhouse and business that included workshops. I had 100 tomato varieties to work with, so I started oven-drying them and taught my students the method, too.
—Sue Gronholz, Beaver Dam, WI

Prep: 15 min. • **Bake:** 5 hours
Makes: 4 servings

  8 plum tomatoes
     Ice water
  ¼ cup olive oil
  ¼ cup minced fresh basil
  4 garlic cloves, minced
  ½ tsp. salt
  ¼ tsp. pepper

1. Preheat oven to 250°. Fill a large saucepan two-thirds with water; bring to a boil. Cut a shallow "X" on the bottom of each tomato. Place tomatoes, a few at a time, in boiling water just until skin at the "X" begins to loosen, about 30 seconds. Remove and immediately drop into ice water. Pull off and discard skins.
2. Cut tomatoes in half lengthwise. Combine tomatoes, oil, basil, garlic, salt and pepper; toss to coat. Transfer tomatoes, cut side up, to a greased 15x10x1-in. baking pan. Roast until tomatoes are soft and slightly shriveled, about 5 hours. Cool completely; refrigerate.
4 tomato halves: 147 cal., 14g fat (2g sat. fat), 0 chol., 302mg sod., 6g carb. (3g sugars, 2g fiber), 1g pro. **Diabetic exchanges:** 3 fat, 1 vegetable.

DAD'S CREAMED PEAS & PEARL ONIONS

ROASTED HERBED SQUASH WITH GOAT CHEESE

Cooking for my family is a hobby that brings me so much joy. My young daughter (and all our Christmas Eve party guests) heartily approved of this new potluck favorite. Any type of winter squash would work well in this standout recipe.

—Lindsay Oberhausen, Lexington, KY

Prep: 25 min. • **Cook:** 30 min.
Makes: 10 servings

- 2 medium acorn squash (about 1½ lbs. each), peeled and cut into 2-in. cubes
- 1 large butternut squash (5 to 6 lbs.), peeled and cut into 2-in. cubes
- 3 Tbsp. olive oil
- 2 Tbsp. minced fresh thyme
- 2 Tbsp. minced fresh rosemary
- 1 Tbsp. kosher salt
- 1 tsp. coarsely ground pepper
- 1 log (11 oz.) fresh goat cheese, crumbled
- 2 Tbsp. coarsely chopped fresh parsley
- 1 Tbsp. maple syrup, warmed slightly

1. Preheat oven to 425°. Toss squashes with oil and seasonings. Transfer to 2 foil-lined 15x10x1-in. baking pans. Roast the squash, stirring once, until soft and some pieces are caramelized, 30-35 minutes. Switch position of pans midway through roasting to ensure even doneness. If a darker color is desired, broil 3-4 in. from heat 2-4 minutes.

2. Cool slightly. To serve, add goat cheese to squash; gently toss. Sprinkle with parsley; drizzle with maple syrup.

Note: To save time, first cut squash into rings, then peel each ring.

1 cup: 251 cal., 8g fat (3g sat. fat), 21mg chol., 715mg sod., 43g carb. (10g sugars, 10g fiber), 7g pro.

DAD'S CREAMED PEAS & PEARL ONIONS

When I was growing up, it was a tradition to make creamed peas with pearl onions for every Thanksgiving and Christmas dinner. My dad would not be a happy camper if he didn't see this dish on the table. It was his favorite! I made it for my own family while our kids were growing up, and my daughter now makes it for her family.

—Nancy Heishman, Las Vegas, NV

Takes: 25 min. • **Makes:** 6 servings

- 5 cups frozen peas (about 20 oz.), thawed and drained
- 2 cups frozen pearl onions (about 9 oz.), thawed and drained
- 2 celery ribs, finely chopped
- ¾ cup chicken broth
- ½ tsp. salt
- ½ tsp. pepper
- ½ tsp. dried thyme
- ½ cup sour cream
- 10 bacon strips, cooked and crumbled
- ¾ cup salted cashews

In a large skillet, combine first 7 ingredients; bring to a boil. Reduce the heat to medium; cook, uncovered, until onions are tender and most of liquid is evaporated, 8-10 minutes, stirring occasionally. Remove from heat; stir in sour cream. Top with bacon and cashews.

¾ cup: 322 cal., 18g fat (6g sat. fat), 19mg chol., 783mg sod., 26g carb. (10g sugars, 7g fiber), 14g pro.

ROASTED HERBED SQUASH
WITH GOAT CHEESE

CARAMEL-PECAN MONKEY BREAD
PAGE 184

Odds & Ends

At *Taste of Home*, we believe it's the little things that put meals and menus over the top. Take everything from special-occasion buffets to after-school snacks to new heights with these easy ideas.

SPICY
ALMONDS

SPICY ALMONDS

We like to venture out into the Selkirk mountain range surrounding our family cabin. These nuts never tasted better than when we enjoyed them together at the peak at the end of an amazing hike. Almonds are extremely nutritious, and, when dressed up with a wonderful blend of spices, they go from ordinary to awesome!
—Gina Myers, Spokane, WA

Prep: 10 min. • **Bake:** 30 min. + cooling
Makes: 2½ cups

  1   **Tbsp. sugar**
1½ **tsp. kosher salt**
  1   **tsp. paprika**
  ½   **tsp. ground cinnamon**
  ½   **tsp. ground cumin**
  ½   **tsp. ground coriander**
  ¼   **tsp. cayenne pepper**
  1   **large egg white, room temperature**
2½ **cups unblanched almonds**

Preheat the oven to 325°. In a small bowl, combine the first 7 ingredients. In another small bowl, whisk egg white until foamy. Add almonds; toss to coat. Sprinkle with the spice mixture; toss to coat. Spread in a single layer in a greased 15x10x1-in. baking pan. Bake for 30 minutes, stirring every 10 minutes. Spread on waxed paper to cool completely. Store in an airtight container.
¼ cup: 230 cal., 20g fat (2g sat. fat), 0 chol., 293mg sod., 9g carb. (3g sugars, 4g fiber), 8g pro.

> I love the combo of flavors in these nuts, but sometimes I'll skip the cayenne, add a dash of curry powder or use seasoned salt in place of the kosher salt.
>
> **—MARK HAGEN, EXECUTIVE EDITOR**

LEMONADE ICED TEA

LEMONADE ICED TEA

I have always loved iced tea with lemon, and this great thirst-quencher just takes it one step further. Lemonade gives the beverage a nice color, too. I dress up each glass with a slice of lemon on the rim.
—Gail Buss, New Bern, NC

Prep: 15 min. + chilling
Makes: 12 servings (3 qt.)

  3   **qt. water**
  9   **tea bags**
  ¾   **to 1¼ cups sugar**
  1   **can (12 oz.) frozen lemonade concentrate, thawed**
        Lemon slices, optional

In a Dutch oven, bring water to a boil. Remove from the heat; add tea bags. Cover and steep for 5 minutes. Discard tea bags. Stir in sugar and lemonade concentrate. Cover and refrigerate until chilled. Serve over ice. If desired, garnish with lemon slices.
1 cup: 100 cal., 0 fat (0 sat. fat), 0 chol., 1mg sod., 26g carb. (25g sugars, 0 fiber), 0 pro.

BASIL CITRUS COCKTAIL

This irresistible cocktail is fruity, fantastic and low in calories. Muddling the basil really brings out the flavor and makes the drink seem extra special.
—*Taste of Home* Test Kitchen

Takes: 10 min. • **Makes:** 1 serving

  6   **fresh basil leaves**
1½ **to 2 cups ice cubes**
  2   **oz. white grapefruit juice**
  2   **oz. mandarin orange juice**
  ¾   **oz. gin**
  ½   **oz. Domaine de Canton ginger liqueur**

1. In a shaker, muddle the basil leaves.
2. Fill shaker three-fourths full with ice. Add the juices, gin and ginger liqueur; cover and shake until condensation forms on outside of shaker, 10-15 seconds. Strain into a chilled cocktail glass.
1 serving: 136 cal., 0 fat (0 sat. fat), 0 chol., 0 sod., 14g carb. (7g sugars, 0 fiber), 1g pro.

PUMPKIN PATCH PUNCH

Oranges are smartly disguised as tiny pumpkin garnishes in this citrus-ade.
—*Taste of Home* Test Kitchen

- -

Prep: 15 min. + chilling • **Makes:** 12 servings

4	medium lemons
4	medium limes
4	medium oranges
3	qt. water
1½	to 2 cups sugar
	Additional oranges and lime peel

1. Squeeze juice from the fruit; pour into a gallon container. Add water and sugar; mix well. Refrigerate until chilled.
2. To make pumpkins, cut the top and bottom thirds from desired amount of oranges. Using a paring knife, insert a small piece of lime peel for a pumpkin stem.
3. Just before serving, transfer punch to serving pitchers and add ice if desired. Top each serving with a pumpkin.

1 serving: 25 cal., 0 fat (0 sat. fat), 0 chol., 1mg sod., 7g carb. (3g sugars, 1g fiber), 1g pro.

STRAWBERRY FREEZER JAM

STRAWBERRY FREEZER JAM

A friend gave me this recipe when we lived in Germany. It comes together easily with a few items, and it's great on ice cream, too!
—Mary Jean Ellis, Indianapolis, IN

- -

Prep: 40 min. + freezing • **Makes:** 4½ pints

2	qt. fresh strawberries
5½	cups sugar
1	cup light corn syrup
¼	cup lemon juice
¾	cup water
1	pkg. (1¾ oz.) powdered fruit pectin

1. Wash and mash berries, measuring out enough mashed berries to make 4 cups; place in a large bowl. Stir in sugar, corn syrup and lemon juice. Let stand 10 minutes.
2. In a Dutch oven, combine the strawberry mixture and water. Stir in the pectin. Bring to a full rolling boil over high heat, stirring constantly. Boil 1 minute, stirring constantly. Remove from heat; skim off foam.
3. Carefully pour mixture into jars or freezer containers, leaving ½-in. headspace. Cover and let stand overnight or until set, but not longer than 24 hours. Refrigerate for up to 3 weeks or freeze up to 12 months.

2 Tbsp.: 79 cal., 0 fat (0 sat. fat), 0 chol., 3mg sod., 20g carb. (20g sugars, 0 fiber), 0 pro.

Ten years ago my best friend and I started a tradition of picking fresh strawberries at one of our local farms. I turn the sweet berries into this luscious jam that's perfect on toast and biscuits.

—AMY GLANDER, EDITOR

DROP DOUGHNUTS

Remember this recipe after your next big dinner because it's a great way to use up leftover mashed potatoes. No one guesses that potatoes are the secret ingredient! The light and fluffy doughnuts are great in the morning with coffee, served as an after-school snack or enjoyed as a late-night treat. They're just perfect to bring to a brunch. The recipe was created by my neighbor's mother-in-law, and I'm so glad they shared it with me.

—Marilyn Kleinfall, Elk Grove Village, IL

- -

Takes: 25 min. • **Makes:** 3½ dozen

- ½ cup mashed potatoes (made with milk and butter)
- ¼ cup sugar
- 1 large egg, lightly beaten
- ½ cup sour cream
- ½ tsp. vanilla extract
- 1½ cups all-purpose flour
- ½ tsp. baking soda
- ¼ tsp. baking powder
  Oil for deep-fat frying
  Additional sugar or confectioners' sugar, optional

1. In a large bowl, combine the potatoes, sugar, egg, sour cream and vanilla. Combine dry ingredients; stir in potato mixture.

2. Heat oil in an electric skillet or deep-fat fryer to 375°. Drop teaspoons of batter, a few at a time, into hot oil. Fry until golden brown on both sides. Drain on paper towels. If desired, roll in sugar while warm.

1 doughnut: 42 cal., 2g fat (1g sat. fat), 5mg chol., 29mg sod., 5g carb. (1g sugars, 0 fiber), 1g pro.

DROP
DOUGHNUTS

CARAMEL-PECAN
MONKEY BREAD

MARINA'S GOLDEN CORN FRITTERS

When it comes to these fritters, just one bite takes me back to when my kids were young. They're all grown up now, but the tradition lives on at get-togethers, when I sometimes triple the recipe. Serve the fritters with maple syrup or agave nectar.
—Marina Castle Kelley, Canyon Country, CA

Takes: 30 min. • **Makes:** 32 fritters

- 2½ cups all-purpose flour
- 3 tsp. baking powder
- 2 tsp. dried parsley flakes
- 1 tsp. salt
- 2 large eggs, room temperature
- ¾ cup 2% milk
- 2 Tbsp. butter, melted
- 2 tsp. grated onion
- 1 can (15¼ oz.) whole kernel corn, drained
  Oil for deep-fat frying

1. In a large bowl, whisk flour, baking powder, parsley and salt. In another bowl, whisk eggs, milk, melted butter and onion until blended. Add to the dry ingredients, stirring just until moistened. Fold in corn.
2. In an electric skillet or deep fryer, heat oil to 375°. Drop the batter by tablespoonfuls, several at a time, into hot oil. Fry 2-3 minutes on each side or until golden brown. Drain on paper towels.

2 fritters: 162 cal., 8g fat (2g sat. fat), 28mg chol., 327mg sod., 18g carb. (2g sugars, 1g fiber), 4g pro.

CARAMEL-PECAN MONKEY BREAD

Kids will get a kick out of pulling off gooey pieces of this delectable monkey bread. It's hard to resist the caramel-coated treat.
—*Taste of Home* Test Kitchen

Prep: 20 min. + chilling
Bake: 30 min. + cooling • **Makes:** 20 servings

- 1 pkg. (¼ oz.) active dry yeast
- ¼ cup warm water (110° to 115°)
- 1¼ cups warm 2% milk (110° to 115°)
- 2 large eggs, room temperature
- 5 Tbsp. plus ½ cup melted butter, divided
- 1¼ cups sugar, divided
- 1 tsp. salt
- 5 cups all-purpose flour
- 1 tsp. ground cinnamon

CARAMEL
- ⅔ cup packed brown sugar
- ¼ cup butter, cubed
- ¼ cup heavy whipping cream
- ¾ cup chopped pecans, divided

OPTIONAL GLAZE
- 4 oz. cream cheese, softened
- ¼ cup butter, softened
- 1½ cups confectioners' sugar
- 3 to 5 Tbsp. 2% milk

1. Dissolve yeast in warm water. Add milk, eggs and 5 Tbsp. melted butter; stir in ¼ cup sugar, salt and 3 cups flour. Beat on medium speed for 3 minutes. Stir in enough of the remaining flour to form a firm dough.
2. Turn onto a floured surface; knead until smooth and elastic, 6-8 minutes. Place in a greased bowl, turning once to grease the top. Refrigerate, covered, overnight.
3. Punch dough down; shape into 40 balls (about 1¼ in. diameter). Pour remaining melted butter in a shallow bowl. In another shallow bowl, combine cinnamon and the remaining sugar. Dip balls in butter, then roll in sugar mixture.
4. For caramel, bring brown sugar, butter and cream to a boil in a small saucepan over medium heat. Cook and stir 3 minutes. Pour half of the caramel into a greased 10-in. fluted tube pan; layer with half the pecans and half the dough balls; repeat. Cover and let rise until doubled, about 45 minutes.
5. Preheat oven to 350°. Bake until golden brown, 30-40 minutes. (Cover loosely with foil for last 10 minutes if top browns too quickly.) Cool 10 minutes before inverting onto a serving plate.
6. For optional glaze, beat the cream cheese and butter until blended; gradually beat in confectioners' sugar. Add enough milk to reach desired consistency. Drizzle glaze over warm bread.

2 pieces: 334 cal., 15g fat (8g sat. fat), 52mg chol., 207mg sod., 45g carb. (21g sugars, 1g fiber), 5g pro.

MARINA'S GOLDEN
CORN FRITTERS

TASTE OF HOME
TEST
KITCHEN
RECIPE OF THE YEAR
★★★★

PEAR CIDER

A wonderful alternative to traditional apple cider, our perfectly spiced, pear-flavored beverage will warm you from head to toe.
—*Taste of Home* Test Kitchen

- -

Prep: 5 min. • **Cook:** 3 hours
Makes: 20 servings (3¾ qt.)

- 12 cups unsweetened apple juice
- 4 cups pear nectar
- 8 cinnamon sticks (3 in.)
- 1 Tbsp. whole allspice
- 1 Tbsp. whole cloves

1. In a 6-qt. slow cooker, combine juice and nectar. Place cinnamon sticks, allspice and cloves on a double thickness of cheesecloth; bring up corners of cloth and tie with string to form a bag. Place in slow cooker.
2. Cover and cook on low until heated through, 3-4 hours. Discard spice bag. Serve warm cider in mugs.
¾ cup: 100 cal., 0 fat (0 sat. fat), 0 chol., 6mg sod., 25g carb. (24g sugars, 0 fiber), 0 pro.

HOMEMADE PEANUT BUTTER

We eat a lot of peanut butter, so I decided to make my own. I checked the price of peanut butter up here against the cost of making my own, and I quickly realized that mine was much cheaper—with the added value of knowing what goes into it! In addition, I think mine is a lot tastier.
—Marge Austin, North Pole, AK

- -

Takes: 15 min. • **Makes:** about 1 cup

- 2 cups unsalted dry roasted peanuts
- ½ tsp. salt
- 1 Tbsp. honey

Process peanuts and salt in a food processor until desired consistency, about 5 minutes, scraping down sides as needed. Add honey; process just until blended. Store in an airtight container in refrigerator.
1 Tbsp.: 111 cal., 9g fat (1g sat. fat), 0 chol., 75mg sod., 5g carb. (2g sugars, 2g fiber), 4g pro. **Diabetic exchanges:** 2 fat.

SWIFT STRAWBERRY SALAD

A simple blend of syrup, orange juice and caramel topping forms the light dressing for fresh berries and crunchy cashews in this sensational salad.
—*Taste of Home* Test Kitchen

- -

Takes: 10 min. • **Makes:** 6 servings

- 4 cups sliced fresh strawberries
- 2 Tbsp. caramel ice cream topping
- 2 Tbsp. maple syrup
- 1 Tbsp. orange juice
- ⅓ cup salted cashew halves

Place strawberries in a large bowl. Mix the caramel topping, syrup and orange juice; drizzle over strawberries. Top with cashews.
⅔ cup: 116 cal., 4g fat (1g sat. fat), 0 chol., 59mg sod., 20g carb. (14g sugars, 3g fiber), 2g pro.

SWIFT STRAWBERRY SALAD

SWIRLED PEPPERMINT
MARSHMALLOWS

APRICOT HABANERO JAM

This jam is excellent warmed and brushed over a baking pork roast. It has an appealing spicy-sweet taste.
—Megan Taylor, Greenfield, WI

Prep: 15 min. • **Process:** 10 min. + standing
Makes: 11 half-pints

- 3½ lbs. fresh apricots
- 6 Tbsp. bottled lemon juice
- 2 to 4 habanero peppers, seeded
- 1 pkg. (1¾ oz.) powdered fruit pectin
- 7 cups sugar

1. Pit and chop apricots; place in a Dutch oven or stockpot. Stir in lemon juice. Place habaneros in a blender; add a small amount of apricot mixture. Cover and process until smooth. Return to the pan. Stir in pectin. Bring to a full rolling boil over high heat, stirring constantly. Stir in sugar; return to a full rolling boil. Boil and stir 1 minute.
2. Remove from heat; skim off foam. Pour hot mixture into 11 hot sterilized jars, leaving ¼-in. headspace. Remove air bubbles and adjust headspace, if necessary, by adding hot mixture. Wipe rims. Center lids on jars; screw on bands until fingertip tight.
3. Place jars into canner with simmering water, ensuring that they are completely covered with water. Bring to a boil; process 10 minutes. Remove jars and cool. For best results, let processed jam stand at room temperature for 2 weeks to set up.
Notes: Wear disposable gloves when cutting hot peppers; the oils can burn skin. Avoid touching your face. The processing time listed is for altitudes of 1,000 feet or less. Add 1 minute to the processing time for each 1,000 feet of additional altitude.
2 Tbsp.: 130 cal., 0 fat (0 sat. fat), 0 chol., 1mg sod., 33g carb. (31g sugars, 1g fiber), 0 pro.

SWIRLED PEPPERMINT MARSHMALLOWS

The fluffy, airy texture of these handmade marshmallows will remind you of glistening snowflakes. They make great gifts from the kitchen, too, come the holidays.
—*Taste of Home* Test Kitchen

Prep: 55 min. + standing • **Makes:** 1½ lbs.

- 2 tsp. butter
- 3 envelopes unflavored gelatin
- 1 cup cold water, divided
- 2 cups sugar
- 1 cup light corn syrup
- ¼ tsp. salt
- ¾ tsp. peppermint extract
- 10 to 12 drops food coloring
- ¼ cup confectioners' sugar
- ¼ cup finely ground peppermint candies

1. Line a 13x9-in. pan with foil and grease the foil with butter; set aside.
2. In a large metal bowl, sprinkle gelatin over ½ cup water; set aside. In a large heavy saucepan, combine the sugar, corn syrup, salt and remaining water. Bring to a boil, stirring occasionally. Cook, without stirring, until a candy thermometer reads 240° (soft-ball stage).
3. Remove from heat and gradually add to gelatin. Beat on high until mixture is thick and the volume is doubled, about 15 minutes. Beat in extract. Spread into prepared pan. Drop food coloring over candy; cut through with a knife to swirl. Cover and let stand at room temperature for 6 hours or overnight.
4. Combine confectioners' sugar and peppermint candies. Using foil, lift the marshmallows out of pan. With a knife or pizza cutter coated with cooking spray, cut into 1-in. squares; toss in confectioners' sugar mixture. Store in an airtight container in a cool, dry place.
1 marshmallow: 24 cal., 0 fat (0 sat. fat), 0 chol., 8mg sod., 6g carb. (6g sugars, 0 fiber), 0 pro.

PUPPY CHOW

PUPPY CHOW

This snack mix is perfect for a late-night treat or a pick-me up any time of the day. I sometimes take a batch to work, and it's always eaten up quickly. It's a slightly different cereal snack because of the chocolate and peanut butter.
—Mary Obeilin, Selinsgrove, PA

Takes: 15 min. • **Makes:** about 6 cups

 1 cup (6 oz.) semisweet
    chocolate chips
 ¼ cup creamy peanut butter
 6 cups Corn or Rice Chex
 1 cup confectioners' sugar

1. In a large microwave-safe bowl, melt the chocolate chips on high for 30 seconds. Stir; microwave 30 seconds longer or until the chips are melted. Stir in the peanut butter. Gently stir in the cereal until well coated; set aside.
2. Place confectioners' sugar in a 2-gallon plastic storage bag. Add cereal mixture and shake until well coated. Store in an airtight container in the refrigerator.
½ cup: 194 cal., 7g fat (3g sat. fat), 0 chol., 170mg sod., 33g carb. (19g sugars, 1g fiber), 3g pro.

TEST KITCHEN TIP

No confectioners' sugar on hand? Make your own! Just combine 1 cup granulated sugar with 1 tsp. cornstarch. It's so easy!

FLAVORFUL STRAWBERRY-RHUBARB JAM

I consider this sweet flavorful jam summer in a jar! The fruity concoction calls for only a handful of ingredients, and it is simply scrumptious, if you ask me.
—Peggy Woodward, Senior Food Editor

Prep: 10 min. • **Process:** 5 min.
Makes: about 6 pints

 4 cups fresh strawberries, crushed
 2 cups chopped fresh rhubarb
 ¼ cup bottled lemon juice
 1 pkg. (1¾ oz.) powdered fruit pectin
 5½ cups sugar

1. In a Dutch oven, combine strawberries, rhubarb and lemon juice; stir in pectin. Bring to a full rolling boil, stirring constantly. Stir in sugar; return to a full rolling boil. Boil and stir 1 minute.
2. Remove from heat; skim off foam. Ladle the hot mixture into 6 hot sterilized pint jars, leaving ¼-in. headspace. Remove air bubbles and adjust headspace, if necessary, by adding hot mixture. Wipe rims. Center lids on jars; screw on bands until fingertip tight.
3. Place jars into canner with simmering water, ensuring that they are completely covered with water. Bring to a boil; process for 5 minutes. Remove jars and cool.
Note: The processing time listed is for altitudes of 1,000 feet or less. Add 1 minute to the processing time for each 1,000 feet of additional altitude.
2 Tbsp.: 99 cal., 0 fat (0 sat. fat), 0 chol., 1mg sod., 25g carb. (24g sugars, 0 fiber), 0 pro.

FLAVORFUL STRAWBERRY-RHUBARB JAM

FRIED ICE CREAM
DESSERT BARS, PAGE 196

Cookies, Brownies & Bars

At the *Taste of Home* offices, a week rarely goes by without someone bringing in a plate of delicious yumminess—we're almost as dedicated to sharing our favorite recipes with our co-workers as with our readers! Topping the list are the bite-sized indulgences you'll find in this chapter!

FUDGY BROWNIES
WITH PEANUT BUTTER
PUDDING FROSTING

FUDGY BROWNIES WITH PEANUT BUTTER PUDDING FROSTING

How to dress up your favorite box brownies? Top them with a peanut butter pudding layer and finish with fudge frosting. These are perfect for a potluck, bake sale or yummy after-dinner treat.
—Amy Crook, Syracuse, UT

- -

Prep: 20 min. • **Bake:** 25 min. + chilling
Makes: 2½ dozen

- 1 pkg. fudge brownie mix (13x9-in. pan size)
- 1½ cups confectioners' sugar
- ½ cup butter, softened
- 2 to 3 Tbsp. peanut butter
- 2 Tbsp. cold 2% milk
- 4½ tsp. instant vanilla pudding mix
- 1 can (16 oz.) chocolate fudge frosting

1. Prepare and bake brownies according to the package directions. Cool on a wire rack.
2. Meanwhile, in a small bowl, beat the confectioners' sugar, butter, peanut butter, milk and pudding mix until smooth. Spread over brownies. Refrigerate for 30 minutes or until firm. Frost with chocolate fudge frosting just before cutting.
1 brownie: 236 cal., 12g fat (4g sat. fat), 23mg chol., 145mg sod., 31g carb. (23g sugars, 1g fiber), 2g pro.

TEST KITCHEN TIP

Unless otherwise specified, *Taste of Home* recipes are tested with lightly salted butter. Unsalted, or sweet, butter is sometimes used to achieve an especially buttery flavor, such as in shortbread cookies or buttercream frosting. In this kind of recipe, added salt would detract from the buttery taste desired.

PUMPKIN SPICE COOKIES

PUMPKIN SPICE COOKIES

These big soft spice cookies created by our staff have a sweet frosting that makes them an extra-special treat. Enjoy!
—*Taste of Home* Test Kitchen

- -

Prep: 15 min. • **Bake:** 20 min./batch + cooling
Makes: about 2½ dozen

- 1 pkg. yellow cake mix (regular size)
- ½ cup quick-cooking oats
- 2 to 2½ tsp. pumpkin pie spice
- 1 can (15 oz.) pumpkin
- 1 large egg, room temperature
- 2 Tbsp. canola oil

FROSTING
- 3 cups confectioners' sugar
- 1 tsp. grated orange zest
- 3 to 4 Tbsp. orange juice

1. Preheat oven to 350°. Combine cake mix, oats and pie spice. In another bowl, beat pumpkin, egg and oil; stir into dry ingredients just until moistened.
2. Drop by 2 tablespoonfuls onto baking sheets coated with cooking spray; flatten with the back of a spoon. Bake until edges are golden brown, 18-20 minutes. Remove to wire racks to cool.
3. For frosting, combine confectioners' sugar, orange zest and enough orange juice to achieve desired consistency. Spread over cooled cookies.
1 cookie: 118 cal., 2g fat (0 sat. fat), 6mg chol., 109mg sod., 26g carb. (18g sugars, 1g fiber), 1g pro.

SOFT PEANUT BUTTER COOKIES

This is the recipe I turn to when I want to offer friends and family the best soft and chewy peanut butter cookies. You can use either creamy or crunchy peanut butter with delicious results. My family can't get enough!
—Emma Lee Granger, La Pine, OR

- -

Prep: 15 min. • **Bake:** 15 min./batch
Makes: about 5 dozen

- 1 cup butter-flavored shortening
- 1 cup creamy peanut butter
- ¾ cup sugar
- ¾ cup packed brown sugar
- 2 large eggs, room temperature
- 1 tsp. vanilla extract
- ½ tsp. water
- 2¼ cups all-purpose flour
- 1 tsp. baking soda
- 1 tsp. salt

1. Preheat oven to 350°. In a large bowl, cream the shortening, peanut butter and sugars until light and fluffy, about 4 minutes. Add 1 egg at a time, beating well after each addition. Beat in vanilla and water. Combine the flour, baking soda and salt; gradually add to the creamed mixture and mix well.

2. Drop by tablespoonfuls 2 in. apart onto ungreased baking sheets. Flatten with a fork. Bake until golden brown, 12-15 minutes. Remove to wire racks to cool.

1 cookie: 105 cal., 6g fat (1g sat. fat), 7mg chol., 91mg sod., 11g carb. (6g sugars, 0 fiber), 2g pro.

STRAWBERRY RHUBARB
CHEESECAKE BARS

STRAWBERRY RHUBARB CHEESECAKE BARS

These bars layer buttery pecan shortbread crust with a rich and creamy filling and sweet-tart jam. If you want to serve larger squares, just cut them into nine bars.
—Amanda Scarlati, Sandy, UT

- -

Prep: 30 min. + chilling
Bake: 15 min. + cooling • **Makes:** 16 servings

- 1 cup all-purpose flour
- ⅓ cup packed brown sugar
  Dash kosher salt
- ½ cup cold butter, cubed
- ⅓ cup finely chopped pecans

FILLING
- 1 pkg. (8 oz.) cream cheese, softened
- ¼ cup sugar
- 2 Tbsp. 2% milk
- 1 Tbsp. lemon juice
- ½ tsp. vanilla extract
  Dash kosher salt
- 1 large egg, room temperature, lightly beaten

JAM
- ½ cup sugar
- 2 Tbsp. cornstarch
- 1⅓ cups chopped fresh strawberries
- 1⅓ cups sliced fresh or frozen rhubarb
- 1 Tbsp. lemon juice

1. Preheat oven to 350°. Line an 8-in. square baking pan with parchment, letting the ends extend up the sides of the pan. In a small bowl, mix flour, brown sugar and salt; cut in butter until crumbly. Stir in pecans.

2. Press into the bottom of prepared pan. Bake until edges just begin to brown, 12-15 minutes. Cool completely on a wire rack.

3. To make the filling, in a large bowl, beat cream cheese and sugar until smooth. Beat in milk, lemon juice, vanilla and salt. Add egg; beat on low speed just until blended. Pour over the crust. Bake until the filling is set, 15-20 minutes. Cool on a wire rack for 1 hour.

4. For the jam, in a small saucepan, mix sugar and cornstarch. Add strawberries, rhubarb and lemon juice. Bring to a boil. Reduce heat; simmer, uncovered, until mixture begins to thicken, 6-8 minutes. Cool completely. Spread over filling. Refrigerate until set, 8 hours or overnight.

5. Using parchment, carefully remove the cheesecake from the baking pan. Cut into bars to serve.

Note: If using frozen rhubarb, measure rhubarb while still frozen, then thaw completely. Drain in a colander, but do not press liquid out.

1 bar: 215 cal., 13g fat (7g sat. fat), 41mg chol., 113mg sod., 24g carb. (15g sugars, 1g fiber), 3g pro.

ROOT BEER COOKIES

When it's too difficult to take along root beer floats on a picnic, take these cookies instead! The flavor is even better the next day—but the hard part is convincing my family to wait that long before sampling!
—Violette Bawden, West Valley City, UT

- -

Prep: 20 min. • **Bake:** 10 min./batch + cooling
Makes: 6 dozen

- 1   cup butter, softened
- 2   cups packed brown sugar
- 2   large eggs, room temperature
- 1   cup buttermilk
- ¾   tsp. root beer concentrate or extract
- 4   cups all-purpose flour
- 1   tsp. baking soda
- 1   tsp. salt
- 1½ cups chopped pecans

FROSTING
- 3½ cups confectioners' sugar
- ¾   cup butter, softened
- 3   Tbsp. water
- 1¼ tsp. root beer concentrate or extract

1. Preheat oven to 375°. In a bowl, cream butter and brown sugar. Add 1 egg at a time, beating well after each addition. Beat in buttermilk and root beer concentrate. Combine the flour, baking soda and salt; gradually add to the creamed mixture. Stir in pecans.
2. Drop by tablespoonfuls 3 in. apart onto ungreased baking sheets. Bake for 10-12 minutes or until lightly browned. Remove to wire racks to cool. In a small bowl, combine the frosting ingredients; beat until smooth. Frost cooled cookies.
Note: This recipe was tested with McCormick root beer concentrate.
1 cookie: 130 cal., 6g fat (3g sat. fat), 17mg chol., 96mg sod., 18g carb. (12g sugars, 0 fiber), 1g pro.

CHOCOLATE MAPLE BARS

We run a maple syrup operation, and I'm always looking for new ways to incorporate maple syrup into my cooking and baking. These bars are delicious!
—Cathy Schumacher, Alto, MI

- -

Prep: 20 min. • **Bake:** 25 min. + cooling
Makes: 3 dozen

- ½   cup shortening
- ¾   cup maple syrup
- ½   cup sugar
- 3   large eggs, room temperature
- 3   Tbsp. 2% milk
- 1   tsp. vanilla extract
- 1¼ cups all-purpose flour
- ¼   tsp. baking powder
- ¼   tsp. salt
- 1½ oz. unsweetened chocolate, melted
- ½   cup chopped pecans
- ½   cup sweetened shredded coconut

FROSTING:
- ¼   cup butter, softened
- 1   cup confectioners' sugar
- ½   cup baking cocoa
- ½   cup maple syrup
- 1   cup miniature marshmallows

1. In a large bowl, cream the shortening, maple syrup and sugar until light and fluffy, 5-7 minutes. Beat in the eggs, milk and vanilla. Combine flour, baking powder and salt; add to creamed mixture and mix well. Remove half of the batter to another bowl.
2. Combine melted chocolate and pecans; stir into 1 bowl of batter. Spread into a greased 13x9-in. baking pan. Add coconut to remaining batter. Spread carefully over chocolate batter.
3. Bake at 350° for 25 minutes or until a toothpick inserted in the center comes out clean. Cool completely on a wire rack.
4. For frosting, in a small bowl, beat the butter until smooth. Gradually add the confectioners' sugar and cocoa. Gradually add syrup, beating until smooth. Fold in marshmallows. Frost bars.
1 bar: 143 cal., 7g fat (3g sat. fat), 21mg chol., 43mg sod., 20g carb. (14g sugars, 1g fiber), 2g pro.

ROOT BEER
COOKIES

FRIED ICE CREAM DESSERT BARS

Fried ice cream is such a delicious treat, but it can be a hassle to make individual servings. This recipe gives you the same fabulous flavor in an easy and convenient bar form.

—Andrea Price, Grafton, WI

Prep: 25 min. + freezing
Cook: 5 min. + cooling • **Makes:** 16 servings

- ½ cup butter, cubed
- 2 cups crushed cornflakes
- 1½ tsp. ground cinnamon
- 3 Tbsp. sugar
- 1¾ cups heavy whipping cream
- ¼ cup evaporated milk
- ⅛ tsp. salt
- 1 can (14 oz.) sweetened condensed milk
- 2 tsp. vanilla extract
  Optional: Honey, whipped cream and maraschino cherries

1. Grease a 9-in. square baking pan; set aside. In a large skillet, melt butter over medium heat. Add cornflakes and cinnamon; cook and stir until golden brown, about 5 minutes. Remove from heat; stir in sugar. Cool completely.

2. In a large bowl, beat cream, evaporated milk and salt until it begins to thicken. Gradually beat in condensed milk and vanilla until thickened.

3. Sprinkle half the cornflake mixture onto the bottom of the prepared pan. Pour filling over the crust; sprinkle with the remaining cornflake mixture. Cover pan and freeze overnight. Cut into bars. If desired, serve with honey, whipped cream and cherries.

1 bar: 276 cal., 18g fat (11g sat. fat), 55mg chol., 187mg sod., 27g carb. (18g sugars, 0 fiber), 4g pro.

HAZELNUT MACARONS

You don't have to be an expert in French cooking to whip up these sandwich cookies. The crisp, chewy macarons take attention to detail, but they're not hard to make—and they're simply a delight, both for personal snacking and giving as gifts.
—*Taste of Home* Test Kitchen

Prep: 50 min. • **Bake:** 10 min./batch + cooling
Makes: about 5 dozen

- 6 large egg whites
- 1½ cups hazelnuts, toasted
- 2½ cups confectioners' sugar
  Dash salt
- ½ cup superfine sugar
  COFFEE BUTTERCREAM
- 1 cup sugar
- 6 Tbsp. water
- 6 large egg yolks
- 4 tsp. instant espresso powder
- 1 tsp. vanilla extract
- 1½ cups butter, softened
- 6 Tbsp. confectioners' sugar

1. Place egg whites in a small bowl; let stand at room temperature for 30 minutes.
2. Preheat oven to 350°. Place hazelnuts and confectioners' sugar in a food processor; pulse until the nuts are finely ground.
3. Add salt to egg whites; beat on medium speed until soft peaks form. Gradually add superfine sugar, 1 Tbsp. at a time, beating on high until stiff peaks form. Fold in the hazelnut mixture.

4. Using a pastry bag, pipe 1-in.-diameter cookies 2 in. apart onto parchment-lined baking sheets. Bake until lightly browned and firm to the touch, 9-12 minutes. Transfer cookies on the parchment to wire racks; cool completely.
5. For the buttercream, in a heavy saucepan, combine sugar and water. Bring to a boil; cook over medium-high heat until the sugar is dissolved. Remove from heat. In a small bowl, whisk a small amount of the hot syrup into the egg yolks; return all to pan, whisking constantly. Cook until thickened, 2-3 minutes, stirring constantly; remove from heat. Stir in espresso powder and vanilla; cool completely.
6. In a stand mixer with whisk attachment, beat butter until creamy. Gradually beat in cooled syrup. Beat in the confectioners' sugar until fluffy. Refrigerate until the mixture firms to a spreading consistency, about 10 minutes.
7. Spread about 1½ tsp buttercream onto the bottom of each of half the cookies; top with the remaining cookies. Store in airtight containers in the refrigerator.

Note: To toast whole hazelnuts, bake in a shallow pan in a 350° oven until fragrant and lightly browned, 7-10 minutes, stirring occasionally. Wrap hazelnuts in a tea towel; rub with towel to loosen skins.

1 sandwich cookie: 117 cal., 8g fat (3g sat. fat), 31mg chol., 67mg sod., 12g carb. (11g sugars, 0 fiber), 1g pro.

FRIED ICE CREAM
DESSERT BARS

PINEAPPLE COCONUT TASSIES

PINEAPPLE COCONUT TASSIES

While these cookies may sound and look fancy, they're rather easy to make. Their simplicity makes them an ideal choice for baking with children. My granddaughter enjoys helping me measure the ingredients. Children also can help shape the dough into balls, then you can finish them together.
—Connie Shuff, York, PA

Prep: 40 min. • **Bake:** 20 min./batch + cooling
Makes: 40 cookies

- 1 cup unsalted butter, softened
- ½ cup confectioners' sugar
- 1 tsp. vanilla extract
- 2 cups cake flour
- 2 Tbsp. cornstarch
- ½ tsp. salt

FILLING
- 1½ cups sweetened shredded coconut
- 1 cup pineapple ice cream topping
- ½ cup sugar
- ¼ cup chopped macadamia nuts
- 1 large egg, room temperature
- 2 tsp. cornstarch

ICING
- ½ cup confectioners' sugar
- 1 Tbsp. 2% milk
- ½ tsp. coconut extract

1. Preheat oven to 350°. Cream butter and confectioners' sugar until light and fluffy. Beat in vanilla. In another bowl, whisk flour, cornstarch and salt; gradually beat into the creamed mixture. Shape dough into 1-in. balls; press evenly onto bottom and up sides of 40 greased and floured mini muffin cups.
2. In a small bowl, mix coconut, ice cream topping, sugar, macadamia nuts, egg and cornstarch. Place 1 Tbsp. in each cup. Bake until edges are golden and filling is puffed, 20-25 minutes. Cool in pans 5-10 minutes. Carefully remove to wire racks to cool.
3. In a small bowl, combine icing ingredients. Drizzle over cookies; let dry completely.

1 cookie: 136 cal., 7g fat (4g sat. fat), 17mg chol., 48mg sod., 19g carb. (9g sugars, 0 fiber), 1g pro.

PEANUT BUTTER BLONDIE BARS

Here's an easy after-school special moms and dads will love. If you don't want the kids to catch you snacking, be sure to wash down the evidence with a glass of milk!
—*Taste of Home* Test Kitchen

Prep: 10 min. • **Bake:** 25 min. + cooling
Makes: 16 servings

- 2 large eggs, room temperature
- ¾ cup packed brown sugar
- ½ cup creamy peanut butter
- ¼ cup butter, melted and cooled
- 3 Tbsp. 2% milk
- 1 cup all-purpose flour
- 1 tsp. baking powder
- ⅛ tsp. salt
- 4 peanut butter cups, chopped

1. Preheat oven to 350°. Grease a 9-in. square baking pan; set aside. In a large bowl, beat eggs and brown sugar for 3 minutes. Add the peanut butter, butter and milk; mix well. Combine the flour, baking powder and salt; gradually add to sugar mixture, beating just until blended. Stir in the peanut butter cups.

2. Spread into the prepared pan. Bake for 25-30 minutes or until a toothpick inserted in the center comes out clean. Cool on a wire rack. Cut into bars.

1 bar: 173 cal., 9g fat (3g sat. fat), 34mg chol., 129mg sod., 20g carb. (13g sugars, 1g fiber), 4g pro.

HOLLY BERRY COOKIES

What would Christmas be without tins overflowing with cookies? These festive filled cookies are the all-time favorites of my family. Back when our children were small, we began baking them the day after Halloween and put them away in the freezer.
—Audrey Thibodeau, Gilbert, AZ

Prep: 30 min. + chilling
Bake: 10 min. + cooling • **Makes:** 2 dozen

- 2 cups all-purpose flour
- 1 cup sugar
- 1 tsp. ground cinnamon
- ¾ tsp. baking powder
- ¼ tsp. salt
- ½ cup cold butter, cubed
- 1 large egg, room temperature
- ¼ cup 2% milk
- ⅔ cup seedless raspberry jam
GLAZE
- 2 cups confectioners' sugar
- 2 Tbsp. 2% milk
- ½ tsp. vanilla extract
  Red Hots
  Green food coloring

1. In a large bowl, combine the first 5 ingredients. Cut in butter until the mixture resembles coarse crumbs. In a small bowl, beat egg and milk. Add to the crumb mixture just until moistened. Cover and refrigerate for 1 hour or until dough is easy to handle.

2. Preheat oven to 375°. On a lightly floured surface, roll out dough to ⅛-in. thickness. Cut with a 2-in. round cookie cutter. Place on ungreased baking sheets. Bake until the edges are lightly browned, 8-10 minutes. Cool on wire racks. Spread raspberry jam on the bottoms of half the cookies; top with another cookie.

3. In a small bowl, combine the sugar, milk and vanilla until smooth; spread over the cookies. Decorate with Red Hots before glaze is set. Let dry. Using a small new paintbrush and green food coloring, paint holly leaves on the cookies.

1 cookie: 171 cal., 4g fat (3g sat. fat), 20mg chol., 81mg sod., 32g carb. (23g sugars, 0 fiber), 2g pro.

HOLLY BERRY
COOKIES

EYES-WIDE-OPEN ESPRESSO COOKIES

The chocolate-covered espresso beans that adorn these cookies advertise exactly what's inside—the classic combination of coffee and chocolate in a delicious, invigorating treat!
—*Taste of Home* Test Kitchen

Prep: 25 min. • **Bake:** 10 min./batch
Makes: 45 cookies

- ½ cup butter, softened
- ½ cup sugar
- ¼ cup packed brown sugar
- 1 large egg, room temperature
- 1¼ cups all-purpose flour
- 6 Tbsp. baking cocoa
- 2 tsp. finely ground espresso beans
- ½ tsp. baking soda
- ¼ tsp. salt
- 1 cup (6 oz.) semisweet chocolate chips
- 45 chocolate-covered coffee beans

1. Preheat oven to 350°. In a large bowl, cream the butter and sugars until light and fluffy. Beat in egg. Combine the flour, cocoa, espresso beans, baking soda and salt; gradually add to creamed mixture and mix well. Stir in chocolate chips.

2. Drop by rounded teaspoonfuls 2 in. apart onto parchment-lined baking sheets. Bake for 8-10 minutes or until the surface cracks. Immediately press a coffee bean into the center of each cookie. Cool for 2 minutes before removing from pans to wire racks. Store in an airtight container.

1 cookie: 71 cal., 4g fat (2g sat. fat), 10mg chol., 44mg sod., 9g carb. (6g sugars, 0 fiber), 1g pro.

LEMON BLUEBERRY WHOOPIE PIES

When I take these soft, cakey cookies studded with juicy blueberries and filled with cream cheese frosting to potlucks, they're always the first thing gone! Be sure to continually scrape the bowl with a spatula while making the batter and frosting.
—Kathy Martino, Pittsburgh, PA

Prep: 30 min. • **Bake:** 10 min./batch + cooling
Makes: 1 dozen

- ½ cup butter, softened
- ½ cup sugar
- 1 large egg, room temperature
- 1 tsp. vanilla extract
- 1¼ cups plus 1 Tbsp. all-purpose flour, divided
- ½ tsp. baking powder
- ¼ tsp. baking soda
- ¼ tsp. salt
- ¼ cup buttermilk
- 1 cup fresh or frozen blueberries
- 2 tsp. grated lemon zest

FILLING

- ¼ cup butter, softened
- ¼ cup cream cheese, softened
- 1 Tbsp. honey
- 1 tsp. grated lemon zest
- ½ tsp. vanilla extract
- 1½ cups confectioners' sugar

1. Preheat oven to 350°. Line baking sheets with silicone baking mats or parchment.

2. In a large bowl, cream butter and sugar until light and fluffy. Beat in egg and vanilla. In another bowl, whisk 1¼ cups flour, baking powder, baking soda and salt; add to creamed mixture alternately with buttermilk, beating well after each addition. In another bowl, toss blueberries and lemon zest with remaining flour; gently fold into dough.

3. Drop dough by tablespoonfuls 2 in. apart onto prepared baking sheets. Bake until the edges just begin to brown, 10-12 minutes. Cool on pans for 2 minutes, then remove to wire racks to cool completely.

4. For filling, in a large bowl, beat butter and cream cheese until blended. Beat in honey, lemon zest and vanilla. Gradually beat in confectioners' sugar until smooth. Spread on bottoms of half of the cookies; cover with the remaining cookies. Refrigerate in an airtight container.

Freeze option: Freeze baked and filled whoopie pies in freezer containers (do not stack). To use, thaw before serving.

Note: If using frozen blueberries, use without thawing to avoid discoloring the batter.

1 whoopie pie: 281 cal., 14g fat (8g sat. fat), 51mg chol., 218mg sod., 38g carb. (26g sugars, 1g fiber), 3g pro.

LEMON BLUEBERRY WHOOPIE PIES

TASTE OF HOME
TEST KITCHEN
RECIPE OF THE YEAR
★★★★★

PEANUT BUTTER CUP COOKIES

With the winning combination of chocolate and peanut butter, it's no surprise these are my family's favorite cookies. Because they are so easy to prepare, I'm able to make them at a moment's notice.
—Faith Jensen, Meridian, ID

Prep: 20 min. • **Bake:** 10 min./batch
Makes: 7½ dozen

- 1 cup butter, softened
- ⅔ cup peanut butter
- 1 cup sugar
- 1 cup packed brown sugar
- 2 large eggs, room temperature
- 2 tsp. vanilla extract
- 2¼ cups all-purpose flour
- 1 tsp. baking soda
- ½ tsp. salt
- 2 cups (12 oz.) semisweet chocolate chips
- 2 cups chopped peanut butter cups (about six 1.6-oz. pkg.)

1. Preheat oven to 350°. In a large bowl, cream the butter, peanut butter and sugars until light and fluffy. Beat in eggs and vanilla. Combine the flour, baking soda and salt; gradually add to the creamed mixture and mix well. Stir in chocolate chips and peanut butter cups.

2. Drop by rounded tablespoonfuls 2 in. apart onto ungreased baking sheets. Bake for 10-12 minutes or until the edges are lightly browned. Cool for 2 minutes before removing to wire racks.

Note: Reduced-fat peanut butter is not recommended for this recipe.

1 cookie: 94 cal., 5g fat (3g sat. fat), 10mg chol., 66mg sod., 11g carb. (8g sugars, 1g fiber), 1g pro.

JOE FROGGERS

JOE FROGGERS

Large, soft and chewy, these cookies are made to munch. This classic recipe has a warm blend of spices that seems stronger the second day. Your family will definitely ask you to make them again!
—*Taste of Home* Test Kitchen

Prep: 15 min. + chilling • **Bake:** 15 min./batch
Makes: 1½ dozen

- ½ cup shortening
- 1 cup packed brown sugar
- 1 cup molasses
- ⅓ cup hot water
- 2 Tbsp. rum or 1 tsp. rum extract
- 3½ cups all-purpose flour
- 1½ tsp. salt
- 1½ tsp. ground ginger
- 1 tsp. baking soda
- ½ tsp. ground cloves
- ½ tsp. ground nutmeg
- ¼ tsp. ground allspice
  Sugar

1. In a large bowl, cream shortening and brown sugar until light and fluffy. In a small bowl, whisk molasses, hot water and rum. In another bowl, whisk the flour, salt, ginger, baking soda, cloves, nutmeg and allspice; add to the creamed mixture alternately with the molasses mixture, beating after each addition. Refrigerate, covered, for 4 hours or until easy to handle.

2. Preheat oven to 375°. Shape dough into 1½-in. balls and place 3 in. apart on greased baking sheets. Flatten to ½-in. thickness with bottom of a glass dipped in sugar.

3. Bake until lightly browned, 12-14 minutes. Cool on pans 2 minutes. Remove cookies to wire racks to cool completely. Store in airtight containers.

1 cookie: 238 cal., 6g fat (1g sat. fat), 0 chol., 277mg sod., 44g carb. (25g sugars, 1g fiber), 3g pro.

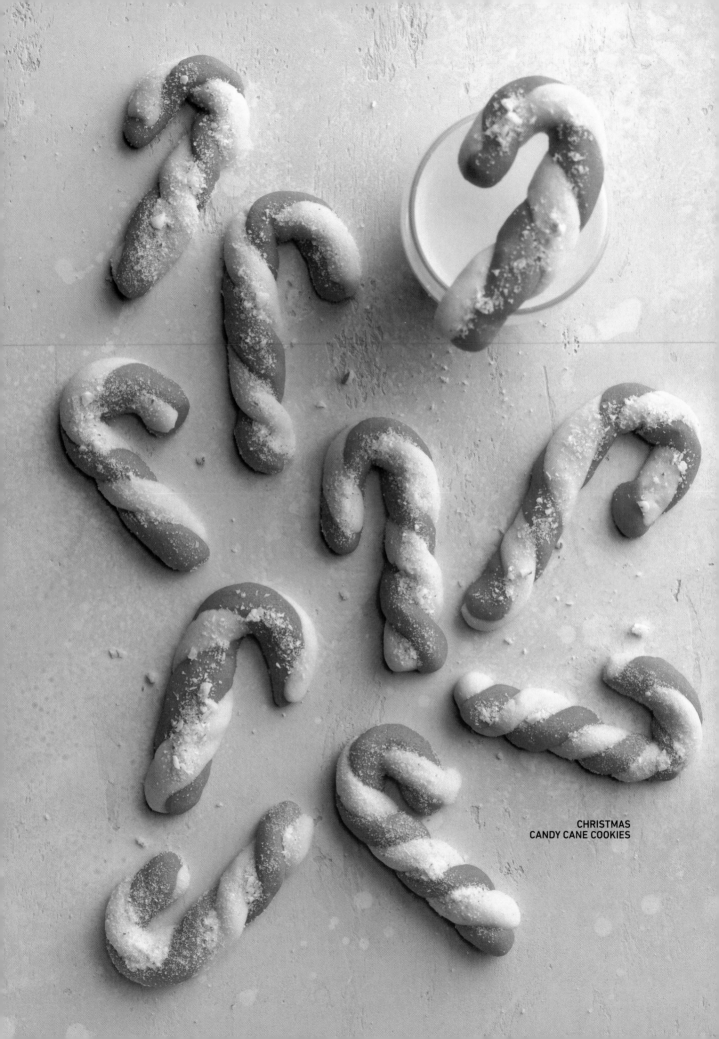

CHRISTMAS
CANDY CANE COOKIES

CHRISTMAS CANDY CANE COOKIES

When I was growing up, we made this cookie every Christmas. Now my family requests this cookie before any others at Christmas.
—Pat Schmeling, Germantown, WI

- -

Prep: 30 min. + chilling • **Bake:** 10 min./batch
Makes: 4 dozen

- ½ cup shortening
- ½ cup butter, softened
- 1 cup confectioners' sugar
- 1 large egg, room temperature
- 1½ tsp. almond extract
- 1 tsp. vanilla extract
- 2½ cups all-purpose flour
- ½ tsp. salt
- ½ tsp. red food coloring
- ½ cup peppermint candy, crushed
- ½ cup sugar

1. Cream the shortening, butter and confectioners' sugar until light and fluffy. Beat in egg and extracts. Combine flour and salt; gradually add to the creamed mixture. Divide dough in half; mix the food coloring into 1 portion. Cover and refrigerate both doughs for 2 hours or until easy to handle.
2. Preheat oven to 375°. Shape 1 tsp. plain dough into a 4-in. rope. Shape 1 tsp. red dough into a 4-in. rope. Place ropes side by side; press together lightly and twist. Place on ungreased baking sheet; curve the top of cookie down to form handle of cane. Repeat with remaining plain and red dough, placing 2 in. apart on baking sheets.
3. Bake 8-9 minutes or until set. Combine crushed candy and sugar; sprinkle warm cookies with candy mixture, then remove to wire racks to cool completely.
1 cookie: 86 cal., 4g fat (2g sat. fat), 9mg chol., 48mg sod., 11g carb. (6g sugars, 0 fiber), 1g pro.

TEST KITCHEN TIP
To make smaller cookies, use just ½ tsp. each of white and red dough to make the candy canes; you'll get a yield of about 8 dozen cookies.

TASTE OF HOME
TEST KITCHEN
RECIPE OF THE YEAR
★★★★★

ULTIMATE FUDGY BROWNIES

ULTIMATE FUDGY BROWNIES

Coffee granules enhance the chocolate flavor in these amazingly fudgy brownies. Add chocolate chips to the batter and you've got a seriously irresistible treat.
—Sarah Farmer, Executive Culinary Director

- -

Prep: 20 min. • **Bake:** 40 min. + cooling
Makes: 16 servings

- 1 cup sugar
- ½ cup packed brown sugar
- ⅔ cup butter, cubed
- ¼ cup water
- 2 tsp. instant coffee granules, optional
- 2¾ cups bittersweet chocolate chips, divided
- 4 large eggs, room temperature
- 2 tsp. vanilla extract
- 1½ cups all-purpose flour
- ½ tsp. baking soda
- ½ tsp. salt

1. Preheat oven to 325°. Line a 9-in. square baking pan with parchment, letting ends extend up the sides of the pan. In a large heavy saucepan, combine the sugars, butter, water and, if desired, coffee granules; bring to a boil, stirring constantly. Remove from heat; add 1¾ cups chocolate chips and stir until melted. Cool slightly.
2. In a large bowl, whisk eggs until foamy, about 3 minutes. Add vanilla; gradually whisk in chocolate mixture. In another bowl, whisk flour, baking soda and salt; stir into chocolate mixture. Fold in remaining chocolate chips.
3. Pour into prepared pan. Bake on a lower oven rack 40-50 minutes or until a toothpick inserted in center comes out with moist crumbs (do not overbake). Cool completely in pan on a wire rack.
4. Lifting with parchment, remove brownies from pan. Cut into squares.
1 brownie: 344 cal., 18g fat (10g sat. fat), 67mg chol., 197mg sod., 47g carb. (35g sugars, 2g fiber), 4g pro.

CHEWY CHOCOLATE-CHERRY BARS

Colorful dried cherries and pistachios star in this take on seven-layer bars. To switch it up even more, try cinnamon or chocolate graham cracker crumbs instead of plain and substitute pecans or walnuts for the pistachios.
—*Taste of Home* Test Kitchen

Prep: 10 min. • **Bake:** 25 min. + cooling
Makes: 3 dozen

- 1½ cups graham cracker crumbs
- ½ cup butter, melted
- 1 can (14 oz.) sweetened condensed milk
- 1½ cups dried cherries
- 1½ cups semisweet chocolate chips
- 1 cup sweetened shredded coconut
- 1 cup pistachios, chopped

1. Preheat oven to 350°. In a small bowl, mix cracker crumbs and butter. Press into a greased 13x9-in. baking pan. In a large bowl, mix the remaining ingredients until blended; carefully spread over the crust.
2. Bake for 25-28 minutes or until the edges are golden brown. Cool in pan on a wire rack. Cut into bars.

1 bar: 164 cal., 9g fat (5g sat. fat), 11mg chol., 77mg sod., 21g carb. (17g sugars, 1g fiber), 2g pro.

SUPER CHUNKY COOKIES

SUPER CHUNKY COOKIES

Chocolate lovers will go crazy over these cookies that feature loads of chocolate! When friends ask me to make "those cookies," I always know exactly which recipe they mean.
—Rebecca Jendry, Spring Branch, TX

Prep: 15 min. • **Bake:** 10 min./batch
Makes: 6½ dozen

- ½ cup butter-flavored shortening
- ½ cup butter, softened
- 1 cup packed brown sugar
- ¾ cup sugar
- 2 large eggs, room temperature
- 2 tsp. vanilla extract
- 2½ cups all-purpose flour
- 1 tsp. baking soda
- ⅛ tsp. salt
- 1 cup miniature semisweet chocolate chips
- 1 cup milk chocolate chips
- 1 cup vanilla or white chips
- 4 oz. bittersweet chocolate, coarsely chopped
- ¾ cup English toffee bits or almond brickle chips
- ½ cup chopped pecans

1. Preheat oven to 350°. In a large bowl, cream the shortening, butter and sugars until light and fluffy. Add 1 egg at a time, beating well after each addition. Beat in vanilla. Combine flour, baking soda and salt; gradually add to the creamed mixture and mix well. Stir in the remaining ingredients.
2. Drop by tablespoonfuls 3 in. apart onto ungreased baking sheets. Bake until lightly browned, 10-12 minutes. Cool cookies 2-3 minutes before removing to wire racks to cool completely.

1 serving: 115 cal., 7g fat (3g sat. fat), 10mg chol., 48mg sod., 14g carb. (10g sugars, 0 fiber), 1g pro. **Diabetic exchanges:** 1 starch, 1 fat.

NEAPOLITAN CRISPY BARS

The multicolored layers in these goodies create quite the buzz. Just wait until people take a bite—the chocolate and strawberry really pop.

—*Taste of Home* Test Kitchen

- -

Prep: 10 min. • **Cook:** 30 min. + cooling
Makes: 1 dozen

- 1 pkg. (10 oz.) large marshmallows, divided
- 3 Tbsp. butter, divided
- 2 cups Cocoa Krispies
- ½ cup miniature semisweet chocolate chips
- 4 cups Rice Krispies, divided
- ¼ cup strawberry preserves
- 5 drops red food coloring, optional

1. In a large saucepan, combine a third of the marshmallows (about 2 cups) and 1 Tbsp. butter. Cook and stir over medium-low heat until melted. Remove from heat; stir in Cocoa Krispies and chocolate chips. Press into a greased 11x7-in. dish.

2. In a saucepan, combine a third of the marshmallows and 1 Tbsp. butter. Cook and stir over medium-low heat until melted. Remove from the heat; stir in 2 cups Rice Krispies. Press into dish over chocolate layer.

3. In a saucepan, combine the remaining marshmallows and butter. Cook and stir over medium-low heat until melted. Remove from heat; stir in preserves and, if desired, food coloring. Stir in the remaining Rice Krispies. Press into the dish; cool. Cut into bars.

1 bar: 228 cal., 5g fat (3g sat. fat), 8mg chol., 159mg sod., 46g carb. (28g sugars, 1g fiber), 2g pro.

ALMOND-TIPPED SHORTBREAD FINGERS

My husband enjoys these cookies so much, he usually can't wait until they're set to start eating them.

—Cindy Sifford, Mount Zion, IL

- -

Prep: 30 min. • **Bake:** 15 min./batch + cooling
Makes: 4 dozen

- 1 cup butter, softened
- ¾ cup packed brown sugar
- 2 tsp. vanilla extract
- 2 cups all-purpose flour
- 6 oz. white baking chocolate, chopped
- 1¼ cups chopped almonds

1. Preheat oven to 325°. In a large bowl, cream butter and brown sugar until light and fluffy. Beat in vanilla. Gradually add flour and mix well. Shape ½ cupfuls of dough into ½-in. thick logs. Cut logs into 2-in. pieces.

2. Place 2 in. apart on ungreased baking sheets. Bake 15-17 minutes or until lightly browned. Remove to wire racks to cool.

3. In a microwave, melt white chocolate; stir until smooth. Dip an end of each cookie into chocolate and allow excess to drip off. Then dip into almonds. Place on waxed paper; let stand until set.

1 cookie: 105 cal., 7g fat (3g sat. fat), 11mg chol., 32mg sod., 10g carb. (6g sugars, 1g fiber), 2g pro.

TEST KITCHEN TIP

For a different look, use melted semisweet chocolate instead of the white baking chocolate and chopped pecans in place of the almonds.

NEAPOLITAN
CRISPY BARS

THUMBPRINT BUTTER COOKIES

These buttery little rounds add beautiful color to a platter of treats. Fill the centers of thumbprints with any fruit preserves you like.
—*Taste of Home* Test Kitchen

Prep: 25 min. • **Bake:** 10 min./batch
Makes: 2½ dozen

6	Tbsp. butter, softened
½	cup sugar
1	large egg, room temperature
2	Tbsp. canola oil
1	tsp. vanilla extract
¼	tsp. butter flavoring
1½	cups all-purpose flour
¼	cup cornstarch
1	tsp. baking powder
¼	tsp. salt
3	Tbsp. apricot or other fruit preserves

1. Preheat oven to 350°. Cream butter and sugar until light and fluffy; beat in the egg, oil, vanilla and butter flavoring. In another bowl, whisk together flour, cornstarch, baking powder and salt; gradually beat into the creamed mixture.

2. Shape dough into 1-in. balls; place 2 in. apart on greased baking sheets. Press a deep indentation in center of each with the end of a wooden spoon handle. Bake until edges are light brown, 8-10 minutes.

3. Remove from pans to wire racks to cool. Fill with preserves.

1 cookie: 75 cal., 3g fat (2g sat. fat), 13mg chol., 52mg sod., 10g carb. (4g sugars, 0 fiber), 1g pro.

DID YOU KNOW?

Dating from the 19th century, thumbprint cookies have also been called *hallongrotta* (Swedish for "Raspberry Cave"), bird's nest cookies, butterballs, or Polish tea cakes.

BIG & BUTTERY CHOCOLATE CHIP COOKIES

Our version of the classic cookie is based on a recipe from a bakery in California called Hungry Bear. It's big, thick and chewy—perfect for dunking.
—Irene Yeh, Mequon, WI

Prep: 35 min. + chilling • **Bake:** 10 min./batch
Makes: about 2 dozen

1	cup butter, softened
1	cup packed brown sugar
¾	cup sugar
2	large eggs, room temperature
1½	tsp. vanilla extract
2⅔	cups all-purpose flour
1¼	tsp. baking soda
1	tsp. salt
1	pkg. (12 oz.) semisweet chocolate chips
2	cups coarsely chopped walnuts, toasted

1. In a large bowl, beat butter and sugars until blended. Beat in eggs and vanilla. In a small bowl, whisk flour, baking soda and salt; gradually beat into butter mixture. Stir in chocolate chips and walnuts.

2. Shape ¼ cupfuls of dough into balls. Flatten each ball to ¾-in. thickness (2½-in. diameter), smoothing edges as necessary. Place in an airtight container, separating layers with waxed paper or parchment; refrigerate, covered, overnight.

3. To bake, place dough portions 2 in. apart on parchment-lined baking sheets; let stand at room temperature 30 minutes before baking. Preheat oven to 400°.

4. Bake until the edges are golden brown (centers will be light), 10-12 minutes. Cool on pans 2 minutes, then remove to wire racks to cool.

Note: To toast nuts, bake in a shallow pan in a 350° oven for 5-10 minutes or cook in a skillet over low heat until lightly browned, stirring occasionally.

1 cookie: 311 cal., 19g fat (8g sat. fat), 38mg chol., 229mg sod., 35g carb. (23g sugars, 2g fiber), 4g pro.

Almond Chocolate Chip Cookies: Reduce vanilla to 1 tsp. and add ¼ tsp. almond extract. Substitute toasted almonds for the walnuts.

Big & Buttery Cranberry Nut Cookies: Substitute dried cranberries for the chocolate chips.

THUMBPRINT
BUTTER COOKIES

PEPPERMINT MELTAWAYS

PEPPERMINT MELTAWAYS

These pretty cookies look festive on a cookie platter; I often cover them with red or green plastic wrap and a bright holiday bow.
—Denise Wheeler, Newaygo, MI

- -

Prep: 30 min. + chilling
Bake: 10 min./batch + cooling
Makes: about 2½ dozen

- 1 cup butter, softened
- ½ cup confectioners' sugar
- ½ tsp. peppermint extract
- 1¼ cups all-purpose flour
- ½ cup cornstarch

FROSTING

- 2 Tbsp. butter, softened
- 2 Tbsp. 2% milk
- ¼ tsp. peppermint extract
- 2 to 3 drops red food coloring, optional
- 1½ cups confectioners' sugar
- ½ cup crushed peppermint candies

1. Cream butter and confectioners' sugar until light and fluffy. Beat in extract. In another bowl, whisk flour and cornstarch; gradually beat into creamed mixture. Refrigerate, covered, 30 minutes or until firm enough to handle.
2. Shape dough into 1-in. balls; place 2 in. apart on ungreased baking sheets. Bake at 350° for 9-11 minutes or until bottoms are light brown. Remove to wire racks to cool.
3. Beat butter until creamy. Beat in milk, extract and, if desired, food coloring. Gradually beat in confectioners' sugar until smooth. Spread over cookies; sprinkle with crushed candies. Store in an airtight container.
1 cookie: 126 cal., 7g fat (4g sat. fat), 18mg chol., 56mg sod., 15g carb. (9g sugars, 0 fiber), 1g pro.

"This recipe has my heart. I make them for parties, and they disappear in an instant. They're so buttery they melt in your mouth. And they're simple to make."
—CHRISTINA HERBST, ASSISTANT DIGITAL EDITOR

CANDY CORN COOKIES

Get a head start on these buttery cookies by making, shaping and chilling the dough ahead of time. When you're ready, just slice and bake the tricolor treats.
—*Taste of Home* Test Kitchen

- -

Prep: 35 min. + chilling • **Bake:** 10 min./batch
Makes: about 5 dozen

- 1½ cups butter, softened
- 1½ cups sugar
- ½ tsp. vanilla extract
- 3 cups all-purpose flour
- 1 tsp. baking soda
- ½ tsp. salt
  Yellow and orange paste food coloring

1. Cream butter and sugar until light and fluffy. Beat in vanilla. In another bowl, whisk together flour, baking soda and salt; gradually beat into creamed mixture.
2. Divide the dough in half. Tint 1 portion yellow. Divide the remaining dough into two-thirds and one-third portions. Color the larger portion orange; leave the smaller portion plain.
3. Shape each portion of dough into two 8-in. logs. Flatten top and push sides in at a slight angle. Place orange logs on yellow logs; push sides in at a slight angle. Top with plain logs, forming a slightly rounded top. Wrap and refrigerate until firm, about 4 hours.
4. Preheat oven to 350°. Unwrap and cut dough into ¼-in. slices. Place 2 in. apart on ungreased baking sheets. Bake until set, 10-12 minutes. Remove from pans to wire racks to cool.
1 cookie: 83 cal., 5g fat (3g sat. fat), 12mg chol., 77mg sod., 10g carb. (5g sugars, 0 fiber), 1g pro.

CINNAMON-SPICE BROWNIES

Gail Mehle of Rock Springs, Wyoming submitted the original recipe for these brownies made with a secret ingredient: cinnamon. The spicy chocolate cinnamon cane sugar adds just a hint of heat.
—*Taste of Home* Test Kitchen

- -

Prep: 20 min. • **Bake:** 40 min. + cooling
Makes: 3 dozen

- ¾ cup baking cocoa
- ½ tsp. baking soda
- ⅔ cup butter, melted, divided
- ½ cup boiling water
- 2 cups sugar
- 2 large eggs, room temperature, beaten
- 1 tsp. vanilla extract
- 1⅓ cups all-purpose flour
- 1 Tbsp. Gustus Vitae spicy chocolate cinnamon cane sugar
- ¼ tsp. salt
- 1 cup (6 oz.) semisweet chocolate chips

FROSTING

- 6 Tbsp. butter, softened
- ½ cup baking cocoa
- 2⅔ cups confectioners' sugar
- 1 to 1½ tsp. ground cinnamon
- ⅓ cup evaporated milk
- 1 tsp. vanilla extract

1. Preheat oven to 350°. In a bowl, combine cocoa and baking soda; blend in ⅓ cup melted butter. Add boiling water, stirring until thickened. Stir in sugar, eggs, vanilla and remaining butter. Add flour, spicy chocolate cinnamon sugar and salt. Fold in chocolate chips. Pour into a greased 13x9-in. baking pan. Bake 40 minutes or until the brownies test done. Cool.
2. For frosting, cream butter in a bowl. Combine cocoa, sugar and cinnamon; add alternately with the milk. Beat to a spreading consistency; add vanilla. Add more milk if necessary. Spread over the brownies.
1 brownie: 138 cal., 7g fat (4g sat. fat), 25mg chol., 83mg sod., 18g carb. (12g sugars, 1g fiber), 2g pro.

CINNAMON-SPICE BROWNIES

LEMON LOVER'S POUND CAKE
PAGE 221

Cakes & Pies

We bake up a lot of sweet treats in our Test Kitchen. And when there's leftovers of a cake or pie, *Taste of Home* staffers happily line up with forks and plates in hand. Now you, too, can whip up oven-fresh, made-at-home bakery pleasures just like these. Turn the page to find a delicious roundup of our favorite cakes and pies—everything from classic layered tortes to flaky, fruit-filled perfection. It's never been easier to have your cake (and pie) and eat it, too!

CITRUS CRANBERRY PIE

CITRUS CRANBERRY PIE

This lattice-topped pie showcases beautiful bright red cranberries. A dollop of orange cream complements the slightly tart flavor.
—*Taste of Home* Test Kitchen

Prep: 30 min. • **Bake:** 50 min. + cooling
Makes: 8 servings

- 3½ cups fresh or frozen cranberries
- 1 cup sugar
- 2 tsp. grated lemon zest
- 1 tsp. grated orange zest
- 1 small navel orange, peeled, sectioned and chopped
- 2 Tbsp. butter, melted
- 2 Tbsp. all-purpose flour
- ¼ tsp. salt
  Pastry for double-crust pie
- 1 large egg, lightly beaten
  Additional sugar

ORANGE CREAM
- 1 cup heavy whipping cream
- 1 Tbsp. sugar
- 2 tsp. grated orange zest
- ½ tsp. orange extract, optional

1. Preheat oven to 450°. Toss together first 8 ingredients.
2. On a lightly floured surface, roll 1 half of dough to a ⅛-in.-thick circle; transfer to a 9-in. pie plate. Trim crust even with rim. Add the pie filling.
3. Roll remaining dough to ⅛-in.-thick circle; cut into strips. Arrange strips over filling in lattice pattern. Trim and seal strips to edge of bottom crust; flute edge. Brush lattice with egg; sprinkle with additional sugar.
4. Bake 10 minutes. Reduce oven setting to 350°; bake 40-45 minutes or until golden brown, covering edges with foil if crust is getting too dark. Cool completely on a wire rack; refrigerate until serving.
5. Meanwhile, beat whipping cream until it begins to thicken. Add remaining ingredients; beat until soft peaks form. Refrigerate until serving. Serve with pie.

Pastry for double-crust pie (9 in.): Mix 2½ cups all-purpose flour and ½ tsp. salt; cut in 1 cup cold butter until crumbly. Gradually add ⅓ to ⅔ cup ice water, tossing with a fork until dough holds together when pressed. Divide in half. Shape each into a disk; cover and refrigerate 1 hour or overnight.

1 piece: 515 cal., 29g fat (15g sat. fat), 85mg chol., 323mg sod., 62g carb. (33g sugars, 2g fiber), 4g pro.

CHOCOLATE CAKE WITH CHOCOLATE FROSTING

CHOCOLATE CAKE WITH CHOCOLATE FROSTING

I once sent this rich chocolate cake to my kids' teachers. It vanished quickly, so I knew I had to make another one!
—Megan Moelbert, Springville, NY

Prep: 40 min. • **Bake:** 30 min. + cooling
Makes: 16 servings

- 2 cups sugar
- 2 cups water
- ⅔ cup canola oil
- 2 Tbsp. white vinegar
- 2 tsp. vanilla extract
- 3 cups all-purpose flour
- ⅓ cup plus 1 Tbsp. baking cocoa, sifted
- 2 tsp. baking soda
- 1 tsp. salt

FROSTING
- 3¾ cups confectioners' sugar
- ⅓ cup baking cocoa
- 1 cup butter, softened
- 1 tsp. vanilla extract
- 3 to 5 Tbsp. 2% milk

1. Preheat oven to 350°. Line bottoms of 2 greased 9-in. round baking pans with parchment; grease parchment.
2. In a large bowl, beat sugar, water, oil, vinegar and vanilla until well blended. In another large bowl, whisk flour, sifted cocoa, baking soda and salt; gradually add to sugar mixture, beating until smooth.
3. Transfer batter to prepared pans. Bake until a toothpick inserted in center comes out clean, 30-35 minutes. Cool in pans for 10 minutes before removing to wire racks; remove parchment. Cool completely.
4. For frosting, sift the confectioners' sugar and cocoa together. In a large bowl, beat butter and vanilla until blended. Beat in the confectioners' sugar mixture alternately with enough milk to reach desired consistency. Spread frosting between layers and over top and sides of cake.

1 slice: 491 cal., 22g fat (8g sat. fat), 31mg chol., 399mg sod., 74g carb. (53g sugars, 1g fiber), 3g pro.

PEACH CAKE

My mom's springtime layer cake is peachy, creamy and easy to assemble. My brother's birthday is in April, and her cake is his special request every year.
—Tamra Duncan, Lincoln, AR

- -

Prep: 15 min. • **Bake:** 30 min. + cooling
Makes: 12 servings

- 1 can (15¼ oz.) sliced peaches, undrained
- 1 pkg. yellow cake mix (regular size)
- ⅓ cup vegetable oil
- 3 large eggs, room temperature
- 1 carton (8 oz.) frozen whipped topping, thawed
- ¾ cup peach yogurt
  Additional drained diced peaches, if desired

1. Drain the peaches, reserving juice. Add enough water to juice to measure 1¼ cups. Cut peaches into 1-in. pieces; set aside.
2. In a large bowl, beat the cake mix, peach juice mixture, oil and eggs on low speed for 30 seconds. Beat on medium for 2 minutes. Pour into 2 greased and floured 9-in. round baking pans. Bake at 350° for 28-33 minutes or until a toothpick inserted in the center comes out clean. Cool the cake in pans for 10 minutes before removing to wire racks to cool completely.
3. In a bowl, combine the whipped topping and yogurt; fold in reserved peaches. Spread topping between layers and over top of cake. Garnish cake with additional diced peaches if desired. Store in refrigerator.
1 piece: 265 cal., 6g fat (5g sat. fat), 47mg chol., 339mg sod., 48g carb. (31g sugars, 1g fiber), 3g pro.

CHOCOLATE CARAMEL HAZELNUT PIE

CHOCOLATE CARAMEL HAZELNUT PIE

I love chocolate, caramel and hazelnuts. So I came up with the recipe for this luscious no-bake pie that has all three flavors. It's a great dessert for a warm summer day.
—Debbie Anderson, Mount Angel, OR

- -

Prep: 25 min. + chilling • **Makes:** 8 servings

- 1½ cups salted caramel pretzel pieces
- 12 Lorna Doone shortbread cookies
- ¼ cup sugar
- 6 Tbsp. butter, melted
- 5 Tbsp. caramel topping, divided

FILLING
- 1 pkg. (8 oz.) cream cheese, softened
- ½ cup Nutella
- 1 jar (7 oz.) marshmallow creme
- 1 carton (8 oz.) frozen whipped topping, thawed
- 1 cup miniature marshmallows
- 1 Snickers candy bar (1.86 oz.), chopped

1. Place pretzel pieces and cookies in a food processor; pulse until fine crumbs form. Add the sugar and melted butter; pulse just until blended. Press onto bottom and sides of a 9-in. pie plate. Drizzle with 3 Tbsp. caramel topping. Freeze while preparing filling.
2. For filling, beat cream cheese and Nutella until smooth. Gradually beat in marshmallow creme. Gently fold in whipped topping and marshmallows. Spoon into crust.
3. Refrigerate until set, 3-4 hours. Top with chopped candy and remaining caramel topping before serving.
1 piece: 663 cal., 35g fat (19g sat. fat), 60mg chol., 327mg sod., 74g carb. (57g sugars, 1g fiber), 6g pro.

TEST KITCHEN TIP
The crust is crunchy, sweet and slightly crumbly. If you don't have a food processor, place ingredients in a zip-top freezer bag and smash with a rolling pin.

TRADITIONAL PUMPKIN PIE

I usually prepare two different desserts for our Thanksgiving dinner, but one of them must be pumpkin pie. My version calls for more eggs than most, making the custard filling especially rich.
—Gloria Warczak, Cedarburg, WI

Prep: 20 min. • **Bake:** 40 min. + chilling
Makes: 2 pies (8 servings each)

- 2 cups all-purpose flour
- ¾ tsp. salt
- ⅔ cup shortening
- 4 to 6 Tbsp. cold water

FILLING
- 6 large eggs, room temperature
- 1 can (29 oz.) solid-pack pumpkin
- 2 cups packed brown sugar
- 2 tsp. ground cinnamon
- 1 tsp. salt
- ½ tsp. each ground cloves, nutmeg and ginger
- 2 cups evaporated milk

DECORATIONS (OPTIONAL)
- Pastry for single-crust pie
- 1 large egg, beaten

1. In a large bowl, combine flour and salt; cut in shortening until crumbly. Gradually add water, tossing with a fork until dough forms a ball. Divide the dough in half. On a floured surface, roll out each portion to fit a 9-in. pie plate. Place the crust in plates; trim crust to ½ in. beyond edge of plate. Flute edges.

2. For filling, beat the eggs in a large bowl. Add the pumpkin, brown sugar, cinnamon, salt, cloves, nutmeg and ginger; beat just until combined. Gradually stir in the milk. Pour into crusts.

3. Bake at 450° for 10 minutes. Reduce heat to 350°; bake until a knife inserted in the center comes out clean, 40-45 minutes longer. Cool pies on wire racks for 1 hour. Refrigerate at least 3 hours before serving. Refrigerate leftovers.

4. If desired, use additional pie crust to make decorations.

For pumpkin pastry cutouts: Roll a small amount of pie dough into a ball; score sides of ball with the blunt side of a knife to create ridges. Place on parchment-lined baking sheet, flatten slightly and insert a whole clove to make the stem. Refrigerate until firm. Brush cutouts with beaten egg and bake at 400° until light golden brown and baked through, 15-20 minutes.

For vine pastry cutouts: Roll out pie dough to ⅛-in. thickness; cut narrow strips of dough in various lengths. Lay strips on parchment-lined baking sheet and shape into coils as desired. Refrigerate until firm. Brush with beaten egg and bake at 400° until light golden brown, 8-10 minutes.

For leaf pastry cutouts: Roll pie dough to ⅛-in. thickness. Cut out leaves using mini leaf-shaped cutters. Using a knife, score leaves to create veins. Refrigerate until firm. Brush with beaten egg and bake at 400° until light golden brown, 8-10 minutes. Arrange baked pumpkins, vines and leaves on surface of the chilled pie.

1 slice: 321 cal., 12g fat (4g sat. fat), 80mg chol., 326mg sod., 47g carb. (32g sugars, 2g fiber), 7g pro.

TRADITIONAL PUMPKIN PIE

SHORTCUT TRES LECHES CAKE

CHOCOLATE HAZELNUT TORTE

Most cake recipes feed a crowd. So we came up with this elegant little cake that serves six. That's enough for two...with just the right amount of leftovers!
—*Taste of Home* Test Kitchen

Prep: 30 min. + chilling
Bake: 25 min. + cooling • **Makes:** 6 servings

- ⅓ cup butter, softened
- 1 cup packed brown sugar
- 1 large egg, room temperature
- 1 tsp. vanilla extract
- 1 cup all-purpose flour
- ¼ cup baking cocoa
- 1 tsp. baking soda
- ⅛ tsp. salt
- ½ cup sour cream
- ½ cup brewed coffee, room temperature

FROSTING
- 7 oz. semisweet chocolate, chopped
- 1 cup heavy whipping cream
- 2 Tbsp. sugar
- ⅓ cup Nutella
    Chocolate curls and hazelnuts, optional

1. In a small bowl, cream butter and brown sugar until light and fluffy, 5-7 minutes. Beat in egg and vanilla. Combine the flour, cocoa, baking soda and salt; gradually add to the creamed mixture alternately with sour cream and coffee. Beat just until combined.
2. Pour into 2 greased and floured 6-in. round baking pans. Bake at 350° until a knife inserted in the center comes out clean, 25-30 minutes. Cool cake for 10 minutes before removing from pans to wire racks to cool completely.
3. For frosting, in a small saucepan, melt chocolate with cream and sugar over low heat; stir until smooth. Remove from the heat; whisk in Nutella. Transfer mixture to a small bowl; cover and refrigerate until frosting reaches spreading consistency, stirring occasionally.
4. Spread frosting between layers and over top and sides of cake. Garnish with chocolate curls and hazelnuts if desired.
1 slice: 768 cal., 45g fat (25g sat. fat), 130mg chol., 386mg sod., 89g carb. (66g sugars, 4g fiber), 9g pro.

SHORTCUT TRES LECHES CAKE

My mom's favorite cake is tres leches, a butter cake soaked in three kinds of milk. I developed a no-fuss version that's rich and tender. It's a great finale to a Mexican meal.
—Marina Castle Kelley, Canyon Country, CA

Prep: 20 min. + chilling
Bake: 30 min. + cooling • **Makes:** 20 servings

- 1 pkg. butter recipe golden cake or yellow cake mix (regular size)
- 3 large eggs, room temperature
- ⅔ cup 2% milk
- ½ cup butter, softened
- 1 tsp. vanilla extract

TOPPING
- 1 can (14 oz.) sweetened condensed milk
- 1 can (12 oz.) evaporated milk
- 1 cup heavy whipping cream

WHIPPED CREAM
- 1 cup heavy whipping cream
- 3 Tbsp. confectioners' sugar
- 1 tsp. vanilla extract

1. Preheat oven to 350°. Grease a 13x9-in. baking pan.
2. In a large bowl, combine cake mix, eggs, milk, softened butter and vanilla; beat on low speed 30 seconds. Beat on medium speed 2 minutes. Transfer to prepared pan. Bake 30-35 minutes or until a toothpick inserted in center comes out clean. Cool in pan on a wire rack 20 minutes.
3. In a 4-cup measuring cup, whisk topping ingredients until blended. Using a skewer, generously poke holes in top of warm cake. Pour milk mixture slowly over cake, filling holes. Cool 30 minutes longer. Refrigerate, covered, at least 4 hours or overnight.
4. In a bowl, beat cream until it begins to thicken. Add confectioners' sugar and vanilla; beat until soft peaks form. Spread over cake.
1 piece: 343 cal., 20g fat (12g sat. fat), 89mg chol., 257mg sod., 36g carb. (28g sugars, 0 fiber), 6g pro.

CHOCOLATE
HAZELNUT TORTE

KEY LIME PIE

Enjoy this pie with a homemade crumb crust and a pudding-like lime filling any time you crave a cool, refreshing dessert. If you can't find Key lime juice, regular lime juice works just fine.
—*Taste of Home* Test Kitchen

- -

Prep: 30 min. + chilling • **Makes:** 4 servings

- ⅔ **cup graham cracker crumbs**
- 2 **Tbsp. sugar**
- 3 **Tbsp. butter, melted**

FILLING

- ½ **cup sugar**
- 2 **Tbsp. all-purpose flour**
- 1 **Tbsp. plus 1½ tsp. cornstarch**
- ⅛ **tsp. salt**
- 1 **cup water**
- 1 **drop green food coloring, optional**
- 2 **large egg yolks, room temperature, beaten**
- 2 **Tbsp. Key lime juice**
- 1 **tsp. butter**
- ½ **tsp. grated lime zest**
  Whipped cream, optional
  Optional: Thinly sliced Key limes and additional grated lime zest

1. In a small bowl, combine cracker crumbs and sugar; stir in the butter. Press onto the bottom and up the sides of a 7-in. pie plate coated with cooking spray. Bake at 325° for 8-10 minutes or until lightly browned. Cool on a wire rack.

2. In a small saucepan, combine the sugar, flour, cornstarch and salt; gradually stir in water and, if desired, food coloring. Cook and stir over medium heat until thickened. Remove from the heat. Stir a small amount of hot filling into egg yolks; return all to the pan, stirring constantly. Bring to a gentle boil; cook and stir 2 minutes longer. Remove from the heat. Gently stir in lime juice, butter and lime zest.

3. Pour into crust. Cool for 15 minutes. Refrigerate for 1-2 hours. Garnish with whipped cream, lime slices and zest if desired. Refrigerate leftovers.

1 piece: 321 cal., 13g fat (7g sat. fat), 132mg chol., 259mg sod., 49g carb. (33g sugars, 1g fiber), 3g pro.

KEY LIME PIE

YUMMY TEXAS PECAN PIE

This ooey-gooey pie's luscious and creamy filling offers that good old familiar flavor so many of us love!
—Laurel Leslie, Sonora, CA

Prep: 20 min. • **Bake:** 70 min.
Makes: 8 servings

- ½ cup sugar
- 3 Tbsp. all-purpose flour
- 1 cup light corn syrup
- 1 cup dark corn syrup
- 3 large eggs, room temperature
- 1 tsp. white vinegar
- ½ tsp. vanilla extract
- 1 cup chopped pecans
  Pastry for single-crust pie

1. In a large bowl, whisk the sugar, flour, corn syrups, eggs, vinegar and vanilla until smooth. Stir in pecans. Line a 9-in. pie plate with pastry; trim and flute edges. Pour filling into crust. Cover edges with foil.

2. Bake at 350° for 35 minutes. Remove foil; bake until puffed and golden (center will still wobble), 35-45 minutes. Cool on a wire rack. Refrigerate leftovers.

1 piece: 543 cal., 20g fat (5g sat. fat), 84mg chol., 215mg sod., 93g carb. (36g sugars, 2g fiber), 5g pro.

COFFEE-CHOCOLATE CAKE

Try this dark, moist cake for your next birthday party or special occasion. The buttercream frosting has an unbeatable homemade taste. Don't be afraid to get creative by adding food coloring or different flavor extracts to make the frosting match a holiday or theme.
—*Taste of Home* Test Kitchen

Prep: 25 min. • **Bake:** 25 min. + cooling
Makes: 12 servings

- 2 cups sugar
- 1 cup canola oil
- 1 cup whole milk
- 1 cup brewed coffee, room temperature
- 2 large eggs, room temperature
- 1 tsp. vanilla extract
- 2 cups all-purpose flour
- ¾ cup baking cocoa
- 2 tsp. baking soda
- 1 tsp. baking powder
- 1 tsp. salt

BUTTERCREAM FROSTING
- 1 cup butter, softened
- 8 cups confectioners' sugar
- 2 tsp. vanilla extract
- ½ to ¾ cup whole milk

1. In a large bowl, beat the sugar, oil, milk, coffee, eggs and vanilla until well blended. Combine the flour, cocoa, baking soda, baking powder and salt; gradually beat into sugar mixture until blended.

2. Pour into 2 greased and floured 9-in. round baking pans. Bake at 325° until a toothpick inserted in the center comes out clean, 25-30 minutes. Cool cake in pans for 10 minutes before removing to wire racks to cool completely.

3. For frosting, in a large bowl, beat butter until fluffy. Beat in the confectioners' sugar and vanilla. Add milk until frosting reaches desired consistency. Spread the frosting between the layers and over top and sides of cake.

1 piece: 859 cal., 36g fat (13g sat. fat), 80mg chol., 621mg sod., 133g carb. (109g sugars, 2g fiber), 5g pro.

COFFEE-CHOCOLATE CAKE

LEMON LOVER'S
POUND CAKE

LEMON LOVER'S POUND CAKE

Everyone raves over this pretty dessert—and it sure doesn't last long. It also freezes beautifully, so why not make two and pop one in the freezer for another day?
—Annettia Mounger, Kansas City, MO

- -

Prep: 20 min. • **Bake:** 55 min. + cooling
Makes: 12 servings

- 1 cup butter, softened
- 3 cups sugar
- 6 large eggs, room temperature
- 5 Tbsp. lemon juice
- 1 Tbsp. grated lemon zest
- 1 tsp. lemon extract
- 3 cups all-purpose flour
- ½ tsp. baking soda
- ¼ tsp. salt
- 1¼ cups sour cream

ICING
- ¼ cup sour cream
- 2 Tbsp. butter, softened
- 2½ cups confectioners' sugar
- 3 Tbsp. lemon juice
- 2 tsp. grated lemon zest

1. In a large bowl, cream butter and sugar until light and fluffy, 5-7 minutes. Add eggs, 1 at a time, beating well after each addition. Stir in lemon juice, zest and extract. Combine the flour, baking soda and salt; add to the creamed mixture alternately with the sour cream. Beat just until combined.
2. Pour batter into a greased and floured 10-in. fluted tube pan. Bake at 350° until a toothpick inserted in the center comes out clean, 55-60 minutes. Cool for 10 minutes before removing from pan to a wire rack to cool completely.
3. For icing, in a small bowl, beat the sour cream and butter until smooth. Gradually add confectioners' sugar. Beat in lemon juice and zest. Drizzle over the cake. If desired, top with additional grated lemon zest. Store in the refrigerator.
1 slice: 658 cal., 26g fat (15g sat. fat), 146mg chol., 286mg sod., 101g carb. (76g sugars, 1g fiber), 8g pro.

CLASSIC CHOCOLATE CAKE

CLASSIC CHOCOLATE CAKE

This recipe appeared on a can of Hershey's Cocoa way back in 1943. I tried it, my boys liked it and I've been making it ever since. I make all my cakes from scratch, and this is one of the best!
—Betty Follas, Morgan Hill, CA

- -

Prep: 15 min. • **Bake:** 35 min.
Makes: 15 servings

- ⅔ cup butter, softened
- 1⅔ cups sugar
- 3 large eggs, room temperature
- 2 cups all-purpose flour
- ⅔ cup baking cocoa
- 1¼ tsp. baking soda
- 1 tsp. salt
- 1⅓ cups whole milk
  Confectioners' sugar or favorite frosting

1. In a bowl, cream butter and sugar until light and fluffy, 5-7 minutes. Add the eggs, 1 at a time, beating well after each addition. Combine flour, cocoa, baking soda and salt; add to creamed mixture alternately with the milk, beating until smooth after each addition. Pour batter into a greased and floured 13x9-in. baking pan.
2. Bake at 350° until a toothpick inserted in center comes out clean, 35-40 minutes. Cool on a wire rack. When the cake is cool, dust with confectioners' sugar or frost with your favorite frosting.
1 piece: 257 cal., 10g fat (6g sat. fat), 67mg chol., 368mg sod., 38g carb. (23g sugars, 1g fiber), 4g pro.

CRANBERRY-CHERRY NUT PIE

This delightful stress-free pie using a basic refrigerated pie crust combines cranberries with convenient cherry pie filling for a fresh, fun flavor.

—*Taste of Home* Test Kitchen

Prep: 20 min. • **Bake:** 40 min.
Makes: 8 servings

- 1 **can (21 oz.) cherry pie filling**
- 2 **cups fresh or frozen cranberries, thawed**
- ¾ **cup sugar**
- ½ **cup chopped walnuts**
- 2 **Tbsp. cornstarch**
- 1 **tsp. vanilla extract**
- ½ **tsp. ground cinnamon**
- ⅛ **tsp. ground allspice**
- 2 **sheets refrigerated pie crust**
- 2 **Tbsp. butter**
- 1 **tsp. 2% milk**
- 1 **Tbsp. coarse sugar**

1. Preheat oven to 375°. For filling, mix first 8 ingredients. Unroll 1 crust into a 9-in. pie plate. Add filling; dot with butter.

2. Unroll remaining crust onto a work surface; make cutout vents using small cookie cutters. Place top crust over filling; seal and flute edge. Decorate top with cutouts. Brush with milk; sprinkle with coarse sugar.

3. Bake on a lower oven rack 40-45 minutes or until crust is golden brown and filling is bubbly. Cover edge of pie with foil during the last 30 minutes if needed to prevent overbrowning. Cool on a wire rack.

1 piece: 482 cal., 21g fat (8g sat. fat), 17mg chol., 223mg sod., 71g carb. (24g sugars, 2g fiber), 3g pro.

MINI PINEAPPLE UPSIDE-DOWN CAKES

These individual pineapple upside-down cakes are an eye-catching addition to my holiday dessert table. A classic yellow cake mix makes them easy to bake anytime.

—Cindy Colley, Othello, WA

Prep: 30 min. • **Bake:** 20 min.
Makes: 2 dozen

- ⅔ **cup packed brown sugar**
- ⅓ **cup butter, melted**
- 1 **can (20 oz.) pineapple tidbits**
- 12 **maraschino cherries, halved**
- 1 **pkg. yellow cake mix (regular size)**
- 3 **large eggs, room temperature**
- ⅓ **cup canola oil**

1. In a small bowl, combine brown sugar and butter until blended. Spoon into 24 greased muffin cups. Drain pineapple, reserving the juice; spoon pineapple into prepared cups. Place a cherry half cut side down in the center of each.

2. In a large bowl, combine the cake mix, eggs, canola oil and reserved pineapple juice. Beat on low speed for 30 seconds. Beat on medium for 2 minutes. Spoon over the pineapple, filling each cup three-fourths full.

3. Bake at 350° for 18-22 minutes or until a toothpick inserted in the center comes out clean. Immediately invert cakes onto wire racks to cool.

1 serving: 184 cal., 8g fat (3g sat. fat), 33mg chol., 170mg sod., 28g carb. (20g sugars, 0 fiber), 1g pro. **Diabetic exchanges:** 1½ starch, 1 fat.

CRANBERRY-CHERRY NUT PIE

BUTTER PECAN LAYER CAKE

Pecans and butter give this cake the same irresistible flavor as the popular ice cream.
—Becky Miller, Tallahassee, FL

Prep: 40 min. • **Bake:** 25 min. + cooling
Makes: 16 servings

- 2⅔ cups chopped pecans
- 1¼ cups butter, softened, divided
- 2 cups sugar
- 4 large eggs, room temperature
- 2 tsp. vanilla extract
- 3 cups all-purpose flour
- 2 tsp. baking powder
- ½ tsp. salt
- 1 cup whole milk

FROSTING
- 1 cup butter, softened
- 8 to 8½ cups confectioners' sugar
- 1 can (5 oz.) evaporated milk
- 2 tsp. vanilla extract

1. Place pecans and ¼ cup butter in a baking pan. Bake at 350° for 10-15 minutes or until toasted, stirring frequently; set aside.

2. In a large bowl, cream sugar and remaining butter until light and fluffy, 5-7 minutes. Add the eggs, 1 at a time, beating well after each addition. Stir in vanilla. Combine the flour, baking powder and salt; add to the creamed mixture alternately with the milk, beating well after each addition. Stir in 1⅓ cups of toasted pecans.

3. Pour into 3 greased and floured 9-in. round baking pans. Bake at 350° until a toothpick inserted in center comes out clean, 25-30 minutes. Cool for 10 minutes before removing from pans to wire racks to cool completely.

4. For the frosting, cream the butter and confectioners' sugar in a large bowl. Add milk and vanilla; beat until smooth. Stir in remaining toasted pecans. Spread frosting between layers and over the top and sides of cake.

1 piece: 814 cal., 42g fat (19g sat. fat), 120mg chol., 375mg sod., 107g carb. (86g sugars, 2g fiber), 7g pro.

BUTTER PECAN
LAYER CAKE

TASTE OF HOME
TEST KITCHEN
RECIPE OF THE YEAR
★ ★ ★ ★ ★

APPLE PIE

EASY CRUNCH BERRY PIE

Here's a fun, simple approach to making a pie that's both company-worthy and kid-friendly. The playful Cap'n Crunch cereal crust is a sweet surprise and makes the perfect complement to a mixed berry no-bake filling.
—*Taste of Home* Test Kitchen

Prep: 30 min. + chilling
Bake: 10 min. + cooling • **Makes:** 8 servings

2¾ cups crushed Cap'n Crunch cereal
½ cup butter, melted
2 cups mixed fresh or frozen unsweetened berries, thawed
¾ cup sugar, divided
1 tsp. lemon juice
1 tsp. grated lemon zest
¼ cup cold water
1 envelope unflavored gelatin
2 pkg. (8 oz. each) cream cheese, softened
½ cup heavy whipping cream
Sweetened whipped cream, optional
Additional mixed fresh berries, optional

1. Preheat oven to 350°. Combine crushed cereal and melted butter. Using the bottom of a glass, press cereal mixture onto bottom and up the sides of a greased 9-in. deep-dish pie plate. Bake until set, 10-12 minutes. Cool completely on a wire rack.
2. Combine berries, ½ cup sugar, lemon juice and zest; let stand 10 minutes. Meanwhile, sprinkle gelatin over cold water; let stand 5 minutes. Transfer berry mixture to a food processor or blender; pulse until smooth. Press through a fine-mesh strainer to remove seeds. Microwave gelatin on high until melted, about 10 seconds; stir into berry mixture.
3. Beat cream cheese and remaining sugar until smooth. Gradually beat in cream and berry mixture. Transfer filling to crust. Refrigerate, covered, until set, about 2 hours. If desired, top with sweetened whipped cream and additional berries.
1 piece: 492 cal., 37g fat (23g sat. fat), 105mg chol., 369mg sod., 37g carb. (29g sugars, 2g fiber), 6g pro.

APPLE PIE

I remember coming home sullen one day because our softball team lost a game. My loving grandma, in her wisdom, suggested a slice of hot apple pie to make me feel better. It did the trick.
—Maggie Greene, Granite Falls, WA

Prep: 20 min. • **Bake:** 45 min.
Makes: 8 servings

½ cup sugar
½ cup packed brown sugar
3 Tbsp. all-purpose flour
1 tsp. ground cinnamon
¼ tsp. ground ginger
¼ tsp. ground nutmeg
6 to 7 cups thinly sliced peeled tart apples
1 Tbsp. lemon juice
Pastry for double-crust pie
1 Tbsp. butter
1 large egg white
Additional sugar

1. In a small bowl, combine the sugars, flour and spices; set aside. In a large bowl, toss apples with lemon juice. Add sugar mixture; toss to coat.
2. Line a 9-in. pie plate with bottom crust; trim even with edge. Fill with apple mixture; dot with butter. Roll remaining crust to fit top of pie; place over filling. Trim, seal and flute edges. Cut slits in crust.
3. Beat egg white until foamy; brush over crust. Sprinkle with sugar. Cover the edges loosely with foil.
4. Bake at 375° for 25 minutes. Remove foil and bake until crust is golden brown and filling is bubbly, 20-25 minutes longer. Cool on a wire rack.
1 piece: 414 cal., 16g fat (7g sat. fat), 14mg chol., 227mg sod., 67g carb. (38g sugars, 2g fiber), 3g pro.

**EASY CRUNCH
BERRY PIE**

CHOCOLATE BAVARIAN TORTE

Whenever I take this impressive layered torte to a potluck, I get oohs and aahs...and so many requests for the recipe. It's so easy!
—Edith Holmstrom, Madison, WI

Prep: 15 min. + chilling
Bake: 30 min. + cooling • **Makes:** 12 servings

1   pkg. devil's food cake mix (regular size)
1   pkg. (8 oz.) cream cheese, softened
⅓ cup packed brown sugar
1   tsp. vanilla extract
⅛ tsp. salt
2   cups heavy whipping cream, whipped
2   Tbsp. grated semisweet chocolate

1. Prepare and bake cake according to package directions, using two 9-in. round baking pans. Cool the cake in pans for 10 minutes before removing to wire racks to cool completely.
2. In a bowl, beat the cream cheese, sugar, vanilla and salt until smooth. Fold in cream.
3. Cut each cake horizontally into 2 layers. Place bottom layer on a serving plate; top with a fourth of the cream mixture. Sprinkle with a fourth of the chocolate. Repeat layers 3 times. Cover cake and refrigerate 8 hours or overnight.

1 piece: 495 cal., 33g fat (16g sat. fat), 111mg chol., 475mg sod., 45g carb. (27g sugars, 1g fiber), 6g pro.

TEST KITCHEN TIP
Heavy cream is a rich cream that ranges from 36% to 40% butterfat and doubles in volume when it is whipped. It's often labeled as either heavy cream or whipping cream.

CHOCOLATE BAVARIAN TORTE

BEE STING CAKE

Bee Sting Cake, or *bienenstich,* originated in Germany. It gets its playful name from the sweet honey-almond topping. The recipe may look daunting, but it's well worth the effort. Take each step at a time, and you'll be surprised how easy it is to make.
—*Taste of Home* Test Kitchen

Prep: 45 min. • **Bake:** 30 min. + cooling
Makes: 8 servings

- ¼ cup sugar
- 3 Tbsp. cornstarch
- ¼ tsp. salt
- 1½ cups whole milk
- 3 large egg yolks
- 2 Tbsp. butter, cubed
- 2 tsp. vanilla extract
- ½ cup heavy whipping cream, whipped

CAKE

- ¼ cup sugar
- 1 envelope (¼ oz.) active dry yeast
- ¼ tsp. salt
- 2¾ cups all-purpose flour, divided
- ¾ cup whole milk
- ⅓ cup butter, cubed
- 2 large eggs, room temperature

ALMOND TOPPING

- ¼ cup butter
- 3 Tbsp. honey
- 2 Tbsp. sugar
- 1 cup sliced almonds

1. For filling, in a small heavy saucepan, mix the sugar, cornstarch and salt. Whisk in the milk. Cook and stir over medium heat until thickened and bubbly. Reduce heat to low; cook and stir 2 minutes longer. Remove from heat. In a small bowl, whisk egg yolks. Whisk a small amount of hot mixture into egg yolks; return all to pan, whisking constantly. Bring to a gentle boil; cook and stir for 2 minutes. Remove from heat. Stir in the butter until melted. Immediately transfer mixture to a clean bowl; stir in vanilla. Cool 30 minutes. Press plastic wrap onto surface of filling; refrigerate until cold.

2. Whisk custard gently. Fold in half the whipped cream. Fold in remaining whipped cream. Cover and refrigerate.

3. While the custard is chilling, make the cake dough. In a large bowl, mix the sugar, yeast, salt and 1 cup flour. In a small saucepan, heat the milk and butter to 120°-130°. Add liquid to the dry ingredients and beat on medium speed for 1 minute. Add eggs; beat on high 1 minute. Stir in enough remaining flour to form a soft dough (dough will be sticky).

4. Turn dough onto a well floured surface; knead until smooth and elastic, 6-8 minutes. Place in a greased bowl, turning once to grease the top. Cover and let rise in a warm place until doubled, about 1 hour.

5. While dough is rising, make the almond topping. In a small saucepan over medium heat, melt butter, honey and sugar. Cook and stir until sugar is dissolved. Remove from heat; stir in almonds. Cool mixture slightly and set aside.

6. Punch down dough. Turn onto a lightly floured surface; roll into a 9-in. circle. Transfer to greased 9-in. springform baking pan, pressing to evenly fill pan with dough. Spoon almond mixture over dough and gently spread to cover entire surface. Cover pan with a kitchen towel; let rise in a warm place until doubled, 25-30 minutes. Preheat oven to 350°. Bake until topping is golden brown, 25-30 minutes. Cool on a wire rack 10 minutes. Loosen sides from pan with a knife. Cool 1 hour longer.

7. Remove cake from base of springform pan. Using a long serrated knife, cut cake horizontally in half; spread the filling over bottom layer. Replace top of cake. Serve immediately. Chill leftovers.

1 piece: 548 cal., 32g fat (16g sat. fat), 178mg chol., 314mg sod., 56g carb. (18g sugars, 3g fiber), 11g pro.

BEE STING CAKE

GINGER-GLAZED
LEMON BUNDT

GINGER-GLAZED LEMON BUNDT

This cake is as gorgeous as a fall day. For extra sparkle, mix half sanding sugar with regular sugar when coating the berries.
—*Taste of Home* Test Kitchen

- -

Prep: 20 min. • **Bake:** 1 hour + cooling
Makes: 12 servings

SUGARED CRANBERRIES
- 3 Tbsp. light corn syrup
- 1 cup fresh or frozen, thawed cranberries
- ⅓ cup sugar

CAKE
- 1 cup butter, softened
- 2 cups sugar
- 4 large eggs, room temperature
- 2 Tbsp. grated lemon zest
- 1 tsp. lemon extract
- 2½ cups all-purpose flour
- 2 tsp. baking powder
- ½ tsp. salt
- 1 cup fat-free vanilla Greek yogurt

GLAZE
- ⅔ cup confectioners' sugar
- 2 Tbsp. butter, melted
- 1 to 3 tsp. lemon juice
- ½ tsp. ground ginger

1. For sugared cranberries, heat corn syrup in microwave until warm; gently toss the cranberries in syrup, allowing excess to drip off. Toss in sugar to coat. Place on waxed paper; let stand until set, about 1 hour.

2. Preheat oven to 325°. Grease and flour a 10-in. fluted tube pan. In a large bowl, cream the butter and sugar until light and fluffy, 5-7 minutes. Add eggs, 1 at a time, beating well after each addition. Beat in lemon zest and extract.

3. In another bowl, whisk flour, baking powder and salt; add to creamed mixture alternately with yogurt, beating well after each addition.

4. Transfer to prepared pan. Bake until a toothpick inserted in the center comes out clean, 60-70 minutes. Cool cake in pan for 10 minutes before removing to a wire rack to cool completely.

5. Mix confectioners' sugar, butter, lemon juice and ginger until smooth. Drizzle over cake. Top with sugared cranberries.

1 slice: 468 cal., 19g fat (12g sat. fat), 108mg chol., 350mg sod., 69g carb. (48g sugars, 1g fiber), 7g pro.

EASY MOCHA CREAM PIE

This luscious cream pie will please coffee and chocolate lovers alike. The homemade crumb crust is excellent with the cool and creamy no-bake mocha filling.
—*Taste of Home* Test Kitchen

- -

Prep: 20 min. + chilling
Bake: 15 min. + cooling • **Makes:** 8 servings

- 2¾ cups chocolate bear-shaped crackers or chocolate wafer crumbs, crushed
- 2 Tbsp. plus ½ cup sugar, divided
- ½ cup butter, melted
- ¼ cup cold water
- 1 tsp. instant coffee granules
- 1 envelope unflavored gelatin
- ½ cup semisweet chocolate chips
- 1½ cups heavy whipping cream, divided
- 2 pkg. (8 oz. each) cream cheese, softened
  - Caramel sundae syrup, optional
  - Chocolate syrup, optional

1. Preheat oven to 350°. Combine crushed crackers and 2 Tbsp. sugar with melted butter. Using the bottom of a glass, press cracker mixture onto bottom and up the sides of a greased 9-in. deep-dish pie plate. Bake until set, 12-15 minutes. Cool crust completely on a wire rack.

2. Meanwhile, mix cold water and coffee granules until blended. Sprinkle the gelatin over coffee mixture; let stand for 5 minutes. Microwave chocolate chips and ¼ cup cream on high until chips are melted; stir until smooth. Stir gelatin into chocolate mixture until smooth. Cool slightly. Beat the cream cheese and remaining sugar until smooth. Gradually beat in remaining cream. Beat in chocolate mixture until blended. Transfer filling to crust. Refrigerate, covered, until set, about 2 hours.

3. If desired, drizzle with caramel and chocolate syrups.

1 piece: 699 cal., 54g fat (31g sat. fat), 139mg chol., 400mg sod., 49g carb. (33g sugars, 3g fiber), 8g pro.

EASY MOCHA CREAM PIE

SHORTBREAD LEMON TART
PAGE 245

Desserts

Life is too short to pass up dessert, and we live by this mantra at *Taste of Home*. So why not surrender to temptation with a homestyle cobbler dolloped with whipped cream or a spoonful of a frosty ice cream delight? Whether you're hosting an classy dinner party or simply seeking the perfect grand finale to a weeknight meal, any one of these indulgences is sure to hit the sweet spot!

BLACK FOREST TART

Cherry pie filling and a melted chocolate drizzle top a rich, fudgy cake made from chocolate cookie crumbs. This tart is best served the day it is made.
—*Taste of Home* Test Kitchen

Prep: 35 min. + chilling
Bake: 25 min. + cooling • **Makes:** 12 servings

1¼ cups chocolate wafer crumbs
¼ cup sugar
¼ cup butter, melted
FILLING
½ cup butter
6 oz. semisweet chocolate, chopped
3 large eggs, room temperature
⅔ cup sugar
1 tsp. vanilla extract
¼ tsp. salt
⅔ cup all-purpose flour
TOPPING
1 can (21 oz.) cherry pie filling
2 oz. semisweet chocolate, chopped
1 Tbsp. heavy whipping cream

1. In a small bowl, combine wafer crumbs and sugar; stir in the butter. Press mixture onto the bottom and up the sides of a lightly greased 11-in. fluted tart pan with a removable bottom.
2. Place pan on a baking sheet. Bake at 350° until lightly browned, 8-10 minutes. Cool on a wire rack.
3. In a microwave, melt the butter and chocolate; stir until smooth. Cool for 10 minutes. In a large bowl, beat the eggs, sugar, vanilla and salt until thickened, about 4 minutes. Blend in chocolate mixture. Stir in flour and mix well.
4. Pour into crust; spread evenly. Bake at 350° until a toothpick inserted in the center comes out clean, 25-30 minutes. Cool tart completely on a wire rack. Spread pie filling over the top.
5. In a microwave, melt chocolate and cream; stir until smooth. Cool for 5 minutes, stirring occasionally. Drizzle over tart. Chill until set.
1 slice: 411 cal., 21g fat (12g sat. fat), 86mg chol., 258mg sod., 54g carb. (36g sugars, 2g fiber), 5g pro.

NEW ENGLAND
INDIAN PUDDING

NEW ENGLAND INDIAN PUDDING

This recipe was inspired by traditional New England Indian pudding. Instead of baking for hours in the oven, my version is made in the slow cooker. Use real molasses—if it's too strong, cut the amount down to ⅓ cup.
—Susan Bickta, Kutztown, PA

Prep: 15 min. • **Cook:** 3½ hours
Makes: 8 servings

1 pkg. (8½ oz.) cornbread/muffin mix
1 pkg. (3.4 oz.) instant butterscotch pudding mix
4 cups whole milk
3 large eggs, lightly beaten
½ cup molasses
1 tsp. ground cinnamon
¼ tsp. ground cloves
¼ tsp. ground ginger
Vanilla ice cream or sweetened whipped cream, optional

1. In a large bowl, whisk cornbread mix, pudding mix and milk until blended. Add eggs, molasses and spices; whisk until combined. Transfer to a greased 4- or 5-qt. slow cooker. Cover and cook on high for 1 hour.
2. Reduce heat to low; stir, making sure to scrape the sides well. Cover and cook 1 hour longer. Stir; cover and cook 1 hour longer. Stir; cover and cook 30-60 minutes longer or until very thick. Serve warm, with ice cream or whipped cream if desired.
⅔ cup: 330 cal., 9g fat (4g sat. fat), 83mg chol., 526mg sod., 51g carb. (36g sugars, 2g fiber), 8g pro.

TEST KITCHEN TIP

Unlike most slow-cooker recipes that advise against lifting the lid and stirring, this one requires you stir it periodically, or the edges will get too dark.

CRANBERRY
CREME BRULEE

MAMA'S BLACKBERRY COBBLER

Alabama has some tasty fresh blackberries. Fifty years ago my mama was going to pick blackberries to make a cobbler, but she went to the hospital to have me instead. This is her mama's recipe.
—Lisa Allen, Joppa, AL

- -

Prep: 15 min. • **Bake:** 45 min.
Makes: 6 servings

½   **cup plus 2 Tbsp. melted butter, divided**
1   **cup self-rising flour**
1½   **cups sugar, divided**
1   **cup 2% milk**
½   **tsp. vanilla extract**
3   **cups fresh blackberries or frozen unsweetened blackberries**

1. Preheat oven to 350°. Pour ½ cup melted butter into an 8-in. square baking dish. In a small bowl, combine flour, 1 cup sugar, milk and vanilla until blended; pour mixture into prepared dish. In another bowl, combine blackberries, remaining ½ cup sugar and remaining 2 Tbsp. melted butter; toss until combined. Spoon over batter.
2. Bake until topping is golden brown and fruit is tender, 45-50 minutes. Serve warm.
¾ cup: 491 cal., 21g fat (13g sat. fat), 54mg chol., 421mg sod., 75g carb. (56g sugars, 4g fiber), 5g pro.

TEST KITCHEN TIP

When making this cobbler, be sure to disperse the berry mixture evenly and all the way to the edges of the dish.

CRANBERRY CREME BRULEE

Love traditional creme brulee? Dress it up for the Christmas season or any time with ruby red cranberries in a sweet-tart sauce. As both the bottom layer and topping, it complements the rich custard.
—*Taste of Home* Test Kitchen

- -

Prep: 35 min. + chilling
Bake: 35 min. + chilling • **Makes:** 8 servings

1   **pkg. (12 oz.) fresh or frozen cranberries**
1   **cup sugar**
¼   **cup water**
⅛   **tsp. salt**
CUSTARD
2½   **cups heavy whipping cream, divided**
10   **large egg yolks**
⅔   **cup sugar**
1   **tsp. vanilla extract**
8   **tsp. superfine sugar**

1. Preheat oven to 325°. In a large saucepan, combine the cranberries, granulated sugar, water and salt. Cook over medium heat for 12-15 minutes or until berries pop, stirring frequently. Remove from the heat. Spoon 2 Tbsp. sauce into each of eight 6-oz. broiler-safe ramekins or custard cups; refrigerate for 10 minutes. Cover and refrigerate remaining sauce until serving.
2. For custard, in a small saucepan, heat 1 cup cream over medium heat until bubbles form around the sides of pan; remove from the heat. In a large bowl, whisk the egg yolks and granulated sugar until smooth. Slowly stir in the hot cream. Stir in the vanilla and remaining cream.
3. Place prepared ramekins in a baking pan large enough to hold them without touching. Spoon custard over cranberry sauce. Place pan on oven rack; add 1 in. of very hot water to pan. Bake for 35-40 minutes or until set (centers will still be soft). Immediately remove ramekins from water bath to a wire rack; cool 10 minutes. Refrigerate at least 8 hours or until cold.
4. To caramelize topping with a kitchen torch, gently blot surface of custard with a paper towel to remove any moisture. Sprinkle tops with superfine sugar. Hold torch flame 2 in. above custard surface and rotate it slowly until the sugar is evenly caramelized.
5. To caramelize topping in a broiler, place ramekins on a baking sheet; let stand at room temperature for 15 minutes. Preheat broiler. Gently blot surface of the custard with a paper towel to remove any moisture. Sprinkle tops with superfine sugar. Broil 3-4 in. from heat 1-2 minutes or until sugar is caramelized.
6. Serve the custards with the remaining cranberry sauce.
1 serving: 530 cal., 34g fat (19g sat. fat), 368mg chol., 75mg sod., 54g carb. (50g sugars, 2g fiber), 5g pro.

MAMA'S BLACKBERRY
COBBLER

BEST EVER BREAD PUDDING

The secret to incredible bread pudding with a soft middle and crisp edges starts with leftover dinner rolls. Kathryn Gartmann came up with the rich brown sugar sauce. A big drizzle of it that sauce takes this dessert over the top.
—*Taste of Home* Test Kitchen

Prep: 20 min. + standing • **Bake:** 40 min.
Makes: 15 servings

- 2 large eggs
- 2 large egg yolks
- 2¼ cups half-and-half cream
- 2 cups whole milk
- ½ cup butter, melted
- ¼ cup sugar
- 1 Tbsp. vanilla extract
- 1½ tsp. ground cinnamon
- ½ tsp. ground nutmeg
- ¼ tsp. sea salt
- 20 dinner rolls (1¼ lbs.), cut into 1-in. cubes (18 cups)
- 3 Tbsp. brown sugar

SAUCE
- 1 cup butter, cubed
- 1 cup packed brown sugar
- 1 cup half-and-half cream
- 2 tsp. vanilla extract
- ¼ tsp. sea salt
- ⅛ tsp. baking soda

1. Preheat oven to 350°. Whisk together the first 10 ingredients until blended. Gently stir in bread. Transfer to a greased 3-qt. or 13x9-in. baking dish. Sprinkle with brown sugar; let stand until bread is softened, about 15 minutes. Bake until puffed and a knife inserted in center comes out clean, 40-45 minutes.

2. Meanwhile, for sauce, melt butter in a large heavy saucepan over medium heat. Add the brown sugar; stir until dissolved. Gradually stir in the cream. Bring to a boil. Reduce heat; simmer 15-20 minutes or until thickened, stirring constantly. Remove from heat; add vanilla, sea salt and baking soda, stirring well. Serve the sauce with warm bread pudding.

1 serving: 497 cal., 29g fat (17g sat. fat), 151mg chol., 540mg sod., 49g carb. (26g sugars, 2g fiber), 9g pro.

STRAWBERRY CHEESECAKE TRIFLE

STRAWBERRY CHEESECAKE TRIFLE

Layers of rich pound cake, luscious whipped cream and sweet strawberries combine for a crowd-pleasing dessert that looks as great as it tastes.
—Marnie Stoughton, Glenburnie, ON

Prep: 20 min. + chilling
Makes: 16 servings

- 2 pints fresh strawberries, sliced
- 1 cup sugar, divided
- 2 pkg. (8 oz. each) cream cheese, softened
- 3 Tbsp. orange juice
- 3 cups heavy whipping cream, whipped
- 1 loaf (10¾ oz.) frozen pound cake, thawed and cut into ½-in. cubes
- 3 oz. semisweet chocolate, grated
  Optional: Chocolate curls and additional strawberries

1. In a bowl, toss strawberries with ½ cup sugar; set aside.

2. In a bowl, beat cream cheese, orange juice and remaining ½ cup sugar until smooth. Fold in the whipped cream; set aside.

3. Drain strawberries, reserving juice; set the berries aside. Gently toss cake cubes with reserved juice. Place half of the cake cubes in a 4-qt. trifle dish or serving bowl. Top cake with a third of the cream cheese mixture, half of the strawberries and half of the grated chocolate. Repeat layers. Top with remaining cream cheese mixture. Garnish with chocolate curls and strawberries if desired. Cover and refrigerate for at least 4 hours.

1 cup: 344 cal., 25g fat (15g sat. fat), 104mg chol., 129mg sod., 28g carbo. (22g sugars, 1g fiber), 4g pro.

RHUBARB CRUMBLE

I'm not sure how well my crumble keeps after it's made...we usually eat it all the first day! You can make this with all rhubarb if you'd like, but the apples and strawberries make it extra good.

—Linda Enslen, Schuler, AB

- -

Prep: 20 min. • **Bake:** 40 min.
Makes: 8 servings

- 3   cups sliced fresh or frozen rhubarb (½-in. pieces)
- 1   cup diced peeled apples
- ½   to 1 cup sliced strawberries
- ⅓   cup sugar
- ½   tsp. ground cinnamon
- ½   cup all-purpose flour
- 1   tsp. baking powder
- ¼   tsp. salt
- 4   Tbsp. cold butter
- ⅔   cup packed brown sugar
- ⅔   cup quick-cooking oats
       Vanilla ice cream, optional

1. Combine the rhubarb, apples and strawberries; spoon into a greased 8-in. square baking dish. Combine sugar and cinnamon; sprinkle over rhubarb mixture. Set aside.

2. In a bowl, combine flour, baking powder and salt. Cut in cold butter until mixture resembles coarse crumbs. Stir in brown sugar and quick-cooking oats. Sprinkle over rhubarb mixture.

3. Bake at 350° for 40-50 minutes or until lightly browned. Serve warm or cold, with a scoop of ice cream if desired.

1 piece: 227 cal., 6g fat (4g sat. fat), 15mg chol., 191mg sod., 41g carb. (29g sugars, 2g fiber), 2g pro.

RHUBARB CRUMBLE

CREAMY CARAMEL FLAN

A small slice of this impressively rich, creamy flan goes a long way. It's a delightful finish to a special meal or holiday celebration.

—Pat Forete, Miami, FL

- -

Prep: 25 min. + standing
Bake: 50 min. + chilling
Makes: 10 servings

- ¾   cup sugar
- ¼   cup water
- 1   pkg. (8 oz.) cream cheese, softened
- 5   large eggs
- 1   can (14 oz.) sweetened condensed milk
- 1   can (12 oz.) evaporated milk
- 1   tsp. vanilla extract

1. In a heavy saucepan, cook sugar and water over medium-low heat until melted and golden, about 15 minutes. Brush down crystals on the side of the pan with additional water as necessary. Quickly pour into an ungreased 2-qt. round baking or souffle dish, tilting to coat the bottom; let stand for 10 minutes.

2. In a bowl, beat the cream cheese until smooth. Beat in eggs, 1 at a time, until thoroughly combined. Add remaining ingredients; mix well. Pour over the caramelized sugar.

3. Place the dish in a larger baking pan. Pour boiling water into larger pan to a depth of 1 in. Bake at 350° for 50-60 minutes or until center is just set (mixture will jiggle).

4. Remove dish from a larger pan to a wire rack; cool for 1 hour. Refrigerate overnight. To unmold, run a knife around edges and invert onto a large rimmed serving platter. Cut into wedges or spoon onto dessert plates; spoon sauce over each serving.

Note: Pay close attention when melting sugar, as it changes quickly. Be sure to find a pan for the water bath before starting to prepare the recipe.

1 slice: 346 cal., 16g fat (10g sat. fat), 155mg chol., 182mg sod., 41g carb. (40g sugars, 0 fiber), 10g pro.

MANGO ALMOND ICEBOX CAKE

My friend inspired this recipe when she asked me to make a mango cake. It's easy to prepare and has a light and refreshing taste. Strawberries can be used as well.
—Rachel Simoneau, Danbury, CT

- -

Prep: 35 min. + chilling • **Makes:** 12 servings

1	**cup water**
½	**cup sugar**
¼	**tsp. almond extract**
1	**pkg. (16 oz.) frozen mango chunks, thawed**
4	**oz. cream cheese, softened**
½	**cup confectioners' sugar**
½	**tsp. vanilla extract**
2	**cups heavy whipping cream**
22	**crisp ladyfinger cookies**
1	**pkg. (5 oz.) miniature meringue cookies, coarsely crushed**
1	**cup sliced almonds**

1. For syrup, place water in a microwave-safe bowl; microwave on high 30 seconds. Stir in sugar and extract until sugar is dissolved; cool completely.
2. Finely chop ¼ cup mango chunks; place in a large bowl. Add the cream cheese, confectioners' sugar and vanilla; beat until blended. In another bowl, beat cream until stiff peaks form; fold into mango mixture.
3. To assemble, line bottom of a 9-in. springform pan with 11 ladyfingers; slowly drizzle with half of the syrup. Layer with half of each of the following: cream mixture, meringue cookies, remaining mango and almonds. Repeat layers. Refrigerate cake, covered, 8 hours or overnight. To serve, loosen sides of cake from the pan with a knife; remove rim.
1 slice: 389 cal., 22g fat (11g sat. fat), 71mg chol., 72mg sod., 45g carb. (38g sugars, 2g fiber), 5g pro.

CARAMEL APPLE CUPCAKES

CARAMEL APPLE CUPCAKES

Bring these extra special cupcakes to your next event and watch how quickly they disappear! With a caramel topping and spice cake base, they make the perfect fall treat.
—Diane Halferty, Corpus Christi, TX

- -

Prep: 25 min. • **Bake:** 20 min. + cooling
Makes: 1 dozen

1	**pkg. spice or carrot cake mix (regular size)**
2	**cups chopped peeled tart apples (about 2 medium)**
20	**caramels**
3	**Tbsp. 2% milk**
1	**cup finely chopped pecans, toasted**
12	**wooden skewers (4½ in.)**

1. Preheat oven to 350°. Line 12 jumbo muffin cups with paper liners.
2. Prepare cake mix batter according to the package directions; fold in apples. Fill prepared cups three-fourths full. Bake until a toothpick inserted in center comes out clean, about 20 minutes. Cool 10 minutes before removing from pans; cool completely on a wire rack.
3. In a small saucepan, cook caramels and milk over low heat until smooth, stirring constantly. Spread over cupcakes. Sprinkle with pecans. Insert a wooden skewer in each.
Note: To toast nuts, bake in a shallow pan in a 350° oven for 5-10 minutes or cook in a skillet over low heat until nuts are lightly browned, stirring occasionally.
1 cupcake: 365 cal., 19g fat (3g sat. fat), 48mg chol., 315mg sod., 48g carb. (30g sugars, 1g fiber), 5g pro.

MOIST CARROT CUPCAKES

If your kids think they don't like carrots, just wait until these cinnamon-scented, lightly frosted cupcakes hit the table.
—*Taste of Home* Test Kitchen

Prep: 20 min. • **Bake:** 15 min. + cooling
Makes: 10 cupcakes

- ⅔ cup sugar
- 3 Tbsp. canola oil
- 1 large egg, room temperature
- ¼ cup unsweetened applesauce
- 1 tsp. vanilla extract
- 1 cup all-purpose flour
- ¾ tsp. baking soda
- ¾ tsp. ground cinnamon
- ¼ tsp. salt
- 1½ cups shredded carrots

CREAM CHEESE FROSTING

- 6 oz. reduced-fat cream cheese
- ⅔ cup confectioners' sugar
- ¼ tsp. vanilla extract

1. In a large bowl, beat the sugar, oil and egg until well blended. Beat in applesauce and vanilla. Combine the flour, baking soda, cinnamon and salt; gradually beat into sugar mixture until blended. Stir in carrots.
2. Fill paper-lined muffin cups half full. Bake at 350° for 15-20 minutes or until a toothpick inserted in the center comes out clean. Cool for 10 minutes before removing from pan to a wire rack to cool completely.
3. In a small bowl, combine the frosting ingredients; beat until smooth. Frost the cupcakes. Refrigerate leftovers.
1 cupcake: 226 cal., 8g fat (3g sat. fat), 33mg chol., 244mg sod., 34g carb. (23g sugars, 1g fiber), 4g pro.

BLACK BOTTOM BRANDY BITES

The idea for these bite-sized beauties started with miniature chocolate bottles of brandy. For an extra dash of fabulous, I place chocolate in the bottom of each pastry cup.
—Arlene Erlbach, Morton Grove, IL

Prep: 30 min. • **Bake:** 10 min. + cooling
Makes: 2 dozen

- 2 sheets refrigerated pie crust
- 1½ cups mascarpone cheese
- ¾ cup turbinado sugar or sugar, divided
- ⅓ cup brandy
- ½ tsp. ground ginger, divided
- ½ tsp. vanilla extract
- ½ cup miniature semisweet chocolate chips, divided
- 1¼ tsp. pumpkin pie spice

1. Preheat oven to 425°. Bring pie crusts to room temperature.
2. Stir together mascarpone cheese and ½ cup sugar. Add brandy, ¼ tsp. ginger and vanilla; stir until well blended. Fold in ¼ cup chocolate chips; cover and refrigerate.
3. Combine pumpkin pie spice, remaining sugar and remaining ginger until well blended. On a lightly floured surface, unroll crusts; sprinkle evenly with sugar mixture. Lightly roll to help sugar mixture adhere. Cut into 24 circles with a 2½-in. biscuit or round cookie cutter; discard scraps. Lightly press circles, sugar side up, into 24 mini muffin cups coated with cooking spray. Pierce once with a fork.
4. Bake 10 minutes or until golden brown; remove from oven. Immediately sprinkle ¼ tsp. of chocolate chips into each cup; spread to cover bottom. Cool in pan for 15 minutes before removing to a wire rack.
5. When the cups are completely cool, refrigerate until the chocolate is set, about 20 minutes. Spoon brandy mixture into cups, or into a pastry bag fitted with a star tip and pipe mixture into cups. Sprinkle with the remaining chips and, if desired, additional pie spice. Refrigerate, covered, until serving.
1 tartlet: 244 cal., 18g fat (10g sat. fat), 38mg chol., 77mg sod., 17g carb. (9g sugars, 0 fiber), 3g pro.

BLACK BOTTOM BRANDY BITES

CRANBERRY PEAR COBBLERS

These individual fruit cobblers feature a hint of ginger and cinnamon. Served warm and topped with ice cream, their homestyle flavor is sure to satisfy anyone's craving.
—*Taste of Home* Test Kitchen

Prep: 15 min. • **Bake:** 45 min.
Makes: 2 servings

- 2 small pears, peeled and cut into ¾-in. pieces
- ¼ cup dried cranberries
- 3 Tbsp. sugar
- 1½ tsp. all-purpose flour
- 1 tsp. grated fresh gingerroot
- ¼ tsp. ground cinnamon
- 1 Tbsp. butter

TOPPING
- 3 Tbsp. sugar
- 1 tsp. grated fresh gingerroot
- ½ cup all-purpose flour
- ¼ tsp. baking soda
- ⅛ tsp. salt
- 8 tsp. cold butter
- ¼ cup buttermilk

1. In a bowl, combine the first 6 ingredients. Spoon into two 10-oz. custard cups coated with cooking spray. Dot with butter. Bake at 350° for 15-20 minutes or until the fruit is hot and bubbly.

2. For topping, combine sugar and ginger in a blender; cover and process until crumbly. Set aside 1½ tsp. of the mixture. Add the flour, baking soda and salt to the blender; cover and process for 20 seconds or until combined. Add butter; process until mixture resembles coarse crumbs.

3. Transfer to a small bowl; stir in buttermilk. Drop by rounded tablespoonfuls onto hot fruit filling; sprinkle with reserved sugar mixture. Bake for 30-35 minutes or until topping is golden brown. Serve warm.

1 serving: 584 cal., 21g fat (13g sat. fat), 55mg chol., 541mg sod., 98g carb. (63g sugars, 5g fiber), 5g pro.

BLACKBERRY DAIQUIRI SHERBET

One summer I decided to make homemade sherbet—one of my favorite treats—using the blackberries growing in my mother's garden. I love the flavor of rum in daiquiris, and the two blend together beautifully!
—Shelly Bevington, Hermiston, OR

Prep: 15 min.
Process: 30 min. + freezing
Makes: 1¼ qt.

- 3 cups fresh or frozen blackberries, thawed
- 1 cup sugar
- ¼ tsp. salt
- 1 can (12 oz.) evaporated milk
- 2 Tbsp. lime juice
- 1 tsp. rum extract
- ½ tsp. citric acid

1. Place the blackberries, sugar and salt in a food processor; process until smooth. Press through a fine-mesh strainer into a bowl; discard seeds and pulp. Stir the remaining ingredients into puree.

2. Fill cylinder of ice cream maker no more than two-thirds full; freeze according to the manufacturer's directions. Transfer sherbet to freezer containers, allowing headspace for expansion. Freeze sherbet until firm, 8 hours or overnight.

½ cup: 147 cal., 3g fat (2g sat. fat), 12mg chol., 96mg sod., 28g carb. (26g sugars, 2g fiber), 3g pro.

TEST KITCHEN TIP
Don't swap the rum extract for actual rum. It might seem like a fun idea, but alcohol will keep the sherbet from freezing solid.

STRAWBERRY
PRETZEL DESSERT

STRAWBERRY PRETZEL DESSERT

Need to bring a dish to pass this weekend? You can't go wrong with this sweet-salty sensation. Expect the raves to roll in!
—Aldene Belch, Flint, MI

- -

Prep: 20 min. • **Bake:** 10 min. + chilling
Makes: 16 servings

- 2 cups crushed pretzels (about 8 oz.)
- ¾ cup butter, melted
- 3 Tbsp. sugar

FILLING
- 2 cups whipped topping
- 1 pkg. (8 oz.) cream cheese, softened
- 1 cup sugar

TOPPING
- 2 pkg. (3 oz. each) strawberry gelatin
- 2 cups boiling water
- 2 pkg. (16 oz. each) frozen sweetened sliced strawberries, thawed
- Optional: Additional whipped topping and pretzels

1. In a bowl, combine the pretzels, butter and sugar. Press into an ungreased 13x9-in. baking dish. Bake at 350° for 10 minutes. Cool on a wire rack.
2. For filling, in a small bowl, beat whipped topping, cream cheese and sugar until smooth. Spread mixture over pretzel crust. Refrigerate until chilled.
3. For topping, dissolve gelatin in boiling water in a large bowl. Stir in sweetened strawberries; chill until partially set. Carefully spoon over filling. Chill until firm, 4-6 hours. Cut into squares; serve with additional whipped topping and pretzels if desired.
1 piece: 295 cal., 15g fat (10g sat. fat), 39mg chol., 305mg sod., 38g carb. (27g sugars, 1g fiber), 3g pro.

This is, by far, my favorite Taste of Home *recipe. It's easy and ideal for any occasion. Best of all, the sweet fruity gelatin and salty-crunchy crust are amazing together.*

—BRIANNA GRIEPENTROG, DIGITAL DESIGNER

MOM'S HAZELNUT & CHOCOLATE BREAD PUDDING

MOM'S HAZELNUT & CHOCOLATE BREAD PUDDING

Mom combined her love of hazelnut spread and bread pudding into one delicious recipe. I adapted it for my slow cooker to save time in the kitchen. It's a great make-ahead treat. We especially enjoy it for game-day parties.
—Jo Hahn, Newport News, VA

- -

Prep: 10 min. • **Cook:** 4 hours.
Makes: 12 servings

- ¼ cup unsalted butter
- 2 Tbsp. semisweet chocolate chips
- 8 cups cubed challah or brioche
- ½ cup chopped hazelnuts
- 4 large eggs
- 1½ cups fat-free milk
- ½ cup fat-free half-and-half
- ½ cup hazelnut spread
- ¼ cup sugar
- ½ tsp. vanilla extract
- ¼ tsp. salt
- Sweetened whipped cream, optional

1. Microwave butter and chocolate chips until melted, 30-45 seconds; stir until smooth. Cool. In a 3- or 4-qt. slow cooker coated with cooking spray, combine the bread cubes and hazelnuts. In a large bowl, combine next 7 ingredients, mixing well. Add the chocolate mixture to bowl; whisk until smooth.
2. Pour egg mixture over the bread and hazelnuts, gently pressing bread cubes to help them absorb liquid. Cook, covered, on low until a knife inserted in center comes out clean, 4-5 hours. Serve warm, dolloped with whipped cream if desired.
½ cup: 259 cal., 14g fat (4g sat. fat), 85mg chol., 190mg sod., 28g carb. (15g sugars, 1g fiber), 7g pro.

SPUMONI BAKED ALASKA

For a dazzling yet refreshing end to a rich holiday meal, try this freezer finale. Its cool, intriguing interior and Christmasy color scheme are bound to garner oohs and aahs.
—*Taste of Home* Test Kitchen

Prep: 50 min. + freezing • **Bake:** 5 min.
Makes: 12 servings

½ cup butter, cubed
2 oz. unsweetened chocolate, chopped
1 cup sugar
1 tsp. vanilla extract
2 large eggs, room temperature
¾ cup all-purpose flour
½ tsp. baking powder
½ tsp. salt
1 cup chopped hazelnuts
2 qt. vanilla ice cream, softened, divided
½ cup chopped pistachios
½ tsp. almond extract
6 drops green food coloring, optional
⅓ cup chopped maraschino cherries
1 Tbsp. maraschino cherry juice
1 Tbsp. rum

MERINGUE

8 large egg whites, room temperature
1 cup sugar
1 tsp. cream of tartar

SPUMONI BAKED ALASKA

1. Preheat oven to 350°. In a microwave-safe bowl, melt butter and chocolate; stir until smooth. Stir in sugar and vanilla. Add eggs, 1 at a time, beating well after each addition. Combine the flour, baking powder and salt; gradually stir into chocolate mixture. Stir in the hazelnuts.
2. Spread into a greased 8-in. round baking pan. Bake until a toothpick inserted in the center comes out with moist crumbs (do not overbake), 35-40 minutes. Cool 10 minutes before removing from pan to a wire rack to cool completely.
3. Meanwhile, line an 8-in. round bowl (1½ qt.) with foil. In a smaller bowl, place 1 qt. ice cream; add the pistachios, almond extract and, if desired, food coloring. Quickly spread ice cream over bottom and up sides of foil-lined bowl, leaving the center hollow; cover and freeze for 30 minutes.
4. In a small bowl, combine cherries, cherry juice, rum and remaining 1 qt. ice cream. Pack ice cream into hollow center of 8-in. bowl; cover and freeze.

5. In a large heavy saucepan, combine egg whites, sugar and cream of tartar. With a hand mixer, beat on low speed 1 minute. Continue beating over low heat until egg mixture reaches 160°, about 8 minutes. Transfer to a bowl; beat until stiff glossy peaks form and sugar is dissolved.
6. Place brownie on an ungreased foil-lined baking sheet; top with inverted ice cream mold. Remove foil. Immediately spread the meringue over ice cream, sealing to edges of brownie. Freeze until ready to serve, up to 24 hours.
7. Preheat oven to 400°. Bake until meringue is lightly browned, 2-5 minutes. Transfer to a serving plate; serve immediately.
1 piece: 554 cal., 29g fat (13g sat. fat), 94mg chol., 314mg sod., 68g carb. (52g sugars, 3g fiber), 11g pro.

TEST KITCHEN TIP

If beads form on top of the meringue or meringue is sticky, it may have been baked at too high of a temperature, or was underbaked. For best results, meringue should not be made on a hot or humid day.

SHORTBREAD LEMON TART

For a change from ordinary lemon bars, we added orange zest to both the crust and filling and turned the recipe into a tart. It's a refreshing finish to a heavy meal.
—*Taste of Home* Test Kitchen

Prep: 20 min. • **Bake:** 25 min. + cooling
Makes: 10 servings

 3   large eggs
1¼ cups sugar
 ¼ cup lemon juice
 1 Tbsp. grated orange zest
 ¼ cup butter, melted
CRUST
 1 cup all-purpose flour
 ⅓ cup confectioners' sugar
 ½ cup ground almonds
 1 tsp. grated lemon zest
 1 tsp. grated orange zest
 ½ cup cold butter, cubed
    Additional confectioners' sugar
    Fresh raspberries, optional

1. Let eggs stand at room temperature for 30 minutes.
2. Preheat oven to 350°. Whisk together eggs, sugar, lemon juice and orange zest. Whisk in butter until smooth. Set aside.
3. For crust, pulse first 6 ingredients in a food processor until mixture forms a ball. Press dough onto the bottom and up the sides of an ungreased 9-in. fluted tart pan with removable bottom.
4. Pour lemon mixture into crust. Bake until center is almost set, 25-30 minutes. Cool on a wire rack. Just before serving, sprinkle with confectioners' sugar and, if desired, fresh raspberries.

1 serving: 330 cal., 18g fat (9g sat. fat), 101mg chol., 158mg sod., 40g carb. (29g sugars, 1g fiber), 4g pro.

SHORTBREAD
LEMON TART

EGGNOG MOUSSE

AMARETTO CHERRIES WITH DUMPLINGS

Treat everyone to a dessert of comfort food—warm tart cherries drizzled with amaretto and topped with fluffy dumplings. A scoop of vanilla ice cream is the perfect finishing touch.

—*Taste of Home* Test Kitchen

- -

Prep: 15 min. • **Cook:** 7¾ hours
Makes: 6 servings

2	cans (14½ oz. each) pitted tart cherries
¾	cup sugar
¼	cup cornstarch
⅛	tsp. salt
¼	cup amaretto or ½ tsp. almond extract

DUMPLINGS

1	cup all-purpose flour
¼	cup sugar
1	tsp. baking powder
½	tsp. grated lemon zest
⅛	tsp. salt
⅓	cup 2% milk
3	Tbsp. butter, melted
	Vanilla ice cream, optional

1. Drain cherries, reserving ¼ cup juice. Place cherries in a 3-qt. slow cooker.
2. In a small bowl, mix sugar, cornstarch and salt; stir in reserved juice until smooth. Stir into cherries. Cook, covered, on high for 7 hours. Drizzle the amaretto over the cherry mixture.
3. For the dumplings, in a small bowl, whisk the flour, sugar, baking powder, lemon zest and salt. In another bowl, whisk milk and melted butter. Add to the flour mixture; stir just until moistened.
4. Drop by tablespoonfuls on top of the hot cherry mixture. Cook, covered, 45 minutes or until a toothpick inserted in the center of dumplings comes out clean. If desired, serve warm with ice cream.

1 cup equals: 441 cal., 8g fat (5g sat. fat), 19mg chol., 268mg sod., 85g carb., 3g fiber, 4g pro.

EGGNOG MOUSSE

Guests will always find room for this light, fluffy, mouthwatering mousse. It makes an elegant, refreshing finish for heavier meals, and it's also a great way to use up any extra eggnog in the fridge.

—*Taste of Home* Test Kitchen

- -

Prep: 15 min. + chilling • **Makes:** 4 servings

2	tsp. unflavored gelatin
2	cups reduced-fat eggnog
2	Tbsp. sugar
⅛	tsp. ground cinnamon
⅛	tsp. ground nutmeg
½	tsp. vanilla extract
1	cup reduced-fat whipped topping, divided
	Additional ground nutmeg, optional

1. In a small saucepan, sprinkle gelatin over eggnog; let stand for 1 minute. Heat over low heat, stirring until gelatin is completely dissolved. Stir in the sugar, cinnamon and nutmeg until sugar is dissolved. Transfer to a small bowl; stir in vanilla. Refrigerate until mixture begins to thicken.
2. Beat mixture until light and fluffy. Beat in ¾ cup whipped topping. Divide among 4 dessert dishes. Refrigerate mousse until firm. Garnish with the remaining whipped topping; sprinkle with additional ground nutmeg if desired.
¾ cup: 165 cal., 6g fat (4g sat. fat), 97mg chol., 80mg sod., 21g carb. (17g sugars, 0 fiber), 7g pro. **Diabetic exchanges:** 1 starch, ½ reduced-fat milk.

AMARETTO CHERRIES
WITH DUMPLINGS

BLUEBERRY GRAHAM DESSERT

When you're short on time but long for cheesecake, give this fruity parfait a try. Ricotta and cream cheeses give every bite cheesecake flavor without the effort or bake time. Instead of making individual servings, you can also layer ingredients in a glass serving bowl.
—*Taste of Home* Test Kitchen

- -

Takes: 15 min. • **Makes:** 4 servings

¾ cup graham cracker crumbs
    (about 12 squares)
¼ cup chopped walnuts
2 Tbsp. sugar
¼ tsp. ground cinnamon
2 Tbsp. butter
3 oz. cream cheese, softened
⅓ cup confectioners' sugar
½ cup ricotta cheese
2 tsp. lemon juice
4 cups fresh blueberries
    Whipped cream, optional

1. In a large bowl, combine cracker crumbs, walnuts, sugar and cinnamon. Stir in butter; set aside. In another large bowl, beat the cream cheese and confectioners' sugar until smooth. Beat in the ricotta cheese and lemon juice.

2. Place ½ cup blueberries in each of 4 dessert dishes. Top with cream cheese mixture, crumbs and remaining blueberries. Garnish with whipped cream if desired. Refrigerate until serving.

1 serving: 430 cal., 23g fat (11g sat. fat), 51mg chol., 255mg sod., 53g carb. (35g sugars, 4g fiber), 9g pro.

BLUEBERRY GRAHAM DESSERT

APPLE DUMPLING BAKE

I received this recipe from a friend, then tweaked it to suit our tastes. Mountain Dew is the secret ingredient in this rich apple dessert that's a snap to make.
—Chris Shields, Monrovia, IN

- -

Prep: 15 min. • **Bake:** 35 min.
Makes: 8 servings

- 2   medium Granny Smith apples
- 2   tubes (8 oz. each) refrigerated crescent rolls
- 1   cup sugar
- ⅓   cup butter, softened
- ½   tsp. ground cinnamon
- ¾   cup Mountain Dew soda
     Vanilla ice cream

1. Preheat oven to 350°. Peel, core and cut each apple into 8 wedges. Unroll both tubes of crescent dough; separate each tube into 8 triangles. Wrap a triangle around each wedge. Place triangles in a greased 13x9-in. baking dish.
2. In a bowl, mix sugar, butter and cinnamon until blended; sprinkle over the dumplings. Slowly pour Mountain Dew around the rolls (do not stir).
3. Bake, uncovered, until golden brown and apples are tender, 35-40 minutes. Serve warm with ice cream.
2 dumplings: 414 cal., 20g fat (9g sat. fat), 20mg chol., 510mg sod., 55g carb. (35g sugars, 1g fiber), 4g pro.

MACAROON-TOPPED RHUBARB COBBLER

Crumbled macaroons are a unique addition to this cobbler's topping. Serve hearty helpings alone or with vanilla ice cream.
—*Taste of Home* Test Kitchen

- -

Takes: 30 min. • **Makes:** 4 servings

- 4   cups sliced fresh or frozen rhubarb (1-in. pieces)
- 1   large apple, peeled and sliced
- ½   cup packed brown sugar
- ½   tsp. ground cinnamon, divided
- 1   Tbsp. cornstarch
- 2   Tbsp. cold water
- 8   macaroons, crumbled
- 1   Tbsp. butter, melted
- 2   Tbsp. sugar
     Vanilla ice cream, optional

1. In a large cast-iron or other ovenproof skillet, combine the rhubarb, apple, brown sugar and ¼ tsp. cinnamon; bring to a boil. Reduce heat; cover and simmer until rhubarb is very tender, 10-13 minutes. Combine the cornstarch and water until smooth; gradually add to the fruit mixture. Bring to a boil; cook and stir until thickened, about 2 minutes.
2. In a small bowl, combine the crumbled cookies, butter, sugar and remaining cinnamon. Sprinkle over fruit mixture.
3. Broil 4 in. from the heat until lightly browned, 3-5 minutes. If desired, serve warm with ice cream.
Note: If using frozen rhubarb, measure it while still frozen, then thaw completely. Drain in a colander, but do not press liquid out.
1 serving: 368 cal., 12g fat (7g sat. fat), 8mg chol., 45mg sod., 62g carb. (55g sugars, 5g fiber), 3g pro.

MACAROON-TOPPED RHUBARB COBBLER

**NOT-FRIED
ICE CREAM CAKE**

NOT-FRIED ICE CREAM CAKE

We created this no-fry ice cream cake to mimic the popular deep-fried dessert you'll find in many Mexican restaurants. It's a no-fuss treat that feeds a crowd, and it's conveniently made ahead.
—*Taste of Home* Test Kitchen

- -

Prep: 20 min. + freezing
Makes: 16 servings

- 1 cup cornflake crumbs
- ⅓ cup sugar
- ⅓ cup butter, melted
- ¾ tsp. ground cinnamon
- ½ gallon butter pecan ice cream, softened, divided
- 4 Tbsp. honey, divided

1. In a small bowl, combine the cornflake crumbs, sugar, butter and cinnamon; set aside ½ cup. Press remaining crumb mixture into a greased 9-in. springform pan. Spoon half of the ice cream over crust. Sprinkle with reserved crumb mixture; drizzle with 2 Tbsp. honey. Cover and freeze for 2 hours.
2. Top with remaining ice cream. Cover and freeze for 8 hours or overnight.
3. Remove cake from the freezer 5 minutes before serving. Remove sides of pan; drizzle with remaining honey.
1 slice: 256 cal., 16g fat (7g sat. fat), 35mg chol., 189mg sod., 27g carb. (22g sugars, 0 fiber), 4g pro.

TEST KITCHEN TIP
For extra fun and flavor, add a dollop of whipped cream and a maraschino cherry to each slice of this ice cream cake. You can also drizzle with chocolate syrup or serve with fresh berries.

OMA'S APFELKUCHEN

OMA'S APFELKUCHEN

For more than 150 years, members of my husband's German family have shared this scrumptious apple cake recipe. Try it with any apples you have on hand. I like to use Granny Smith.
—Amy Kirchen, Loveland, OH

- -

Prep: 20 min. • **Bake:** 45 min. + cooling
Makes: 10 servings

- 5 large egg yolks
- 2 medium tart apples, peeled, cored and halved
- 1 cup plus 2 Tbsp. unsalted butter, softened
- 1¼ cups sugar
- 2 cups all-purpose flour
- 2 Tbsp. cornstarch
- 2 tsp. cream of tartar
- 1 tsp. baking powder
- ½ tsp. salt
- ¼ cup 2% milk
  Confectioners' sugar

1. Preheat oven to 350°. Let the egg yolks stand at room temperature for 30 minutes. Starting ½ in. from 1 end, cut apple halves lengthwise into ¼-in. slices, leaving them attached at the top so they fan out slightly. Set aside.
2. Cream butter and sugar until light and fluffy, 5-7 minutes. Add egg yolks, 1 at a time, beating well after each addition. In another bowl, sift the flour, cornstarch, cream of tartar, baking powder and salt twice. Gradually beat into creamed mixture. Add milk; mix well (batter will be thick).
3. Spread batter into a greased 9-in. springform pan wrapped in a sheet of heavy-duty foil. Gently press apples, round side up, into batter. Bake until a toothpick inserted in the center comes out with moist crumbs, 45-55 minutes. Cool on a wire rack 10 minutes. Loosen sides from pan with a knife; remove foil. Cool 1 hour longer. Remove rim from pan. Dust with confectioners' sugar.
1 slice: 422 cal., 23g fat (14g sat. fat), 148mg chol., 177mg sod., 50g carb. (28g sugars, 1g fiber), 4g pro.

Recipe Index

Equivalents & Substitutions

EQUIVALENT MEASURES

3 teaspoons = 1 tablespoon		**16 tablespoons** = 1 cup	
4 tablespoons = ¼ cup		**2 cups** = 1 pint	
5⅓ tablespoons = ⅓ cup		**4 cups** = 1 quart	
8 tablespoons = ½ cup		**4 quarts** = 1 gallon	

FOOD EQUIVALENTS

Macaroni	1 cup (3½ ounces) uncooked = 2½ cups cooked
Noodles, Medium	3 cups (4 ounces) uncooked = 4 cups cooked
Popcorn	⅓-½ cup unpopped = 8 cups popped
Rice, Long Grain	1 cup uncooked = 3 cups cooked
Rice, Quick-Cooking	1 cup uncooked = 2 cups cooked
Spaghetti	8 ounces uncooked = 4 cups cooked
Bread	1 slice = ¾ cup soft crumbs or ¼ cup fine dry crumbs
Graham Crackers	7 squares = ½ cup finely crushed
Buttery Round Crackers	12 crackers = ½ cup finely crushed
Saltine Crackers	14 crackers = ½ cup finely crushed
Bananas	1 medium = ⅓ cup mashed
Lemons	1 medium = 3 tablespoons juice + 2 teaspoons grated zest
Limes	1 medium = 2 tablespoons juice + 1½ teaspoons grated zest
Oranges	1 medium = ¼-⅓ cup juice + 4 teaspoons grated zest

Cabbage	1 head = 5 cups shredded	**Green Pepper**	1 large = 1 cup chopped
Carrots	1 pound = 3 cups shredded	**Mushrooms**	½ pound = 3 cups sliced
Celery	1 rib = ½ cup chopped	**Onions**	1 medium = ½ cup chopped
Corn	1 ear fresh = ⅔ cup kernels	**Potatoes**	3 medium = 2 cups cubed

Almonds	1 pound = 3 cups chopped	**Pecan Halves**	1 pound = 4½ cups chopped
Ground Nuts	3¾ ounces = 1 cup	**Walnuts**	1 pound = 3¾ cups chopped

EASY SUBSTITUTIONS

WHEN YOU NEED...		USE...
Baking Powder	1 teaspoon	½ teaspoon cream of tartar + ¼ teaspoon baking soda
Buttermilk	1 cup	1 tablespoon lemon juice or vinegar + enough milk to measure 1 cup (let stand 5 minutes before using)
Cornstarch	1 tablespoon	2 tablespoons all-purpose flour
Honey	1 cup	1¼ cups sugar + ¼ cup water
Half-and-Half Cream	1 cup	1 tablespoon melted butter + enough whole milk to measure 1 cup
Onion	1 small, chopped (⅓ cup)	1 teaspoon onion powder or 1 tablespoon dried minced onion
Tomato Juice	1 cup	½ cup tomato sauce + ½ cup water
Tomato Sauce	2 cups	¾ cup tomato paste + 1 cup water
Unsweetened Chocolate	1 square (1 ounce)	3 tablespoons baking cocoa + 1 tablespoon shortening or oil
Whole Milk	1 cup	½ cup evaporated milk + ½ cup water

Cutting Techniques

MINCING AND CHOPPING

Holding the handle of a chef's knife with one hand, rest the fingers of your other hand on the top of the blade near the tip. Using the handle to guide and apply pressure, move knife in an arc across the food with a rocking motion until pieces of food are the desired size. Mincing results in pieces no larger than ⅛ in., and chopping produces ¼- to ½-in. pieces.

DICING AND CUBING

Using a utility knife, trim each side of the fruit, vegetable or other food, squaring it off. Cut lengthwise into evenly spaced strips. The narrower the strips, the smaller the pieces will be. Stack the strips and cut lengthwise into uniformly sized strips. Arrange the square-shaped strips into a pile and cut widthwise into uniform pieces.

MAKING BIAS OR DIAGONAL CUTS

Holding a chef's knife at an angle to the length of the food, slice as thick or thin as desired. This technique is often used in stir-fry recipes.

MAKING JULIENNE STRIPS

Using a utility knife, cut a thin strip from one side of vegetable. Turn so flat side is down. Cut into 2-in. lengths, then cut each piece lengthwise into thin strips. Stack the strips and cut lengthwise into thinner strips.

CUTTING WEDGES

Using a chef's knife or serrated knife, cut the produce in half from stem end to blossom end. Lay halves cut side down on a cutting board. Set knife at the center of one the halves and cut in half vertically, then cut each quarter in half vertically. Repeat with other half.

ZESTING

Pull a citrus zester across limes, lemons or oranges, being careful not to remove the bitter white pith. The small holes in the zester will yield thin, narrow strips of zest. Use full strips to garnish or, if recipe instructs, chop into fine pieces and use as directed.

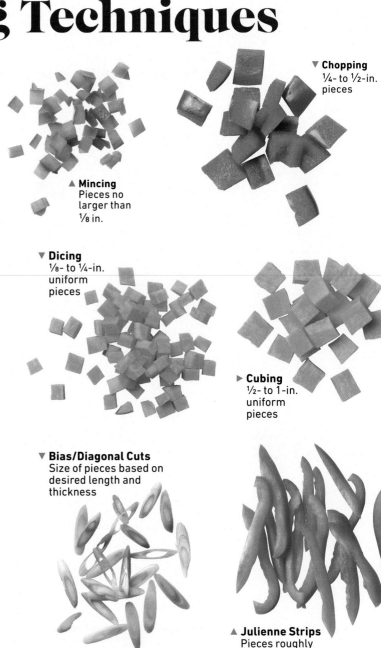

▲ **Mincing**
Pieces no larger than ⅛ in.

▼ **Chopping**
¼- to ½-in. pieces

▼ **Dicing**
⅛- to ¼-in. uniform pieces

▶ **Cubing**
½- to 1-in. uniform pieces

▼ **Bias/Diagonal Cuts**
Size of pieces based on desired length and thickness

▲ **Julienne Strips**
Pieces roughly 2 in. long

▲ **Wedges**
Size of wedges based on desired thickness

▲ **Zesting**
Size of strips or chopped zest based on desired preference